P9-CAD-753

POST
GRAD

POST GRAD

Five Women and Their First Year Out of College

Caroline Kitchener

An Imprint of *HarperCollins*Publishers

This is a work of nonfiction. The events and experiences detailed herein are all true and have been faithfully rendered as remembered by the author, to the best of her ability, or as they were told to the author by people who were present. Some names and identifying characteristics have been changed in order to protect the privacy of individuals involved.

HarperCollins books may be purchased for educational, business, or sales promotional use. For information, please email the Special Markets Department at SPsales@harpercollins.com.

FIRST EDITION

Designed by Jane Treuhaft

Library of Congress Cataloging-in-Publication Data has been applied for.

ISBN 978-0-06-242949-0

17 18 19 20 21 LSC 10 9 8 7 6 5 4 3 2 1

FOR MILLY,

who stood beside me at graduation and always

CONTENTS

Introduction

Two weeks into my senior year at Princeton, I went to a recruitment event for one of the largest consulting firms in the world. I put on my suit, blew my hair dry, and walked over to Prospect House, a facility typically reserved for Princeton's most exclusive gatherings: award ceremonies, board of trustees meetings, faculty retirement parties. As soon as I walked in, it was clear I wasn't going to get a seat. There must have been more than two hundred students crammed into the main dining room—all in suits, all wearing name tags, all staring intently at the projector screen at the front of the room.

Every year, approximately 30 percent of Princeton graduates go into finance or consulting.[1] I'd always thought that number

1 *Annual Report 2013–2014: Career Services at Princeton University.* Princeton, NJ: Trustees of Princeton University, 2015. https://careerservices.princeton.edu/sites/career/files/Career%20Services%20Annual%20Report%202013-14_Digital_1.pdf.

seemed absurdly high. For the past four years, I'd watched top students I knew in every major—financial engineering, but also English, anthropology, and public policy—compete with one another for a spot at one of the top consulting firms or investment banks. I figured the main draw was the $70,000 to $100,000 starting salary, but I knew there must be more to it than that.

I'd never envisioned a career in consulting before, but listening to the associates describe their experiences—many of them just two or three years older than me—I started to see it: sitting at a desk with a view of downtown Manhattan, going out for drinks with my team after work, working out at the firm's private gym with a girl I knew from college. Up until that point, the months and years after graduation had seemed completely nebulous. I had no idea what to expect—no idea what I'd be doing and no idea whom I'd be doing it with.

But now the consulting firm associates were presenting me with a clear and familiar picture. They spent a good twenty-minute chunk of the presentation discussing mentorship. They all said they had at least three senior people at the firm they could go to for advice—people who were personally invested in their success. Throughout the event, they also casually referred to their "class": the group of thirty or forty first-year college grads who started working at the firm at the same time. Every Friday, the company sponsored a happy hour somewhere in downtown Manhattan, attended by almost all first- and second-year employees. While the young associates acknowledged that they worked long hours—occasionally staying at the office until well after midnight—they said it wasn't that bad because they were doing it with their closest friends. I thought about all the times my friends and I had camped out in the Princeton library until one or two in the morning. Consulting, I thought, sounded just like college.

I'm sure the speakers from the consulting firm wanted me to feel this way. They'd probably spent years honing this presentation, figuring out exactly what would appeal to college seniors. They knew we were anxious about our first year out of college. They knew we wanted a community.

Graduating from college is like leaving a pool and jumping into the ocean. In the ocean, things are uncertain. You have currents you can't control pulling you in different directions, and you lack the community that helped you get through college.

Consulting firms and investment banks (which have a similar recruiting model) rope off a section of the ocean, and create their own little pools. If you reach one of these pools, you're safe. Again, you're surrounded by a cohort of people your own age—friends, potential future life partners—and you have a built-in topic to talk about: work. And while the finance and consulting tracks aren't as popular at most other schools as they are at Princeton, these kinds of pools exist everywhere. When I started interning at Atlantic Media (home of *The Atlantic* magazine) the summer after my junior year, for example, twenty recent college graduates had just started their yearlong fellowships. Immediately, the fellows found themselves in a community similar to the one they had in college, hanging out together after work and on weekends.

As a student at Princeton, it's easy to feel like all of your peers are taking jobs with employers who recruit large numbers of recent grads because those companies are the ones you hear about most. But in reality, even though a large chunk of Princeton grads find their way to the safe harbors of finance and consulting, most of us don't. This book is about five women who, for the first year after graduation, stayed in the ocean. It's about how we built our own communities when we didn't have anyone to do it for us.

DURING MY SENIOR YEAR at Princeton, I started following four women in my graduating class, interviewing them about their time at college and their plans for the future. I intentionally chose women who were very different from one another: with different aspirations, values, and racial, ethnic, and socioeconomic backgrounds. For one year after graduation, I continued interviewing these women, regularly visiting them in their new cities and watching them transition from college to whatever came next: coding for a large real estate company, filming a documentary, applying to medical school, or singing jazz at a prestigious music conservatory.

As a group, women my age have been written about a lot. Journalists and researchers have tried hard to figure us out: what drives us, what scares us, what makes us different from our parents' generation. When I started working on this book, I thought I would study my peers in a similar way—observe the choices they made, and record. But a few months after graduation, I realized I couldn't separate my own experiences from theirs. Most of what they were feeling, I was feeling, too. I decided to make myself the fifth character and tell our stories together.

I didn't write this book to make sweeping generalizations about our generation. I wrote about only five women. Our experiences and identities don't represent all young women in their early twenties, or even all young women in our graduating class. But while I was reporting and writing, I was surprised by how many similarities emerged among the five narratives. As different as we all were, during our first year out of college, we had a lot of the same priorities and concerns. Up until graduation, structured school communities had always determined how we fit into the world. After we left college, we each struggled to figure that out on our own. Even if other recent graduates can't relate to our exact experiences, I think they'll connect to what I see as universal feelings of confusion, self-doubt, and isolation. I hope this book will give some insight into what's hard about this crucial transitional year, particularly for women.

This first post-graduation year is especially important now, as women have started to outpace men in the college classroom but continue to fall behind them in the workplace. In 2015, for the first time since the U.S. Census Bureau started collecting data on higher education, women became more likely than men to get a college degree.[2] A 2011 report released by Princeton's Steering Committee on Undergraduate Women's Leadership found that women at Princeton academically outperform their male peers, graduating with substantially higher grade point averages.[3] Today, women are getting better grades than men at colleges and universities across the country.[4] But somewhere between graduating from college and entering the workplace, women lose this advantage. One year after

2 Ryan, Camille, and Kurt Bauman. *Educational Attainment in the United States: 2015.* Washington, DC: U.S. Census Bureau, 2016. https://www.census.gov/content/dam/Census/library/publications/2016/demo/p20-578.pdf.

3 *Report of the Steering Committee on Undergraduate Women's Leadership.* Princeton, NJ: Trustees of Princeton University, 2011. http://en.calameo.com/read/0008049754788e9221f34.

4 Conger, Dylan, and Mark C. Long. "Why Are Men Falling Behind? Gender Gaps in College Performance and Persistence," *Annals of the American Academy of Political and Social Science* 627, no. 1 (2010): 184–214.

graduation, men earn, on average, 18 percent more than women.[5] And as we get older, that gap continues to grow.[6] In a 2012 report, the American Association of University Women concluded that, while differences in occupation and college major choice account for some of the gender wage gap, they don't account for all of it. About one-third of the gap, according to the report, just comes down to gender.[7] By following five women through the first year out of college, carefully documenting the decisions each of us made, I thought I might be able to begin making some sense of these numbers. Again, I can't draw any overarching conclusions from the lives of only five women, but I was able to observe and report on the subtle ways in which gender seems to influence women's decisions and priorities at this important stage in our lives.

THERE IS A LOT OF PRESSURE inherent to the first year out of college. This is true for all college graduates, but I think it's particularly intense coming out of a school like Princeton. At Princeton, students are surrounded by people with extraordinary professional goals and expectations. Starting freshman year, my teachers, parents, and classmates regularly told me there was nothing I couldn't do. In my first week, one guy on my hall announced he was going to be president, then spent twenty minutes de-

---

5 Corbett, Christianne, and Catherine Hill. *Graduating to a Pay Gap: The Earnings of Women and Men One Year After College Graduation.* Washington, DC: American Association of University Women, 2012. http://www.aauw.org/files/2013/02/graduating-to-a-pay-gap-the-earnings-of-women-and-men-one-year-after-college-graduation.pdf.

6 *The Simple Truth About the Gender Pay Gap.* Washington, DC: American Association of University Women, 2016. http://www.aauw.org/files/2016/02/SimpleTruth_Spring2016.pdf.

7 Corbett and Hill, *Graduating to a Pay Gap.*

tailing exactly how he was going to get there: he would spend two years at a consulting firm where he would specialize in one particular issue, run for local office at age twenty-five, run for Congress at thirty-five, and make his first presidential run before he turned fifty. Students at Princeton not only have lofty aspirations, they have plans. Less than a year after graduation, Ben Taub, a fellow member of the Princeton class of 2014, published a nine-thousand-word investigative piece in *The New Yorker,* the kind of journalistic accomplishment that typically, if you're lucky, tops off the end of a long, successful career. Another one of my classmates, Tim Hwang, cofounded FiscalNote, a company that analyzes legislative data and predicts the outcome of upcoming votes. Five months after graduation, Tim's company had more than $7 million in venture capital funding.[8]

When you're graduating with people like this—along with at least two dozen Rhodes, Marshall, Fulbright, and Gates Cambridge scholars—the first year out of college can feel like a race. People do impressive things while they're still students at Princeton, but professional accomplishments reach an entirely different level as soon as we begin our adult lives, unencumbered by a senior thesis and a rigorous class schedule.

Women in my graduating class were on campus when "Princeton Mom" Susan Patton wrote her infamous letter in the college newspaper, the *Daily Princetonian,* telling undergraduate women to lay off the books and focus on finding a husband.[9] Every woman

---

8 Heath, Thomas. "FiscalNote Snares $7 Million in Investments from Winklevoss, Singapore Wealth Fund," *Washington Post,* November 19, 2014, https://www.washingtonpost.com/business/capitalbusiness/fiscalnote-snares-7m-in-investments-from-winklevoss-singapore-wealth-fund/2014/11/18/95076abe-6f76-11e4-ad12-3734c461eab6_story.html.

9 Patton, Susan A. "Advice for the Young Women of Princeton: The Daughters I Never

I knew at Princeton had a visceral negative reaction to that message. Who was this woman, I remember thinking, and how dare she imply a romantic relationship was the best thing my female friends and I could take away from college? And also that we had to have that romantic relationship with a guy? If anything, Patton made us more determined to focus on our careers. We resented her narrative, and we didn't want to play into it. Coming out of Princeton, there is a lot of shame associated with making sacrifices for a boyfriend or girlfriend. We knew we shouldn't be spending this important year—the first year out in the real world—focusing on a relationship.

Over the course of the first year after graduation, I realized all the women in this book, to varying extents, felt torn. On the one hand, we wanted to challenge ourselves and take risks. In his book *Emerging Adulthood,* Jeffrey Arnett, professor of psychology at Clark University, identifies "self-focus" as one of the characteristics that makes the period between adolescence and adulthood so unique.[10] For most people, this is the time in our lives when we're least tied to other people. We're in a position to decide what's best for ourselves, without factoring in anyone else. And that makes us feel like we should make our own decisions while we still can.

On the other hand, however, the women I interviewed wanted to feel comfortable and loved. This was because everything in our lives—our jobs, our relationships, our home base—felt unstable,

---

Had," letter to the editor, *Daily Princetonian,* March 29, 2013, http://dailyprincetonian.com/opinion/2013/03/letter-to-the-editor-advice-for-the-young-women-of-princeton-the-daughters-i-never-had/.

10 Arnett, Jeffrey Jensen. *Emerging Adulthood: The Winding Road from the Late Teens Through the Twenties,* 2d ed. (New York: Oxford University Press, 2015), 9.

subject to change. Right after graduation, most college grads lose their college community. Even if you're lucky enough to have some semblance of a community around you, with the average twenty- to twenty-four-year-old changing jobs approximately every sixteen months, someone is always moving.[11] If you're not planning a change—grad school, a year abroad, or a job in a new city—your best friend or your boyfriend is. We get lonely. We're alone way more than most of us have ever been before, and we're scared that whatever stability we do have could be yanked out from under us at any moment.

These conflicting emotions created a lot of tension for the women in this book. Again and again, we had to make choices between professional and personal advancement and a relationship. What surprised me was how much we wanted to choose the relationship. Over the course of the year, every woman in this book clung to a romantic partner—either drawing closer to someone she had begun dating in college or starting to date someone new. But we also put a lot of effort into maintaining other existing relationships, particularly with our parents. All five of us were hyperaware of the emptiness that swelled in our lives after graduation, and we desperately wanted to fill it—to rebuild some semblance of the community we used to have in college.

ONE OF THE BIG THINGS that differentiates us—the Millennial generation—from previous generations is that we tend to be older

11 "Employee Tenure News Release," Bureau of Labor Statistics, last modified September 18, 2014, http://www.bls.gov/news.release/archives/tenure_09182014.htm.

when we get married. In 1960, 59 percent of adults between the ages of eighteen and twenty-nine were married. By 2011, that number had dropped to 20 percent.[12] A lot of sociologists and journalists have painted Millennials, particularly Millennial women, as resistant to serious relationships. In her 2013 *New York Times* feature story "Sex on Campus: She Can Play That Game, Too," Kate Taylor interviewed a group of high-achieving women at the University of Pennsylvania.[13] She concluded that these women "envisioned their 20s as a period of unencumbered striving, when they might work at a bank in Hong Kong one year, then go to business school, then move to a corporate job in New York. The idea of lugging a relationship through all those transitions was hard for many to imagine." She quotes sociologist Elizabeth Armstrong, a professor at the University of Michigan focusing on young women's sexuality, who says that, in their twenties, college women see romantic relationships as unnecessary distractions from their goals.

Maybe Taylor and Armstrong are right: when we're in college, especially at elite schools, women deprioritize relationships. But the narratives in this book suggest that might change right after we graduate, when we lose the kind of structured community we've had since kindergarten. The women I interviewed wanted support and stability. We wanted to move closer to the people around us, even if that occasionally meant making personal and professional sacrifices.

---

12 Pew Social and Demographic Trends. *Barely Half of U.S. Adults Are Married—A Record Low.* Washington, DC: Pew Research Center, 2011. http://www.pewsocialtrends.org/files/2011/12/Marriage-Decline.pdf.

13 Taylor, Kate. "Sex on Campus: She Can Play That Game, Too," *New York Times,* July 12, 2013, http://www.nytimes.com/2013/07/14/fashion/sex-on-campus-she-can-play-that-game-too.html?pagewanted=all&_r=0.

While most Millennial women, particularly those graduating from elite colleges, expect to wait until their late twenties or early thirties to get married, we start thinking about our future partner and family long before that.[14] Eighty-six percent of us say we eventually want to get married,[15] and 52 percent say that "being a good parent" is "one of the most important things in [our] lives."[16] That's before the vast majority of us have children. Even though we're far from ready to walk down the aisle, committed romantic relationships are generally important to women in their early twenties. A 2010 sociology study by Robin Simon and Anne Barrett showed that, in early adulthood, being in a relationship has a greater positive emotional impact on women than on men.[17] Young adults—male and female—are less likely to become depressed if they're in a relationship, but the correlation between breakups/being single and depression is significantly more pronounced for women. I'm not saying that women my age need a relationship to be happy. That's certainly not true. Just that, for whatever reason, many of us find it harder to be single in our early twenties than the guys we graduated with.

And we're not just looking for someone we can regularly go to for sex. TV shows like *Girls* and *Gossip Girl* show women in their early twenties having a lot of casual sex. Relationships, when they

---

14 Taylor, "Sex on Campus."

15 Arnett, *Emerging Adulthood,* 85.

16 *Millennials: A Portrait of Generation Next.* Washington, DC: Pew Research Center, 2010. http://www.pewsocialtrends.org/files/2010/10/millennials-confident-connected-open-to-change.pdf.

17 Simon, Robin W., and Anne E. Barrett. "Nonmarital Romantic Relationships and Mental Health in Early Adulthood: Does the Association Differ for Women and Men?" *Journal of Health and Social Behavior* 51, no. 2 (June 2010): 168–182. http://www.jstor.org/stable/pdf/27800379.pdf?_=1460941575504.

do happen, rarely last long without one character cheating on the other. But these images aren't representative of Millennial women. Today, women in their early twenties actually have less casual sex than the previous generation. According to a study by the Archives of Sexual Behavior, Millennials will have had eight sexual partners by the time they turn forty-five, whereas Baby Boomers had an average of eleven.[18] Only 33 percent of women in their twenties say it's okay for two people to have sex if they are not emotionally involved with each other.[19] Right out of college, it seems like most of us want more out of our relationships. We want a meaningful connection and some sense of stability.

At the same time, however, the women I interviewed weren't sure if monogamy was the way to go. After we graduated, three of the five of us had experiences with polyamory, or "poly": having more than one romantic partner. Poly is different from just hooking up with a lot of people at the same time because, in most cases, you're emotionally invested in at least one relationship. You have a boyfriend or girlfriend—whom you call your "primary"—but you also might have a secondary and a tertiary. While only 5 percent of Americans are currently in polyamorous relationships, the poly population is disproportionately young, liberal, and highly educated—characteristics that all the women I interviewed shared.[20]

---

18 Paquette, Danielle. "Why Millennials Have Sex with Fewer Partners Than Their Parents Did," *Washington Post,* May 6, 2015, https://www.washingtonpost.com/news/wonk/wp/2015/05/06/why-millennials-have-sex-with-fewer-partners-than-their-parents-did/.

19 Arnett, Jeffrey Jensen, and Joseph Schwab. *The Clark University Poll of Emerging Adults: Thriving, Struggling, and Hopeful.* Worcester, MA: Clark University, 2012. http://www2.clarku.edu/clark-poll-emerging-adults/pdfs/clark-university-poll-emerging-adults-findings.pdf.

20 Khazan, Olga. "Multiple Lovers, Without Jealousy," *The Atlantic,* July 21, 2014. http://www.theatlantic.com/health/archive/2014/07/multiple-lovers-no-jealousy/374697/.

I think polyamory appealed to so many of the women because it allowed them to simultaneously have a serious relationship and maintain their independence. It seemed like a win-win situation. In a poly relationship, they felt like they could remain "self-focused" and embrace the wide array of personal and professional possibilities presented to them during their first year out. But for everyone who tried it, poly didn't turn out to be such an easy solution. Many of the women I interviewed found that being in an open relationship made their lives less stable than having no relationship at all.

The interesting point is not just that we were all in relationships during our first year out of college. It's that we generally prioritized these relationships to a degree that, before graduation, we never expected we would. Three of us changed or seriously considered changing our professional trajectories to be closer to our romantic partners—either physically or emotionally. Another two started serious relationships after promising themselves they would steer clear of anything that wasn't strictly casual. And everyone, at one point or another, questioned the impact her relationship was having on her post-college life.

Romantic relationships weren't the only ones that mattered to the women I interviewed. During our first year out of college, many of us also fixated on relationships with our parents. I'd always assumed that after college I'd immediately become completely financially independent from my parents and, by extension, less concerned with their opinions on how I was living my life. That didn't happen. One year after graduation, my parents still covered my health insurance and cell phone bill. They also helped me out whenever I had any kind of large, unanticipated expense: a new laptop when mine was stolen or a last-minute flight to see a sick family member. Today, 50 percent of young people aged eighteen to twenty-four depend on their parents for some kind of financial support,[21] and 45 percent of college grads in the same age range moved back in with their parents after graduation.[22]

It's not that we want to rely on our parents. According to a 2012 Clark University poll, 74 percent of eighteen- to twenty-nine-year-olds "would prefer to live independently of their parents, even if it means living on a tight budget."[23] But with the rising costs of housing, health care, and personal technology, we often feel like we have to accept financial help. And that means parents are more involved in our lives at this stage than they used to be: 55 percent of eighteen- to twenty-nine-year-olds say they communicate with their parents either every day or almost every day.[24]

For most people my age, this increased communication with parents leads to better relationships.[25] But that's not true across the board. For three of the five women in the book, myself included, relationships with parents deteriorated at some point during the first year out. This happened because our parents disagreed with our personal or professional decisions. The girls who stayed on a parent-approved path, on the other hand, got closer to their parents as the year went on.

---

21 *Millennials: A Portrait of Generation Next.*

22 Weissmann, Jordan. "Here's Exactly How Many College Graduates Live Back at Home," *The Atlantic,* February 26, 2013, http://www.theatlantic.com/business/archive/2013/02/heres-exactly-how-many-college-graduates-live-back-at-home/273529/.

23 Arnett and Schwab, *Clark University Poll of Emerging Adults.*

24 Ibid.

25 Arnett, *Emerging Adulthood,* 49–82.

With one possible exception, we all cared a lot about what our parents thought. We spent an extraordinary amount of time agonizing over our relationships with them and how our decisions would make them feel. When we chose to go against what they wanted, we didn't do it lightly. Most of us desperately sought their approval. Without the familiar pillars of our friends, teachers, and mentors from college to keep us grounded, reminding us of who we were and what we wanted, we saw our parents as guideposts. If they didn't agree with what we were doing, we thought maybe we shouldn't be doing it.

Between parents and romantic partners, all five of us struggled to figure out how dependent we could be and how independent we should be. It was a hard balance to strike. Often we spent just as much (if not more) time thinking about what we were supposed to want as what we actually wanted.

Before I graduated, I wish someone had told me how difficult the upcoming year would be. But no one talked about it. I knew a lot of older students, but it wasn't until I started writing this book, and opening up about the things that were hard for me, that I heard anyone call their first year out one of the most challenging years of their lives. Coming out of an elite school, no one wants to be the first to say that life after college isn't what they expected. No one talks about the isolation, the identity crisis, or the all-consuming panic that sets in when you realize you have no idea what you want to do with the rest of your life and no one around to point you in the right direction. No one admits how much you want to lean on the people around you.

Like I said, I know the experiences of the women in this book won't resonate with everyone. Almost one million women graduate from college in the United States every year, and I only wrote about five. But there is one thing I think will ring true for every recent grad who reads these stories: the first year out of college is a hard year. For me, it was the hardest year. It helps to know that it's hard for everyone else, too.

CHAPTER ONE

Graduation

It was 9:45 A.M., and I was still in the bathroom, desperately trying to figure out how to pin my graduation cap to my head. In fifteen minutes, my class would start processing into the chapel for baccalaureate, the religious ceremony that would kick off Princeton's three-day graduation. With five bobby pins clenched between my teeth, and ignoring my phone as it vibrated on top of the toilet, I repeatedly dug one of the pins into my scalp, willing it to gain just enough traction to get me through the next hour. When my phone started to ring for the fourth consecutive time, I gave up, shoved the bobby pins into the pocket underneath my shiny black polyester robe, and sprinted toward Nassau Hall.

I scanned the faces of the hundreds of people on the quad, peering under caps, looking for my best friend, Katherine. I couldn't believe how many of them I didn't recognize. The line started to move, and I panicked. I was dangerously close to being the weird loner sitting between two groups of strangers, holding my cap on my head through the whole ceremony.

Whatever way I looked at it, that day seemed incredibly significant. Everything in my life up until that point had been preparation: years devoted to making myself a better worker, a better friend, and generally a more competent member of society. It was the beginning of my adult life. I definitely didn't want to start it alone.

When I finally found Katherine at the front of the line, I gave her a big hug.

"Hey, Caroline," she said, laughing. "Is everything okay?"

"Yeah," I said, still hugging her. "I'm glad I found you."

As we started to move forward, I spotted my dad in the crowd, standing on top of a table with his Nikon around his neck, flailing his arms to make me look in his direction.

"Smile," Katherine said, squeezing my hand. "Here we go."

■ ◆ ■ ◆ ■

Denise Aboya stood next to her father as he addressed everybody in the room: Denise's mom, her brothers and little sister, her grandparents, her cousins, her aunts and uncles, and many people she'd always called aunts and uncles. There were more than forty of them, and they were all there to celebrate her.

Some of the women wore floor-length African wrappers: bright yellow, orange, and burgundy patterned fabrics with matching beaded necklaces and head ties. Most of the people at the party weren't actually related—just part of the same tribe in Bamenda, a city in northwestern Cameroon. Many of them had arrived in the United States more than twenty years ago and settled into American suburbs to raise their children. Their homes were scattered across the East Coast and Midwest, but they found one another.

Every once in a while they came together to talk, sing, and worship, gathered around vats of jollof rice and meat smothered in garlic, ginger, and habanero pepper. This was one of those times.

"We have many different last names," Denise's father said, "but if you look far back in the tree, I'm sure all of us are related. We are one.

"At the ceremony tomorrow, there will be seats at the front reserved for us," Mr. Aboya continued, speaking slowly and deliberately, with a strong Cameroonian accent. "We will be sitting next to the former vice president of the United States, Al Gore."

"Mm-hmm," said one of Denise's aunts, closing her eyes and lifting her hand to the ceiling. "We are praising, we are praising."

The rest of the room murmured in agreement: "Yes, sir."

"Nothing less for us!" shouted Denise's fourteen-year-old sister, Joanna.

Denise appreciated how excited they all were to be here. After baccalaureate, a few of her aunts had scavenged the seating area for any left-behind pamphlets and napkins, stockpiling as many as possible just because they had the Princeton seal.

My parents did the same thing. They have a box of Princeton memorabilia at our house: envelopes, coasters, pins. Every couple of months while I was in college, my dad would ask me to buy him a new pack of Princeton pens. "They just write better than any other pen I've ever had," he'd say. But they were your standard black Bic ballpoints, and I knew better. When I got into Princeton, my parents couldn't understand why I didn't immediately send in my deposit. It was the first time I felt like they might actually force me to do something. My high school English teacher said it was because of the "gold ring." "Having a kid who goes to Princeton," he told me, "is like wearing one all the time." A lot of Princeton parents have worn these gold rings for years—they went to Princeton or another Ivy, as did their parents, as did their parents. But for Denise and me—and our families—this was a new thing. My dad never went to college, and my mom went to a two-year art school. Denise's parents both attended state universities in Illinois. So Princeton was a big deal. Graduation was a big deal. And this raised the stakes for what came after it.

"We are sitting in this place of honor," Denise's father continued, "because tomorrow Denise will be receiving one of the most prestigious awards at Princeton University."

Denise thought about what her mom told her the day she started high school: stand up straight, shoulders back. Denise had been a chronic sloucher. She'd always been tall—almost six feet by the time she turned sixteen. Growing up, she hated the way her head popped up above everyone else's. She hated attention from the basketball coaches at her all-white, suburban middle school—guys who refused to accept the towering black girl's complete lack of coordination. Standing in her uncle's living room, in front of her whole family, Denise was sorely tempted to give in to old instincts: to hunch her shoulders, look at the ground, and make herself small. It was too much. She believed that all this—graduating from Princeton with honors and the special award—happened because of God and the people around her. It felt like a lie to take the credit. She wasn't even sure she'd want the praise and recognition if she thought she deserved it, because taking the credit came with a whole slew of expectations: success, wealth, Harvard Medical School.

Her father kept talking, directing everyone toward Denise and her accomplishments. She hated it, but he wasn't the kind of guy you stopped midconversation. Mr. Aboya is six-foot-three, with wide shoulders and a torso like a punching bag chock-full of heavy cement. Unshakable. "He's a *man,*" Denise says to describe him.

"Denise has made us very proud. And being our first child, we thank her so much because—"

"The rest will follow suit!" yelled one of Denise's aunts.

"Amen," said one of her uncles.

Another aunt yelled, "Let them follow!"

The room was full of children. Denise knew many of her parents' friends had brought their kids along tonight, hoping they'd be inspired to follow her example.

After Denise's dad finished speaking, her grandfather stood up. Back in Bamenda, Vincent Aboya was the *tita,* the "prince." As he got to his feet, the room fell instantly silent. He stood still for a minute before starting to speak, taking his time to choose his words. It was a noble kind of pause. He knew they would wait.

"When Denise started Princeton, I told her father that if I have to come back to America again, it will be for Denise's graduation," he said. "And here I am."

Everyone clapped. Vincent had been to America five times in his life. The trip was expensive and the visa application difficult. But he had come, and Denise understood the weight of that honor.

"Denise has lifted the Aboya name high," he said, making eye contact with his granddaughter. "We know more great things will come."

■ ◆ ■ ◆ ■

As the rest of our class screamed the lyrics to the incessantly peppy pop song "Call Me Maybe" at ten o'clock the night after baccalaureate, Alex sat in her dorm room, staring at her computer screen, trying to finish a research paper. After moving out a few days before, her room was completely empty except for a pillow and blanket, a fluorescent desk lamp, and a stack of old library books. Alex picked at the chicken sandwich she'd bought at the campus store for dinner, trying to ignore the singing. Even though she couldn't see it, she knew exactly what was happening on the other side of the quad. Singers lined the steps of Blair Arch, arms draped on shoulders, falling over one another to jump and dance every time the chorus came on. They tried to outdo one another with hand gestures, miming the phone—"call me"—and the question—"maybe?"

Every year, for an hour over graduation weekend, the senior class crowds onto the same staircase and sings songs that defined their four years at Princeton—a tradition called "Senior Step Sing." Ponytailed girls in tank tops pass around spiked bottles of Minute Maid orange juice. Some show up drunk—more leave drunk—but most are just high on the last moments of intense togetherness. This particular graduation ritual is specially designed to manufacture nostalgia: seniors stand next to hundreds of people they've never spoken to, reflecting on a common college experience that, in reality, was different for every person in the class. Wanting to feel like a part of something before they have to scatter.

Alex wasn't in the mood. She didn't want to pretend she felt any strong connection to her graduating class. Her friend Jay was the only person she felt like celebrating with, and Jay was out with her parents. If Alex went to Senior Step Sing, she knew she'd be draping her arms around strangers or people she vaguely recognized from class. Alex took three years off before starting senior year—everyone she'd known before she left was gone. Now her friends were mostly graduate students and post docs at Princeton. Her girlfriend, Bethany, was working on her PhD.

Alex took a picture of her sad face—big eyes, bottom lip out—and sent it to Bethany on WhatsApp, a messaging application they always used to keep in touch: "Miss you, Cat Cat." If I'm with Alex when she texts Bethany, she'll typically show me the message, usually with a big, goofy grin on her face. She wrinkles her nose and says, "We're gross." But she keeps smiling.

Alex has a great smile. After spending a few weeks sitting across from her in a women's studies seminar in the fall of our senior year, it's what made me send a slightly creepy e-mail asking her to hang out outside of class. I'd never met Alex before or talked with her about anything except the course, "Women in Higher Education in the Contemporary United States," but I knew that I wanted to know her. A lot of people at Princeton are so consumed with their own big goals and hectic daily schedules that they rarely take the time to look you in the eye, connect, and listen. Even responding to a classmate's question in class, many students will talk mostly to the teacher, primarily concerned with the academic brownie points they're scoring for their answer. Alex isn't like that. When she'd respond to me in class, she'd lean forward slightly, make eye contact, and smile. I could always tell she genuinely cared about what I had to say.

Alone in her dorm room, Alex couldn't help thinking about her parents, at a Comfort Inn less than a mile away. She hadn't seen them for almost a year. It was hard not to wonder why they had come all this way, from their tiny town in Arkansas, just to sit by themselves in a hotel room.

Alex's parents came to the baccalaureate ceremony that morning, but it hadn't gone well. Daniel Grady, Alex's dad, is a Southern Baptist minister, and baccalaureate is a religious celebration of graduation that draws on all kinds of different faiths: Judaism, Christianity, Hinduism, Buddhism, Taoism. She thought he'd be interested in this part of graduation—that he'd appreciate the nod to faith from a secular school. But when Alex found him waiting for her outside the chapel, he had his head in his hands. As he looked up at her, scowling and rubbing his temples, she remembered all those times he'd called other religions "cults." He'd always said the Southern Baptist faith was the only way to heaven.

"Dad," she said, gesturing to Jay, "I want you to meet my best friend from college."

"Nice to meet you, Mr. Grady," Jay said, reaching out her hand.

Daniel grunted, ignored the handshake, and looked away.

After our class swarmed out of the chapel, families rushed to find their graduate and steer him or her away to an archway or a marble staircase or a strategically placed oak tree. There were pictures, hugs, and congratulations before the families dispersed to whatever restaurant they made reservations at three months ago. Jay went to find her parents, leaving Alex alone with her mom and dad.

"Baby, your daddy's not feeling too well," Emily Grady, Alex's mom, said. "I think we're just gonna head back to the hotel, have a little rest. We'll see you tomorrow, okay?"

In the car on the way back to the hotel, no one said anything. When they arrived, Daniel jumped out of the backseat and slammed the door before Alex even put the car into park. Alex's mom turned to her, tears in her eyes.

"I'm so sorry he's being a jerk, honey. It's my fault. It's all my fault."

After assuring her mom that Daniel's behavior had nothing to do with her, Alex hugged her good-bye and started the drive back to campus.

"Fuck you, Dad," she said. "Fuck you."

It felt good to curse her dad, alone in her car. Right now, she wished he would just leave. She'd asked him to come to graduation, on the phone back in April. She'd made an event of it—practiced what she'd say beforehand, how she'd convince him. "I feel like there is this huge hole in my life where my parents are supposed to be," she'd said. And he melted. He bought tickets to graduation and started planning a family vacation to Europe—a particularly grand gesture for her father, who never spent money on vacations. For a while, Alex thought he might have forgiven (or forced himself to forget) what he found out in December. But then he changed again. He did that a lot. He made Alex feel loved and whole and supported, and then, just when she started to get comfortable, he'd take it back. Slamming the car door without saying good-bye, he was taking it back.

■ ◆ ■ ◆ ■

For two years, Michelle Sullivan belonged to the most exclusive group at Princeton University: the Ivy Club. Ivy is one of Princeton's eleven eating clubs—mansions where upperclassmen eat, drink, and party.

Ivy is the oldest and arguably most prestigious of these clubs, described by F. Scott Fitzgerald as "detached and breathlessly aristocratic," with an endowment larger than a lot of small liberal arts colleges. Every night inside the brick Jacobethan building, waiters serve dinner to 150 undergraduates on white tablecloths. To become one of these 150 people, you go through a series of ten interviews with older club members. If just one gives you the thumbs-down, you're out. If you get into Ivy, you're special—rich, beautiful, social—and you're made to feel it. On the night of initiations, all new members are given a silver Tiffany necklace and a silk Brooks Brothers tie.

Rushing to get in line at baccalaureate, Michelle debated which group of friends to seek out and sit with. The night before, she'd eaten dinner with her friends from Ivy, Claire and Rebecca, her best friends for her first three years of college. Claire had been texting Michelle all morning, updating her on where their group was standing in line.

But Michelle didn't want to sit with her Ivy friends. She wasn't even sure they actually wanted to sit with her. So much of the Ivy world was about keeping up appearances. It was about being nice to people's faces and judging them hard right after they left. Michelle knew her Ivy friends talked about her. From their perspective, she'd done the most egregious thing she could conceivably do at Princeton: leave Ivy for Terrace, the club known as a haven for hippie stoners that you didn't even have to apply to get into. By trading in her Tiffany necklace for a communal bong, she'd spat in the faces of the proudest people on campus.

Michelle fit into Ivy. She had the pedigree for it. She'd been groomed by the best prep schools in London and shuttled to voice and piano lessons by parents who didn't go to work—who devoted all their energy to raising Michelle and her brother. In London, her extended family is essentially royalty. Her family owns an international hotel chain, worth almost $2 billion. Her relatives are always on television, cutting ribbons and chatting on talk shows. When she walks down the street with her grandmother, people take selfies and ask for autographs.

So Michelle could talk to the Ivy people. Well versed in the language of the elite, she understood what topics were too controversial for the dinner table. She knew it was never okay to discuss money problems. She'd mastered the appropriate way to talk about her sexuality to seem flirtatious but not easy: preferably only around boys, after a few drinks, while laughing a lot. She knew these scripts. By the time she left Ivy, breaking them had become a kind of obsession.

"For me, boundaries are made to be crossed," Michelle told me. "I get this urge to do something crazy."

Michelle's Ivy friends didn't understand this. They took themselves seriously—in Michelle's opinion, too seriously. Claire wouldn't go to sleep at night until she finished exactly seven *New York Times* articles, so that when she talked to her dad, he'd think his daughter was smart and well informed. The Ivy girls were from important families, so they felt they had important obligations. Michelle wanted to be around people who were relaxed and off-the-cuff: people who talked loudly about sex in public places, who made her laugh so hard that she snorted, and who could always come up with something fun to do on a Saturday night (just getting drunk didn't count; she wanted real experiences). If you didn't do these things, according to Michelle, you were "vanilla." Serious. Dull.

I used to find all this slightly intimidating. I listened to Michelle talk about vanilla people and nodded my head—throwing in a "ugh, I know" and "that's the worst" every once in a while for good measure. But the whole time I'd be wondering whether she thought that I was vanilla, too. I was in Tower, an eating club with a reputation for being extremely straitlaced. While some other eating clubs happily blow their budget on beer and eat hot dogs for the last few weeks of school, Tower members order every meal from a computer in the dining room, choosing from more than seventy different options for lunch and dinner. Tower is overwhelmingly type A, home to the debaters, the student government, the theater directors, and the editors of the newspaper. In Michelle's world, that wasn't cool. And I didn't want her to associate me with it.

I'll never be a party girl. I'm not going to suggest we take vodka shots on a Monday night, and I'm at peace with that. I'd rather sit around drinking tea with a few good friends, while watching my favorite TV show, *Gilmore Girls,* and working on a craft project. "Popular" isn't something I'm too worried about. "Boring" or "vanilla," on the other hand, is much more concerning. I think I was so bothered by Michelle badmouthing her Ivy friends because, on the surface, I looked like them. I went to a private all-girls school in a Connecticut commuter town. My dad lived on Nantucket, a popular summer vacation spot for Wall Street men—and their daughters. These facts have a tendency to come up fairly early in conversations with new people, and I'm always afraid I'm being judged for them. I started to get over the insecurity I felt around Michelle when I realized that her instincts probably aren't all that different from my own. She's used to people writing her off as a privileged rich girl with a narrow perspective on the world. Calling the Ivy girls "vanilla" may have just been a way of convincing other people that she wasn't.

When Michelle located where her Terrace friends were standing in line, she thought about Sam, the guy she'd been dating for the last two years. In his free time, Sam played double bass, smoked a lot of pot, and read books by authors like Jack Kerouac and Hermann Hesse. He wasn't in Ivy or any other eating club. He was above that somehow, cooking his own meals in a housing complex with other kids who had decided against the eating-club scene. When they started hooking up, Sam had been embarrassed by Michelle. She'd go over to his dorm, and if his friends were around, he would make up some reason for why she had to go home. He didn't want them to know he was dating the kind of Princeton princess they liked to make fun of.

This was new for Michelle. Usually guys loved her. They loved how upfront she was about what she wanted. But Sam judged her in a way that made her judge herself. He was intimidatingly alternative—an encyclopedia of which music was cool-weird and which had crossed over to become cliché-weird. He told her that people in Ivy were shallow, Bon Iver (her favorite band) was melodramatic, and her college a cappella group was juvenile. Michelle had wanted to make him want her. She'd wanted to prove she wasn't just another Ivy girl. She was rich—that couldn't be helped. But she changed other things.

As she approached her Terrace friends, Michelle wondered if these decisions had really been her own. Did she want to ditch Claire and her old friends from Ivy? Did she actually think they were boring? She'd spent the last two years painstakingly trying to mold herself into Sam's perfect girl. She'd tried so hard to be different and exciting, but she wasn't entirely sure it was real.

A month ago, Sam told her he wanted to break up before the summer. Graduation would be their last weekend together.

■ ◆ ■ ◆ ■

Olivia Surat wouldn't talk to me over graduation. She was angry, and I understood why. A few days before baccalaureate, I made her stay a night in the campus hospital. She tried to get out of it, and I told the nurses she was lying.

Of the four women I interviewed for this book, Olivia is the only one I knew before I started working on it. One night in September of senior year, I talked to Olivia in the Tower dining room for three hours about how she thought monogamy was a social construct. She told me about her poly (polyamorous) community in New York City and her obsession with meeting people through online dating websites, "just to make friends." She wore a beanie, fingerless gloves, and dark colors—black, gray, and olive green—even in the spring, even at meals. She wanted to teach me Thai massage. Olivia was the least vanilla person I had ever met. I couldn't decide if I had a crush on her, or was just completely fascinated by her willingness to adopt a lifestyle so opposed to what most Princeton students had been taught to want.

The week before graduation, the whole senior class divides into groups of eight or ten and rents houses somewhere, mostly in Myrtle Beach, South Carolina, or the Outer Banks, North Carolina. Olivia came with me to Nantucket.

I knew she was having a hard time before we left. She was on the verge of failing two classes, her bulimia was getting bad again, and if she didn't get a job before the end of May, she would have to go back to Malaysia after graduation. And then there was Leon. She'd been dating him for three months. He was what the polyamorous community would call her "primary"—basically the same concept as a boyfriend, minus the exclusivity. When Leon started dating Olivia, he decided (rather conveniently, I thought) that he was poly, too. A few days before we left for Nantucket, he decided (again, quite conveniently) that no girl was off-limits and kissed Allison, one of Olivia's best friends. Olivia found an e-mail he wrote to Allison right after the kiss, saying how sexy she was and how he couldn't remember the last time he felt that deep of a connection to another person. "It really hurt because he never said those things to me," Olivia told me right after she read it.

The night Olivia arrived on Nantucket, the two of us went out for a walk before dinner.

"I love him, Caroline," she said. "I need him in my life every day."

"I know it feels like that now, but he's really not—"

"Of course it makes sense that he'd want her. Allison is so much more confident than I am. She's always in control, and Leon wants to be dominated."

I couldn't blame Olivia for feeling inadequate next to this particular girl. Allison was supremely organized and competent. At Princeton, she was known for starting a nonprofit at age twenty. But it was clear to me that Olivia had certain qualities that set her apart.

"Listen to me," I said, and stopped walking. "Most people would never take the kind of risks you have. If you stayed in Malaysia, you could have started your own business, easy. You had the connections and everything—but you chose to leave, because you wanted to be somewhere else. You take risks to make yourself happy, and I bet that's going to lead to a better life." I paused and she nodded. "Do you think Allison would have left her home if she didn't know she'd be successful? I don't think I would have been that brave."

"Yeah, no, I guess you're right," she said.

I remember feeling pretty good about my pep talk as we walked back to the house. Like that was all she needed. Problem solved.

Halfway through dinner, I saw Olivia in the kitchen, downing a full glass of red wine in two gulps while everyone else was at the table. I just figured she wanted to get a little drunk, which didn't seem like a bad thing. A few minutes later, she left to make a call.

I don't know how I let so much time go by without wondering where she was. But when I went into my bedroom to check my phone an hour later, I had a voice mail from the Nantucket Police Department. Olivia was in the emergency room. A family down the road found her passed out in their bushes with a carving knife in her purse—the one from our kitchen.

When we got to the hospital, the nurses wouldn't let me go in to see her right away. They said they needed to get her cleaned up. I didn't really want to think about what that meant. They asked me for her personal information and I had to say "I don't know" over and over again. Her parents' names, her home address, her home phone number, her insurance information, her emergency contact—I didn't know any of it.

"Her parents live in Malaysia," I told them. "They don't speak English and she doesn't have contact with them."

One nurse scowled and rolled her eyes. I'm sure she didn't believe that a twenty-two-year-old could actually be completely estranged from her parents. It didn't seem fair to me for Olivia to be this alone this early. I thought about my dad waiting in the car outside, anxious to hear how his daughter's friend was doing, and listed myself as Olivia's emergency contact.

The doctors kept Olivia in the hospital overnight and we left Nantucket the next morning. Her teeth and lips were still purple from the wine. She kept asking about Leon: Has he called? Has he texted me? Is he worried? Do you think he still loves me? I didn't want to talk about him. All I could think about was getting Olivia back to Princeton—to the doctors and counselors at our university health center whom she could see for free until she graduated. That would just be a couple of days, but still. I needed someone else to care about what was happening to her. On the seven-hour car ride back to Princeton, Olivia seemed happy with this plan. She said she'd see whatever doctor the nurses suggested.

But when we pulled up outside the health center, Olivia immediately started trying to convince me to go back to my dorm. It was late, she said, and she could check herself in. I told her I wanted to make sure she was okay.

"Caroline, I can handle myself," she said. She was aggressive in a way I'd never seen her be before, and I realized she'd never had any intention of going to the health center. She wanted to come back to Princeton to see Leon.

When I finally coerced her into going inside with me, it got worse. She tried to get me to leave. I wouldn't. I sat outside the door while she talked to the nurses. I heard her tell them she was fine, she just drank too much the night before. On the phone, I'd told the nurses about the knife. When they asked Olivia about it, she told them it was a pocketknife, something she always carried with her.

"She's lying," I told the nurse in the hall.

They decided to hold her for the night. Before I left, I asked a nurse if I could go into her room and say good-bye.

"I'm sorry, honey," she said. "I don't think she wants to see you."

■ ◆ ■ ◆ ■

When you graduate from Princeton, you don't just walk across a stage and get a diploma. It's a three-day event. The first day is baccalaureate, the last is actual graduation, and the one in the middle is Class Day. This is when the school pulls out the big guns: comedian Steve Carell, President Bill Clinton, and, for us, in 2014, Vice President Al Gore—whomever they can get to upstage the comparable celebrations going on at Harvard and Yale. Two of the funniest people in the senior class give speeches, the presidents of the a cappella groups sing the school song, and students are honored with a few prestigious awards. There is less pomp and circumstance to Class Day than the two events it's sandwiched between. There are no robes. It doesn't feel like it's put on for the parents or the professors. It's for us—the graduates.

Which was why Alex was so sad to be missing it. On Monday morning, like the night before, she wasn't with our class. This time, as we all lined up in our matching class jackets, she was sitting at the Comfort Inn, trying hard to avoid making eye contact with her dad. Her parents sat on the bed and Alex sat cross-legged on the chair a few feet away.

"Okay, Alex, let's talk about the elephant in the room," said Daniel. He put on his glasses, like he did at the pulpit after his regular pre-sermon discussion of football and the weather. The glasses went on, the dimples faded. It was time to get serious.

"We're never going to approve of this, you need to know that. You've brought your mother and me a lot of shame."

Alex stared at the wall.

"Why didn't you tell us sooner?" Daniel asked. "We would have fixed this."

"How? What exactly would you have done to fix this?"

"We would have gotten you help."

"Do you mean you would have sent me to a reparative camp? A Southern Baptist psychologist? Exodus International?" Exodus International is an "ex-gay camp" where zealous Christian parents send their children to "pray the gay away."

"We would have done any or all of those things. I would have done something to help it go away."

In that moment, Alex realized that all the years of fear and hiding had been justified. A part of her had always wondered whether her secrecy had been an unnecessary precaution. She used to think that maybe she wasn't giving her parents enough credit—maybe they'd accept her if she were just honest with them. But now she knew she'd been right all along.

Alex kept staring. Emily, Alex's mom, buried her head in her sweater, sobbing.

"We still love you, but we don't want to be a part of this," Daniel continued. He stood up, leaned toward Alex, and wagged his large forefinger in her face. "You're never to talk to us about any person you're with. We never want to know a name. And don't you dare drag your mom into this. Do you hear me?"

Alex knew her dad was trying to push her buttons, so she focused on the small triumph of knowing something he didn't. Her mom did want to meet Bethany, and she had, yesterday. So while he talked at her, she thought about those precious thirty minutes: half an hour when two of the most important people in her life had met each other, laughed with each other, appreciated each other. Bethany had called it a "stealth heist." Alex and her mom had dropped her dad off at Panera and said they were going to the art museum. Then they drove to the crosswalk on Washington Street in downtown Princeton, stopping just long enough for Bethany to jump into the car. Alex knew her dad would be furious if he found out, which made telling him tempting. But she couldn't. Her mom still wanted to be with her dad, and she had to respect that, even if she didn't understand it.

Emily Grady would do anything for her daughter. When I met her in person, she said Alex was her best friend. "She loves me, despite all my warts," she said. Like her husband, Emily is a conservative Southern Baptist. But unlike her husband, she wasn't willing to write off her daughter for making choices that didn't align with her personal values.

Emily is a short, heavyset woman with a thick southern drawl. When she told me about her job as a pediatric nurse, she called the patients her "babies" and explained that she "just loves to hug on them." Every year, Emily is one of the nurses who volunteers to work on Christmas, so the young nurses can stay at home with their children. By nature, she is kind, quiet, and always eager to make other people happy. Those characteristics make it easy for her husband to push her around. "When I married Daniel, I didn't know who I was, so I was who Daniel thought I should be," Emily told me. After more than thirty years of marriage, that hadn't changed much. She was still afraid to stand up to her husband. So when he started yelling at Alex in the hotel room, she didn't say anything.

"Alex, listen to me," her dad said. "Look at me. Your mother and I feel like you've abandoned us."

In all the time I've known Alex, I've never heard her raise her voice. Bethany calls Alex's typical method of dealing with conflict "eskimoting." It's a cross between a robot, completely detached, and an Eskimo, who will traditionally leave his community when he gets old or sick, shutting out everyone who loves him. Given the choice of fight or flight, Alex almost always chooses the latter. She'd rather push people away than engage. But this time, she yelled.

"How can you say I abandoned you when you're the one who abandoned me? I couldn't move my head for two months, did you know that? I just had to lie in bed, Skyping into my classes or just missing them, and you took away my health care."

That past December, Alex's doctor diagnosed her with cervical dystonia, a rare disease that makes the muscles in your neck involuntarily contract, causing severe pain, migraines, and impeding movement. The doctor told her that, without treatment, she could lose control of her neck muscles for the rest of her life. Alex's dad found out she was gay a few days before she got this diagnosis. His first move was to take her off the family health insurance plan.

"I resent that you would say I'd deny you health care. I never knew you were really sick," he said.

"Oh, come on. You can't do that. I have the e-mails that you sent me. I'll get them out right now."

"No, you don't have to do that. We're talking."

When her dad first found out she was gay, Alex promised herself that she would respond with love. She called it "love-bombing": no matter what he said to her, no matter how absolutely he severed their relationship, she would be waiting for him when he wanted her to be a part of his life again. If he was dying, she'd be sitting by his bed. If he wouldn't let her in the room, she'd be waiting right outside.

For weeks at a time, Alex hadn't been able to move her neck or get out of bed. Dystonia prevented her from finishing her senior thesis, the hundred-page research paper Princeton requires every senior to write, which counted for 20 percent of her departmental GPA. That meant she couldn't officially graduate with the rest of our class. Tomorrow, she would walk across the stage and collect her diploma holder, but she wouldn't receive the actual document until after she finished her thesis later that year. The neurological movement disorder had wreaked havoc on her life for the past six months, and Daniel still refused to acknowledge its severity. Even so, Alex managed to be sympathetic. She knew how hard the situation was for her dad. Eventually, he was going to have to tell all his pastor friends that his only daughter was gay.

But sitting in the hotel room, Alex decided the love-bombing had to stop. It hurt too much for her to keep loving someone who wouldn't even acknowledge his mistakes. She wished she could make a clean break—walk out of the hotel room and stop trying. But for her mom's sake, Alex called a truce. They had to spend the next two weeks touring England and Ireland together.

THE NEXT DAY, as Alex walked to graduation in her cap and gown, a couple approached her on the street. The man asked if she was graduating. When she told him she was, he said, "That's an amazing achievement. Congratulations!" He shook her hand and introduced her to his wife. After they talked for a few minutes about Alex's post-graduation plans, the man looked her in the eye and said, "Your parents must be so proud." As she walked away, Alex thought about how much she wished this total stranger could have been her dad. Over the past three days, Daniel hadn't once said he was proud of her.

■ ◆ ■ ◆ ■

On Class Day, Denise's whole family wore the Bamenda gown, the traditional dress from their home city in Cameroon. The gowns were ankle-length, with yellow and orange geographic shapes—circles, stars, and spirals—hand-embroidered in random patterns against black fabric. They had elaborate collars, ten rings of alternating shades of red, white, yellow, and green. Each gown was slightly different. Denise's younger aunts wore dresses that were sleeveless and formfitting, while her grandfather's stood out with a distinctive leopard-print pattern, signaling his status within the family.

"Each time you see somebody put on this particular outfit, you know exactly where that person came from," said Nahvet, Denise's mom. "If you're from Bamenda, the gown is one thing you want to get. It shows your pride."

Before she met her family that morning, Denise walked up to the folding chairs right by the stage. Two weeks ago, when she found out she'd be receiving an award, Denise told her mom she would get special tickets for Class Day—at the front, next to Al Gore and the university president. "See if you can get fifteen," Nahvet said. Denise hadn't wanted to ask—most students got only four regular tickets—but Nahvet pushed her. Denise sent an e-mail to the Class Day organizers and hadn't heard back. But when she walked up to the stage that morning, she found fifteen seats with her name on them.

When her family arrived, her aunts started dancing around, chanting, "Aboya, reserved! Aboya, reserved! Aboya, reserved!"

Her brothers clapped Denise on the back and said, "You got us at the very front. Everybody will be seeing us!"

Nahvet turned to Denise in shock. "I knew this was a possibility, but . . . Princeton University really saved these seats for our humble family? What on earth did we do to merit this?"

Denise couldn't answer because she honestly didn't know why, out of 1,200 students, she was the one sitting here, being recognized for best exemplifying "clear thinking, moral courage, a patient and judicious regard for the opinions of others." She'd led a lot of activities and events at Princeton, but she felt sure there were other people who'd made a bigger impact.

Denise tried to quiet her mind. "Thank you, God," she prayed silently, closing her eyes. "Thank you for all of this. I know you have some purpose for me. I don't think I understand it yet, but I am so incredibly humbled by everything you've done. I'm going to try really hard and do the most with all you've given me. Thank you. I can't even—"

Nahvet nudged her arm. "It's about to start."

Denise could hear her heart drumming in her ears, in her throat. She turned her head just for a second to look back at her classmates, their families and friends. There must have been at least five thousand people in the audience, and she had to walk across the stage in front of all of them. Denise put her head on her mom's shoulder and whispered, "So many other amazing people must have been nominated, how did it end up being me? How will I stand up?"

Nahvet tilted her head down to look Denise in the eye and

smiled—a knowing smile, reminding Denise once again that, while her mom may be her best friend, she also had an extra twenty-nine years' worth of life experience. Throughout college, Denise called Nahvet at her lowest and most vulnerable moments: whenever she walked out of a test she thought she'd failed, or felt far away from her faith. For almost everyone else, she appeared perpetually strong and confident. But on the phone with her mom, Denise would break down and say, "Mommy, I don't think I can do this." Nahvet would listen, pause, and convince her that, in fact, she could.

When the dean of the college called her name, Denise's family erupted, jumping out of their chairs. Denise felt like she might be sick. Walking up to the podium, she tried hard not to make eye contact with anyone sitting on the stage. She shook hands with the dean, took the plaque, and began walking back toward her seat.

Everyone in the audience started laughing. "Come on back here, Denise," the dean said, chuckling. "You don't get to run away so soon!"

Denise stood next to the dean as she read out a list of her accomplishments. She could feel her hands trembling. The ocean of people in folding chairs extended as far as she could see, continuing past the edge of the quad and up the steps of nearby buildings. They were all staring at her. She didn't know what to do with her face. She knew she should probably smile and look out at the audience, but again, she just wanted to stare at the ground and will the speech to be over. Instead, she looked at her family, focusing on her father. A few months ago, she didn't think he would make it to graduation. He'd had a heart attack and, at one point, the doctors had given him a 20 percent chance of survival. But he was here now. It was the greatest gift God had ever given her, she thought, to be responsible for the look of intense pride in his eyes.

■ ◆ ■ ◆ ■

The morning after graduation, an hour before my dad arrived to start loading my stuff into our car, Olivia knocked on my door. The bed and chair were covered with clothes, posters, and loose-leaf papers I'd squirreled away from past classes, so we sat cross-legged on the floor.

"So how was this weekend?" I asked her, trying not to sound nervous. She hadn't responded to my text messages in a week, and I'd sent a lot of them.

"This weekend was perfect. I was so happy with Leon. So happy. We were so happy."

"That's great, Olivia. I'm really glad you had fun."

"Ah, so much fun," she said, looking down at her cell phone and flicking her finger across the screen. "Look. This picture is us from the night before graduation. We were hooking up in the library and then a guard found us. I didn't have my shirt on." She laughed. "And you know what we did after that?"

"What?"

"We went to the chapel and started hooking up there. It was hilarious."

She kept flipping through pictures from graduation weekend, and I started wondering why she'd stopped by. I had a hard time believing she'd come over just to chat after such a thorough silent treatment. Then she brought up the question I'd been expecting.

"So I can still stay at your house for the next few weeks, right? I was thinking of coming this Saturday."

We'd talked about this a while ago. She didn't have anywhere to go after graduation, and I said she could stay with my family in Connecticut until I left to teach English in China for a month later in the summer. The plan was for her to commute to New York City every day, while she looked for a job and met new people. But then Nantucket happened. My parents knew about the emergency room and the knife. My dad saw it firsthand. If someone my age was staying in our house, my parents saw that person as their responsibility. And after Nantucket, there was no way they were going to agree to take on Olivia.

I had no idea what to do. She was desperate. If she wasn't, she wouldn't have been asking. Olivia comes from a family with a lot of money. In Malaysia, her dad built his own construction company that's now worth over $100 million. Her parents wanted to support her but, last Christmas, she started refusing to take anything from them. She hadn't spoken to them since, and they didn't come to graduation. When I asked her why she was so determined to be financially independent, she said, "I don't like my parents, so I don't want to treat them like people that I like." If she took their money, she said she might feel like she owed them.

So that morning, a few hours before Princeton kicked us out of our dorms, Olivia was looking at a summer with no money, no job, no place to stay, and no health insurance to pay for a psychiatrist or medication. The week before, she'd blasted an e-mail out to a big group of friends and friends of friends in New York City, asking them to let her spend a few nights on a couch or a floor. She had a couple takers, but just enough to get her through two, maybe three weeks, tops. That night she planned to stay with a guy her roommate occasionally hooked up with in New York.

I told Olivia I hadn't had a chance to talk to my parents about it yet. This was true—I just didn't tell her I knew what they were going to say. It wasn't the right time. Earlier that morning, she'd taken Leon to the airport. He was on a plane to San Francisco, where he would start his new life working as a software engineer for the mobile payment platform Square. At least at first, they were going to try to make a long-distance relationship work.

"As soon as I get enough money, I'm going to move out there," Olivia said.

She knew Leon wasn't committed to her. She'd read the e-mail. She understood how intensely he felt about somebody else. I thought she would be making a mistake, leaving all her friends and professional contacts on the East Coast to follow a guy like that to California. But even though I thought this was a bad decision, I understood it. She wanted to hang on to something familiar. For the foreseeable future, Olivia wouldn't have any kind of security in her life: no romantic security or professional security or economic security.

"I literally have no idea what is going to happen to me tomorrow—I don't know where I'm going to sleep, who I'm going to meet, what I'm going to do—but I like that. I don't want my life to be boring right now."

Hearing her say that made me a little jealous. It made me wonder whether my choices were too safe. I certainly didn't want my life to be boring, either.

CHAPTER TWO

June–July

I drove home from graduation in the car alone with my mom. I'd been dreading this drive because I knew something was wrong. Something had been wrong all week. When I got my diploma, she flashed her formal smile—the one she used when she was obligated to look happy. But I knew it meant she was upset, disappointed, or just sad. At graduation, it was tough to stomach that smile. I'd worked so hard. My mom got to hear my name read out on the magna cum laude list and see me win a prize for my senior thesis. But none of that was enough to make her drop her shoulders, loosen the scarf wrapped tightly around her neck, and beam in the easy way I remembered from my high school graduation.

My mom used to be my person. Not my best friend (I never really understood people who said that about their moms—Denise has tried to explain it to me), but the person who meant much more to me than any other. I spent twelve years of my life growing up in Hong Kong, Germany, and England. Until high school, my dad was out of town on business almost every week, and my only siblings, two half sisters from my dad's first marriage, never lived with us. So it was my mom and me, floating alone on our own little island—whatever house or apartment we were renting at the time—surrounded by people who didn't speak our language or eat the breakfast cereal we liked. My mom had had a great job as a graphic designer in New York City, but she stopped working when we left the States. So I was all she had. She was all I had. And I think that ended up with us needing each other so intensely, we didn't know how to take space, or give it.

All of this was a relatively recent revelation. When we came back to the States in my freshman year of high school, my mom tried hard to manage my life. All nonacademic weekend activities required her approval. I could forget about ever going to a house party. She cried when she found out about my first boyfriend. I became a pro at stifling coughs, because the minute she heard one, she would sit down next to me on the couch for thirty minutes, with a box of tissues, telling me to "get it out," whenever she sensed a trace of phlegm. This continuous oversight was frustrating, and led to quite a few shouting matches, but my mom and I stayed close.

I think I willingly tolerated so many rules and restrictions because I valued our relationship so much. I knew my mom wanted me to have the best of everything. Her mother, my grandmother, raised five kids on her own. Growing up, my mom had to take care of herself. No one ever set clear limits or pushed her to reach her full potential. So my mom was determined to push me. To see all the things I could achieve with the most intense kind of parental support. Looking back now, I know I never would have gotten into Princeton without everything she did to keep me on track.

I also just loved hanging out with her. In high school, I would rather have stayed home with my mom on a Tuesday night, eating spaghetti and watching *American Idol,* than have gone out with my friends. No question.

My relationship with my mom changed the summer before my junior year of college. Two big things happened that summer: I found out that my parents were getting divorced, and I started my relationship with my boyfriend, Robert. And because of how everything unfolded, those two events will always be inextricably linked. I spent the first two months of that summer in China, teaching public speaking classes at two different universities. A few days after I came back, my mom and I flew down to Alabama to visit my grandma. In our hotel room one afternoon, I logged on to my mom's computer to check what movies were playing that night and saw an e-mail from a divorce court lawyer.

When I finally yanked my eyes away from the screen and asked her about the e-mail, she snapped: "Why are you looking through my stuff? Why are you on my computer?" It took a good five minutes for her to acknowledge what I saw and start explaining. When I started crying she looked surprised. "This can't come as a surprise to you," she said.

It did. Sure, my parents fought a lot, but I'd always assumed that all parents fought a lot. My mom and dad had been married for almost thirty years. If they'd been together that long, I figured they could work through anything. During particularly loud and emotional arguments, I'd considered the possibility of a divorce but always stopped short of seeing it as something that might actually happen. My dad was sixty-seven years old and my mom was fifty-five. Surely, I thought, it was too late to make any big changes.

But, as my mom explained to me in the hour after I first saw the e-mail, it wasn't too late. She reminded me that she was twelve years younger than my dad and tired of sacrificing the things she wanted for other people. Now it was time for her to start living her own life.

I asked a lot of questions and found out she'd told my dad that she wanted a divorce a few days after I left for China. They'd already told all our family friends, even a few acquaintances. My high school principal knew before I did. I was furious that my mom hadn't told me and even more furious that she seemed to be taking the situation so lightly. She deflected my anger by rounding on me, accusing me of snooping through her computer. I desperately wanted her to acknowledge how much more significant this situation was than me looking at her e-mail.

When my mom left to visit my grandma an hour later, I stayed in the hotel and called Robert. We weren't officially dating, but we had spent most of the summer talking on Skype for about an hour every day. Things were complicated because, at the time, I was dating someone else. To everyone who asked questions—my boyfriend, my parents, my roommates, my students in China—I maintained that Robert and I were just good friends. We participated in mock trial together, an extracurricular competition that simulated a courtroom. Along with our six other team members, we spent hours together every week, plus the occasional tournament weekend away. So it was easy to characterize our relationship as one built out of necessity—he was my "directing attorney," questioning me (or my "witness") in our pretend court of law, and we needed to practice. But the two of us knew better. Over the course of the semester before I left for China, our mock trial partnership and friendship turned into something else entirely.

The problem was that when I started liking Robert, I didn't stop liking my boyfriend. Before I came back to the States, I decided to stay in my existing relationship and tried to cut Robert out of my life. But then I found out about my parents' divorce, and Robert was the first person I wanted to call.

When I told him what happened, he immediately suggested that he drive to Alabama and pick me up. He was at home in Georgia for the summer, a five-hour drive from where my grandmother lived. My knee-jerk reaction was to completely dismiss this idea. I couldn't leave, I thought. My mom wouldn't let me. But then it occurred to me that I didn't have to do what my mom wanted me to do. With a few small exceptions, I'd played the role of obedient daughter my whole life, in large part because my mom and I were so close. I respected her opinion and figured that, even if I went behind her back and did something she told me not to, she knew me so well that she'd eventually find out anyway.

But in that moment, I didn't feel close to my mom. She'd kept news—big, life-altering news—from me for two months, so why shouldn't I keep something from her?

"Yeah, okay. Let's do it," I said to Robert. "Tell me when you're close. I'll make sure Mom isn't here so I can run out with my stuff."

That night, I scribbled a note on a piece of hotel stationery—"I won't be flying home with you . . . I'll find my own way back up to Princeton next week"—and ran out of the hotel, rolling suitcase in tow. I turned my phone off; I knew the calls from my mom would start any minute. Later, I found out that she had spent the next few hours calling every one of my friends (and, in some cases, their parents), asking if they had any idea where I'd gone.

I can't stress enough how out of character this whole episode was for me. I know that's a big part of why my mom resented

Robert as much as she did. When I eventually filled her in on the details of my escape, she rewrote them, telling my dad she was sure Robert had somehow coerced me into going with him. The alternative was that Robert had corrupted her only child, transforming me into someone who didn't respect or listen to her mother, and that wasn't a whole lot better.

The resentment intensified as Robert and I grew closer and it became clear to my mom that he wasn't like the other guys I'd dated. We passed the nine-month mark in our relationship—the point when I'd broken up with my last two boyfriends—and stayed strong, even as I spent a semester abroad. Slowly, I think my mom started to see Robert as someone with the potential to become my new person.

I thought my mom's attitude toward Robert would have to change eventually, but it got worse. She never used his name ("Will *someone* be picking you up after dinner?") and refused to let him stay in our house. Once, Robert dropped me off in Connecticut at midnight. He had to make it all the way back to DC, but it was too late and he needed sleep. Mom made him get a hotel down the street.

Looking back now, I realize my mom probably felt the way she did because of how my relationship with Robert seemed to impact my relationship with her. Whether the two were in any way related, it's true that the closer I got to Robert, the more distant I became from my mom. I'm sure she saw Robert as the thing standing between us, pushing us further and further apart.

Robert went to all the graduation events with my family, and I was pretty sure this was what made Mom so upset. It started in the months leading up to graduation, when I called to tell her who was getting my six tickets: my parents, my sister Milly, my cousin

Amber, my friend Ray, and Robert. Her voice was cold when she finally said something. "Don't you think you should invite more family . . . people who have really been there for you?" It was like she couldn't acknowledge the important role he had in my life.

"I felt like we didn't have any time together. I don't understand why he always had to be there," Mom said when I asked her what was wrong.

"Because he's my boyfriend, Mom, and I wanted him there."

"He's just always around. It's creepy. Doesn't he have anywhere else to be?"

"I don't think there's anywhere else he wanted to be. I would have been really upset if he didn't come to graduation."

"But this was our weekend—yours and mine and your father's. And I couldn't enjoy it with him there."

"Well, that's a problem, because he's going to be around a lot more now that we've graduated—at Thanksgiving and Christmas. You have to get over this."

"No, I don't. I can't change the way I feel about him."

"Then you're going to have to be okay with seeing a lot less of me. He's going to be around for many more years, maybe forever. And I'm not going to want to come home if he's not welcome."

"Then I guess you won't be coming home much."

I spent a long two weeks at my house. Away from home, it was a little easier to accept that my relationship with my mom was broken. That our phone calls were mostly logistical and ended abruptly. That attacks were far more common than compliments or words of support. Away, I could compartmentalize and steer my mind in another direction when things reminded me of the relationship we used to have. At home, that happy history was everywhere. Glass bottles of red Ragú sauce in the kitchen reminded me of spaghetti Bolognese dinners she used to make the night before I had a big test in high school. The sign outside the local shopping center—GOODWIVES—reminded me of our secret plan to replace it with one that read GOODHUSBANDS. The contrast between then and now was extremely painful. I would pretend that nothing had changed, open myself up to her and talk like we used to. But then she would criticize something in my life, and I would get overly defensive. I wasn't sure why, but whenever my mom got particularly aggressive or critical, I would think about sledding with her on this one hill by our house in Germany. I thought about the two of us barreling through three feet of powder snow in our ski pants and rolling around on the ground laughing. I missed that. And I wasn't sure if I'd ever get it back.

■ ◆ ■ ◆ ■

Three days after graduation, Denise was sitting on the New York City subway during rush hour, heading home from a nine-hour training session for her new job. She had a stack of flash cards for the MCAT, the medical school admissions test, in her lap, but couldn't force herself to look at them.

She hadn't stopped since graduation. There was too much to do: train for her new job, find an apartment and move in, finish her personal statement for med school, write the supplemental essays for each individual school, decide whether to take the MCAT a second time. Most people she knew who were applying to med school had their applications done by now. The supplemental essay questions weren't released until July, but it was common to study prompts from past years, predict what the essays would be, and get them done, just so your application could be one of the first submitted. That was how you won the game of rolling admissions, and Denise was way behind.

Since moving to New York, Denise had been thinking about Michael Jackson: how he sold one billion albums, but got depressed because he didn't think he could ever top himself. He could never calm down enough to feel good about all his achievements. She didn't want to be like that, but at the same time, she knew she had to keep going. After graduation, Denise didn't give herself any time to relax and feel proud. She immediately pushed herself to do more, to be better. If she didn't, she was afraid she might lose out on something.

"Why couldn't I just have taken two years off and applied to med school a year after graduation?" Denise asked me over the summer. "Why did it have to be now? Why do I feel like I have to take the MCAT again, when my first score was fine? Where does it end?"

She felt a lot of pressure, but she wasn't sure where it came from exactly. Her mom said she didn't care where she went to medical school, but Denise was pretty sure that wasn't true. Nahvet liked to brag. Her parents emigrated from Cameroon with almost no money. When Denise was born, her mom was halfway through her master's at the University of Illinois. The whole family lived in a small student-housing unit. As soon as Denise was old enough for day care, Nahvet sent her to the local branch of Head Start, a government-funded education program for low-income children. When Head Start wasn't in session, Nahvet would carry Denise to class.

"I've said to Denise, the title of her first book should be 'From Head Start to Princeton,'" Nahvet told me, laughing. "It's incredible."

Denise was convinced her parents thought she was superwoman. In her senior year of high school, they were the ones who convinced her to apply to Princeton. Her original college list didn't include any Ivy League schools. Early on, Washington University in St. Louis offered her a full scholarship, and she hadn't wanted to apply anywhere else. But her parents said she should at least try. The college application process prompted the worst series of fights Denise had ever had with her parents. She told them there was no way she'd get into a school like Princeton. Then she did, with an offer of full financial aid.

"Getting into Princeton was a blessing and a curse," Denise said. "Because now they all think I'm just being humble. I tried to tell them Princeton was a fluke. I've been asking people all around me, 'Please don't be disappointed when I don't get into the medical school you want me to get into.' But I think they still expect me to get into Harvard."

Denise is deeply afraid of failure, but that's something very few people know. On campus, she walked twice as fast as most people, taking long strides with her back perfectly straight and her shoulders back. No one at Princeton would have believed that she used to have a slouching problem. She wears metallic gold sneakers, peacock feather earrings, and colorful beach dresses from African street markets. In conversation with people who know more than her about a subject, Denise isn't afraid to stop them midsentence and say, "Wait a second, I don't understand." Before Denise started freshman year, she and her orientation group had dinner with Shirley Tilghman, Princeton's president at the time. During that dinner, Denise carried the conversation, engaging the president about a book they'd both read, while the other eleven freshmen slumped sheepishly in their seats.

When Denise first told me how afraid she is of failure, I had the same thought she is convinced her parents have: she's just being humble. I couldn't believe that someone so successful and widely respected stayed up at night consumed by fears of rejection. But she does. Denise is accustomed to exceeding expectations. When Denise described her family to me for the first time—her parents and siblings and extended network of aunts, uncles, and cousins—she said, "They are everything. Everything." She was terrified of letting them down.

The subway ride was almost over and there were way too many flash cards in the "I don't know" pile. Denise wanted to use every free second to study, but today she was finding it particularly hard to focus. The guy sitting a few seats down kept looking over. Denise caught his eye and immediately flicked her gaze back down to her flash cards. She was not the kind of girl who flirted on the subway. But then he got up from his seat.

"I just wanted to come over and say hello. I'm Craig."

Denise knew immediately that she wanted to talk to him. He had a baby face: dimples, big eyes, and a chin covered in patchy tufts of fuzz that would have suited an adolescent boy better than a grown man. She had to lean in to hear his voice—a soft, sweet baritone—because it was so close to a whisper. Normally she'd be on her guard with a man who randomly approached her on the subway. Craig was a big guy—tall and solidly built, like her father—and older, maybe in his early thirties. But he had gentle eyes. They made it impossible for her to feel threatened.

Denise and Craig talked for a while. She told him about the organization she was about to start working for, a nonprofit that provided mental heath care for low-income children in Harlem.

"So you have a kind heart," Craig said matter-of-factly.

Denise stared at him for a second, then leaned in closer. "I'd like to think so. Do you?"

"Too kind. People take advantage of it."

This sounds like the beginning of a cheesy romantic comedy. It certainly doesn't seem like the kind of thing that actually happens. It's also strange because, of all the women in this book, Denise is the one I'd least expect to be wooed by a charming stranger on the subway. She gets annoyed when people walk too slowly on the sidewalk. She always has somewhere to be, and she wants to arrive as soon as possible. So in this subway situation, I would have expected her to find a nice way to make the guy go away, then roll her eyes and say to herself, "Nobody has time for that." But Denise decided that Craig was a worthy distraction.

"I'd really like to see you again," Craig said when it was time for Denise to get off the train.

Before she moved to New York, all of Denise's friends prepared her for a terrible dating scene. They said the men she met at bars would only be interested in sleeping with her. So Denise had resigned herself to a boy-less year. She would focus exclusively on getting into a good med school, with nothing else vying for her attention. But Craig had given her a fifteen-minute escape from her fears of inferiority and rejection, and that didn't seem like a bad thing.

When Craig asked for her number, she gave it to him. She hoped she saw him again, too.

■◆■◆■

In January of senior year, right after she decided to become financially independent from her parents, Olivia made a profile on

SeekingArrangement, a website that connects "sugar babies"—young, pretty women—with "sugar daddies"—usually rich, older men. The website claims to be entirely aboveboard: a dating website like any other, the only difference being the "net worth" prominently displayed at the top of every daddy's profile. It advertises "mutually beneficial relationships," in which young women shower men with attention in exchange for "the finer things in life"—fancy dinners, extravagant vacations, or monthly allowances.

As soon as Olivia made her profile, she started getting messages asking how much she charged for an hour of sex. This didn't come as a surprise. Before signing up, Olivia had researched SeekingArrangement. She understood the website's subtext and didn't shy away from calling it sex work.

When Olivia first told me she was having sex for money, I asked if she was sure this was her only option. Her parents still wanted to support her, and I tried to suggest she wait a little longer before becoming fully independent. I wanted her to be safe.

Olivia rolled her eyes.

"Everything you have should be something you earn by yourself," she said. "Complete financial independence is what makes you a real person."

After doing a little research, I found out that more than two million young women have active profiles on SeekingArrangement, and 45 percent of them are in college. Olivia explained that SeekingArrangement intentionally caters to undergraduates: she got a free premium membership by registering as a sugar baby with a .edu account. According to her, a lot of men look for someone they can have intelligent conversations with—a young, smart, attractive woman they can pretend is actually their girlfriend, not just a prop to look pretty on their arm. This arrangement almost always includes sex, but a lot of the time, that's not the main object. After a few "sugar dates," Olivia realized that to be good at this job, she had to convince the daddy that she was genuinely attracted to him and impressed by what he had to say.

The first man Olivia met on the site physically hurt her. After texting for a few days, she agreed to meet him at his apartment one day in late January. As soon as she walked in, he asked for sex. When she knelt down to start giving him a blow job, he grabbed the back of her head and forced his penis deep into her throat. She started crying and he pushed harder, grinning.

"He was really enjoying watching me be tortured," she later told me. "It made my soul sad, that someone would get pleasure from seeing a girl cry."

She pulled away and asked him to stop. He tightened his grip on her head. When he finished, he gave Olivia fifty dollars, barely enough to cover the cost of the cab and train back to Princeton.

It was hard for me to understand why she kept meeting sugar daddies after that. When I suggested a few other ways she could make money, she shrugged and said, "It was just one guy. Most of them aren't like that."

WHEN I WENT TO NEW YORK to visit Olivia after graduation, she told me that SeekingArrangement was still one of her sources of income. She hadn't talked to me about any sugar daddies for a while, and I'd assumed she'd stopped meeting them.

"You look sad and bothered by this," she said.

"Yeah, I guess I am sad," I told her after a long pause. "I'm sad about some of the things you've had to go through."

"You don't get it. I don't want to take being a sugar baby as something sad. Since I've been on SeekingArrangement, I've started to prioritize taking care of myself. This is the first step toward being an adult, and a lesson learned. If I'm sad about it, I feel like an idiot. But I'm stronger for having done this, and life goes on."

Olivia told me she chose to be financially independent because she believed people should work to achieve everything they have in life. "You have to earn your support networks," she said to me more than once. She never had to earn her parents. They were just given to her.

For the first month of the summer, Olivia floated between apartments that belonged to friends and acquaintances. She used the money she made on SeekingArrangement for food and coffee at shops where she'd camp out all day, working on e-mails and job applications. I knew that Olivia didn't have many friends in New York, and I worried about her being alone. At least when she met sugar daddies during the school year, she came back to a campus full of people who cared about her. After bad experiences, she would cuddle up next to Leon, her primary, as he nuzzled her cheek and stroked her hair. But in New York, she had nothing close to that kind of comfort.

"Those first few weeks were the hardest," Olivia said. "I didn't have a job, I didn't have money. But mostly I felt abandoned by Leon. I felt like he should have been there, taking care of me."

Leon was in San Francisco, loving his job, living on a houseboat with ten other people, making lots of new friends. They were still together, but it felt different. Out in California, Leon couldn't care about Olivia in the same way he had for the past three months. If she had a mental breakdown at night, he'd be out with friends or still at work. They talked almost every day, but their conversations and text messages felt stilted. On the Fourth of July, a mutual friend told Olivia that Leon flew back to the East Coast to spend the holiday with his family. She tried not to dwell on the distance she felt on the phone. Leon was a math guy, she told herself—being awkward with anything verbal was just part of who he was. But when Olivia heard about Leon's trip home, she couldn't ignore the fact that he didn't want to see her. She wondered whether the distance made him think he'd taken on too much responsibility for her life. Now maybe he was realizing that he could—and should—let go.

Alone in New York, Olivia couldn't deal with that possibility. She knew distance was what changed their relationship. So she convinced herself that everything would be good again if she and Leon could just be in the same physical space, even for a few days. In the middle of July, she bought a ticket to San Francisco.

■ ◆ ■ ◆ ■

"Michelle! Are you seeing these things?"

Michelle woke up to see her family's Turkish tour guide inches from her face, spraying her forehead with spit.

"Later there is much time for sleep," the tour guide said, laughing when Michelle jumped back in her seat. "Now we pay attention!"

Michelle and her parents were on their own luxury bus, traveling through Istanbul. This was her graduation present: three weeks traveling through Europe, staying at five-star hotels, eating six-course meals at the best restaurants, getting chauffeured around by private drivers and tour guides. In Paris, they had stayed at the Mandarin Oriental in a luxury suite overlooking the Eiffel Tower.

Over the past few days, she'd spent hours browsing the Louvre. She'd toured mosques in Istanbul and taken a hot-air balloon ride in Cappadocia. Michelle had begged for this trip. Even though she'd grown up in London, she'd never done most of the typical European sightseeing. But now that she was on this dream trip, she couldn't enjoy it. She hadn't been sleeping at night. At first, when her parents asked, she blamed her long midday naps on jet lag. But after a week, that stopped working.

"I'm so sorry," Michelle finally said when her mom asked her what was wrong. "I'm loving this, I really am. I'm just having a hard time getting over Sam."

Michelle had known the breakup was coming. Sam, her boyfriend for the past two years, gave her a month's advance notice, and she thought she'd taken the news well. But now she was actually alone, she couldn't think about anything for more than ten minutes without somehow being reminded of Sam. They'd agreed not to talk over the summer, but she had to constantly fight the urge to text or e-mail. She didn't want to look weak.

During the day, Michelle toured the cities and put on a happy face for her parents, but after they went to bed, alone in her hotel room, she gave herself permission to be as sad as she felt. She spent most of her time at night scrolling through relationship-related forums on Reddit, one of the largest online communities, reading about other people who were going through similar breakup situations. A week into the trip, she posted her own question: "Can you break up with a person, spend years apart, but then come back together in a different time and place? Please, someone, tell me that's possible."

For Michelle, breaking up with Sam didn't just mean losing a boyfriend. It left her wondering what parts of her identity were actually her own. In September, Michelle would move to Philadelphia to start her master's in jazz vocals at one of the most competitive music conservatories in the country. When I asked Michelle's friends from Ivy about her decision to go to music school, they all said they were shocked. They knew Michelle loved music—she directed her Princeton a cappella group for four semesters—but before senior year, they said, she didn't seem to take it seriously. Michelle's a cappella group was known as "the drinking group with a singing problem." People joked (probably not for no reason) that it selected new recruits based on looks and alcohol tolerance. In her first two years at Princeton, Michelle, while clearly the most gifted singer in the group, cared a lot more about the social side of a cappella—and the virtually guaranteed ticket into Ivy—than the music.

Michelle's decision to apply to a music conservatory wasn't completely out of the blue. Michelle took jazz classes for three of her four years at Princeton and spent school breaks on international trips with the jazz ensemble. When she graduated, she received a certificate in jazz performance, along with her degree in sociology. But while Michelle was at Princeton, even her fellow musicians didn't seem to think she was serious about music.

"She was in an a cappella group, and she was distanced from the other instrumentalists because she was a vocalist," said one of Michelle's friends from the Princeton jazz community. "When I first met her, I thought, 'Oh, that's Michelle, ditzy vocalist.' To be honest, I don't think people respected her that much in the jazz program until right before she graduated."

Sam, on the other hand, was one of the most driven and well-regarded musicians at Princeton. He started playing the bass at age eight, and by high school, he'd become a compulsive perfectionist.

After every concert, he would obsess over one or two tiny errors that no one, not even his bass teacher, noticed. He cared about this one thing so much that almost everything else on campus—most of all the kind of sloppy arch sings Michelle led with her a cappella group every Thursday night—seemed childish and irrelevant. Before they started dating, Michelle realized that that was how he saw her and her music, and she desperately wanted to prove him wrong.

Michelle knew she changed a lot because of Sam. The confusing part was figuring out what she changed for him—to make him like her—and what she changed for herself. Because Michelle didn't choose to go to music school just to impress some guy. She's too smart for that. Sam shifted her priorities. He gave her a new definition for what was cool, different from any she'd gleaned from people in Ivy. Breaking up with Sam was like losing the picture on the top of the puzzle box. The image that had provided all the instructions for Michelle's new identity was gone, and now she had to improvise.

"She started dating Sam and the next thing you know she's in Terrace and doing music," one of Michelle's friends told me. "Ultimately, those were things she wanted to do. But she was definitely re-forming herself in his image."

Sam wasn't the first guy who prompted Michelle to change pieces of her identity. Before him, she'd dated David: a preppy, buttoned-up, straight-A student who was determined to go from Princeton to a six-figure salary at a New York consulting firm. Over the course of their one-year relationship, Michelle stopped binge drinking (or at least scaled back quite a bit), donned a more conservative wardrobe, and worked on her grades. Michelle started dating Sam almost immediately after David, so she hadn't been single for more than a month since her freshman year at Princeton. Now she knew she owed it to herself to stay single and figure out who she was when she wasn't trying to be something for a guy.

■ ◆ ■ ◆ ■

"She's been acting out real bad. She throws her sister on the floor. Sometimes she threatens me. One time she said she wanted to kill me and throw me on the train tracks."

Denise tried to look unfazed—nodding her head, making just enough eye contact with the mother to seem empathetic but not enough to seem concerned. Three days a week, Denise worked in the psychology wing of a children's hospital in Harlem. Before the kids saw the doctor, she asked their parents questions. The doctor then used Denise's notes to quickly determine the nature of the problem and whether to recommend therapy. Most of the evaluations were fairly routine: parents bringing in kids who were a little late learning to speak or didn't like playing with other kids on the playground. But every once in a while, a parent would come in with a story like this one, and Denise would have a hard time staying composed and professional.

"Have there been any traumatizing events in her life lately?" Denise asked the mother.

"Well, her dad's in jail. Her grandma died a couple weeks ago. And a while back, her uncle did some bad things to her."

Denise lifted her pencil off the clipboard and looked at the little girl playing in the adjacent room. Her hair was in long, braided pigtails, and she smiled at Denise. She couldn't have been older than three.

"Give me one second. I'll be right back. I just have to go get something."

Denise made a beeline for the bathroom, closed the door to the last stall, and sat on the toilet with her head in her hands.

"I just sat there thinking . . . What? What do you mean, he did some bad things to her? Who the fuck touched that little girl? Also, how did we do this to a human being in three years? That shouldn't be long enough to completely fuck a child's life up."

Some days, Denise's job made her feel completely helpless. This was the community she most wanted to serve—low-income, predominantly African American and Latino—but sometimes the problems they faced seemed so big that she doubted she could make any lasting impact. One kid threatened to cut his wrists, another bit a nurse hard enough to make her bleed, another had been to three different day care facilities because he kept punching other children. And Denise met with only the youngest patients in the psychology wing. All of them were under the age of five.

After a few minutes, Denise went back into the examination room and finished the questionnaire. The questions were clearly difficult for the mother to answer. She choked up a couple of times and tried to hide her face from her daughter. Denise wanted to put her clipboard aside and give her a hug. She wished she could give the mother some tissues, ask her how she was doing, and listen. Since she couldn't do any of those things, Denise had been working on her eye contact—she'd been practicing in the mirror, trying to wordlessly convey to the parents that, even though she wasn't a counselor, she could understand what they were going through.

Denise got her job through a Princeton fellowship that places seniors in various service-oriented organizations across the country. Denise's fellowship focused on providing mental health care for children: she spent half the week at the hospital, the other half at an elementary school for students with mental disabilities. There, she spent most of the day managing student records and calling parents from a room full of carpeted cubicles and clunky, tan-colored Microsoft computers. Like the hospital, the administrative job came with a lot of responsibility. If she overlooked a file, or didn't immediately respond to an inquiry from the Department of Education, kids with special needs wouldn't be eligible for the program and would likely get lost in the huge, impersonal Harlem public school system. One day, Denise realized that the office had forgotten to submit federal funding applications for thirty students. In two days, she arranged for every parent to come in and fill out the forms. When one mother couldn't make it in, Denise offered to personally deliver the paperwork to her house.

Denise loved her new job and worked hard to make sure she did it well, eating lunch at her desk and regularly sticking around for two hours after everybody else left. If her job had been the only thing she had to think about, she would have felt like she had a good handle on post-grad life. But it wasn't. In one month, Denise was going to retake the MCAT, and she'd hardly started studying.

■ ◆ ■ ◆ ■

In early July, Alex moved to Redmond, a city thirty minutes outside downtown Seattle, with her older brother, Ben. They decided to make the move into a road trip—Ben and his wife, Tory, in one car, Alex and her girlfriend, Bethany, in another.

When I first met Alex at the beginning of our senior year, she told me that she was Ben in female form. Almost everything Alex did, Ben did first. At age nine, Ben told their Southern Baptist congregation that he'd been saved; a few weeks later, Alex had the same revelation. In high school, Ben, under careful instruction from his father, forged a path for getting out of their small, impoverished town in Arkansas: score high on the ACT, take up the javelin, get straight As in school, enroll in Stanford's online math courses for gifted youth, become a nationally ranked javelin thrower, apply to Ivy League schools. He got into the Wharton School, the business school at the University of Pennsylvania. Two years later, after following Ben's path with dogged precision, Alex got into Princeton. That was how it had always been: Ben tried first, ensuring it was safe for Alex to follow.

So when Alex was deciding what to do after college, it made sense to keep following Ben. She'd already done some freelance programming for the real estate company he worked for. The company wanted Ben to start an independent project, and he needed a partner. The plan fell together so easily. Ben wanted to work from Seattle, so Alex agreed to move out there and live with him and Tory. Living under the same roof, Ben and Alex would have time to start their own company, like they'd always talked about. They would work hard at the real estate company, make a few contacts they could trust, and then, when they were ready, leave with a team to go out on their own. It seemed like a good way for Alex to spend two or three years after graduation. Very secure.

But during the road trip, Alex started to wonder whether she'd made the right decision by following her brother to the Northwest. At first, there were just small problems. Like the walkie-talkies Ben insisted they use. He would constantly tell Alex and Bethany to speed up or slow down, demanding they keep their car where he could see it. Alex knew her brother liked to be in control. But as the trip went on, she started to suspect there was something in particular triggering his need to take charge. She thought it might have something to do with Bethany.

Ben isn't a particularly social guy. He is friendly around certain people, but has no patience for those who put him on edge. "People either give you energy or they are Dementors," Ben told me the first time I met him—a reference to the soul-sucking monsters from the Harry Potter series. Every night I stayed at Alex's house in Redmond, he and Tory would watch TV after dinner, each wearing a set of big, black, noise-canceling Bose headphones. Alex knew she made up 50 percent of Ben's friend network—and that he'd never start a company with someone he didn't trust with his life. Somewhere in between Iowa and Idaho, she realized Ben probably saw Bethany as a threat to his professional dreams. If Alex moved back to the East Coast to be with Bethany, they wouldn't be able to start their company together.

As they got closer and closer to Seattle, Alex increasingly saw the two cars as two camps: she and Bethany versus Ben and Tory. This became especially apparent when they reached Mount Rushmore. Walking from their car to the monument, they came across someone Alex called a "serious redneck": a man wearing a cowboy hat and camouflage, the holes in his pants patched up with duct tape. When he saw Alex and Bethany holding hands, he said to his friend in a thick southern drawl, "I guess those gays are everywhere now." He lifted his right hand, stuck his index finger out, and pointed directly at Alex's chest. Then he pretended to pull the trigger.

Alex couldn't breathe. She associated these kinds of ignorant comments with deep hatred and real danger. For the next few days, she couldn't appreciate anything around her. The experience reaffirmed Alex's conviction that in certain parts of the country, particularly the South and Midwest, she wasn't safe or welcome.

After Mount Rushmore, Alex couldn't hide how unsettled and vulnerable she felt. She just wanted to get to the West Coast. Ben kept saying, "Look, look—Alex, isn't this beautiful?" She'd respond with "sure" or "uh-huh." In the middle of dinner at a diner in rural Montana, Alex finally told Ben what was bothering her. He said she was being ridiculous.

"Well, if you don't want to deal with stuff like that, you know what the solution is," Ben said. "Why do you have to hold hands?"

"Are you serious?" Bethany said, instantly transitioning into what Alex called "Lawyer Bethany." "We are holding hands for that little boy across the street who thinks he is the only gay person in this town."

"I just don't get it," Ben continued, looking at Alex and ignoring Bethany altogether. "You guys don't need to rub your relationship in everyone's faces all the time."

"Well, maybe if you grew up listening to your dad say that people like you should go to reparative therapy, you'd see this is a normal way to feel," Alex said.

"It's just inconsiderate. You can't blame these people for being homophobic—that's just the way they are. You're acting just as bad as they are by judging them." That comment triggered Alex's fight response for the second time in a month.

"No, we're not," she said. "It's fine to judge homophobic people because they deserve it."

Before she went on the road trip, Alex told me Ben accepted her decision to come out 100 percent. She said he was close to completely rejecting religion, as she had, but stayed in the church for Tory, who wanted to raise her children as Christians. Now Alex was starting to suspect that Ben was more devout than she'd wanted to admit. Ben started preaching after-hours at their church in Arkansas at age seventeen and applied to seminary as a senior at UPenn. After he turned down seminary for a job at a real estate company, Alex knew he became a lot less involved with the church. But maybe some of his conservative Southern Baptist views had stuck around. Or maybe he just resented how much sway Bethany seemed to have over his sister. Either way, Alex felt like the people she loved most were suddenly pulling her in two different directions.

Since age six, when she first started thinking she might like girls, Alex had been terrified of homelessness. She grew up hearing her dad say that AIDS was a good thing because it punished gay men—that all gay men molested children and all gay women were molested as children. He once told Alex he could never accept a gay child. He said he wouldn't want that child to hug him.

Alex fixated on homeless people—what they wore, where they slept, how they begged for money—convinced that as soon as her dad found out she was gay, she would have to survive on the side of the street. When Alex was little, the leaders of her church found out that two members of the congregation—family friends—were gay. Alex never saw those two people again, and she had no idea where they went. She assumed they'd lost their jobs, their homes, and their families. After that, she felt like she had to prepare for the same thing to happen to her. Even after graduating from Princeton, Alex continued to obsess over her own security. If she was going to completely break away from her dad, she needed to feel safe, protected by people who would never let her lose everything.

Immediately after Alex's dad found out she was gay, Ben

stepped in as protector. He paid most of Alex's medical bills when she didn't have health insurance, offered her a job and a place to stay, and invited her to his own Christmas dinner when she was disinvited from her dad's.

"Ben is my Superman," Alex told me right after her dad took her off his health care plan.

Alex's relationship with Ben felt different after their argument at the diner in Montana. She used to be so sure that her brother understood her better than anyone else—that living with him would be like living with a best friend. The road trip made her worry she'd made a serious error in judgment. In two weeks, Bethany would leave. If everything went according to plan, Alex would be alone in a house with Ben and Tory for the next year.

■ ◆ ■ ◆ ■

Alex understood the situation with my mom better than anyone else. We both felt torn between our original families and the people we thought might become our families in the future. Alex's dad and brother, as well as my mom, seemed to want us to revert to who we were as teenagers. To us, they seemed determined to maintain their status as the ultimate decision makers, staunchly opposed to us going out alone to create our own, very different lives. Alex's dad wanted the daughter who pretended to be a straight, conservative Christian. Ben wanted the romantically unattached sister who didn't mind pulling sixteen-hour days at a start-up. I wasn't exactly sure what my mom wanted for me, but I knew it involved breaking up with Robert . . . and possibly a nunnery—located somewhere near a top law school.

I spent most of the first two weeks after graduation at home, trying to avoid my mom. I hated doing that, but I felt like I had to. I've never found criticism more difficult to swallow than when it comes from my mother—not because it makes me angrier than criticism from other people, but because I'm more inclined to believe it. Recently, most of our long conversations had turned into her criticizing my decisions: usually my relationship with Robert, but sometimes my friends, this book, and my future as a writer. After graduation, I didn't want to spend time with my mom because I was so unsettled. I'd just lost the community I had for the past four years. In school, surrounded by friends and professors who gave me constant encouragement, I could handle my mom's disapproval. But now I knew her criticism would have more power. She knew me better than anyone else—I cared about her more than anyone else—and it was hard to dismiss her opinion.

My relationship with my mom had become particularly strained lately because of the state of her relationship with my dad. Growing up, I'd always known I had a much better chance of getting my parents to agree with me if they were both part of the conversation. Since my half sisters never lived with us, we were always a unit of three. When my dad didn't agree with me on something, I'd go to my mom, and when Mom didn't agree, I'd go to Dad. Usually I could make at least one of them see my side and convince the other to come around. My dad supported pretty much all the decisions I'd made in the last few years of college; he was excited about the book, he encouraged me to move to DC, and he liked Robert. He tried to talk to my mom—to convince her that I was on the right track—but by that point, she'd stopped listening.

My parents' marital situation was complicated. In November of my senior year, the night before their divorce proceedings were scheduled to begin, they decided to call the whole thing off. At first I was ecstatic. Everything in my family had felt off since they'd split up, and I thought this meant it would all go back to normal. But in the seven months since they'd decided to get back together, they hadn't stopped living in separate houses in separate states. From my perspective, at least (and, admittedly, I made the conscious choice not to ask too many questions), they still lived completely separate lives. The summer after graduation, that left me at home alone with my mom, without backup.

I LEFT TO SPEND the summer in China at the beginning of July. A few days before I got on the plane, my mom and I had the worst fight I can remember. It started with me telling her I was headed to DC for a couple of days to see some friends and look at apartments.

"You just want to be away from me. You only have two weeks at home and you've hardly been here. I don't understand."

At first I tried to deny this. "No," I said, "I really just need to look at housing. Places go up on Craigslist a month or two before you're supposed to move in." Not true, but I didn't want to get into the reasons I was avoiding her.

She ran upstairs to her bathroom and locked the door.

"I just feel like I don't know you anymore," she said. "You're not my daughter. It's like you're dead inside."

I'd started walking up the stairs, but when I heard that, I stopped. My mom and I had had our fair share of fights, but before, there had always been unspoken ground rules. Rule number one: No matter how angry you are, never give the other person reason to doubt that you love her. I couldn't believe my mom had taken it this far. All I could think about was getting out of the house and calling someone I knew who would empathize. I walked down to the bottom of my street, sat under a tree, and dialed Robert's number. It took me a while to relay what had happened—her words hurt even more when I confirmed them with my own voice—but Robert eventually got me to calm down.

"She loves you, I know she does," he said. "You just need to talk and tell her why you're upset. You can't shut her out. She is clearly going through a really hard time right now, and she needs you."

I went home and wrote a letter. I was too emotional to get my point across any other way. When I was done, I sat outside my mom's bedroom door and read it out loud. I told her how important her opinion was to me and how afraid I was of internalizing it, changing everything in my life as a result. I asked her to trust me enough to make my own decisions, even if they turned out to be the wrong ones, because I needed to learn.

"Please say something," I said when I finished.

Neither of us spoke for a while. I sat against the door, clutching my knees to my chest, staring at my letter. Finally I heard her whisper, "I don't have anything to say."

CHAPTER THREE

August

Going to China was a way to pause time. Even after graduation, I hadn't allowed myself to worry about what would come next. I left a lot of decisions unmade—the most important one being where to live—and justified the uncertainty with two words I repeated to myself whenever the future seemed too overwhelming: "after China."

Throughout college, China had been my place to process. After a summer teaching English in Hunan Province my freshman year, I jumped on any low-budget way to go back: Chinese-language study-abroad programs, home stays, and more teaching. Princeton required a constant state of intensity I couldn't sustain without a break. On campus, I could never really relax and think deeply about what I was doing, because if I wasn't doing anything, I felt sure I was doing something wrong. There were too many professors to meet with, lectures by heads of state to attend, people to impress. This urgency to do everything was compounded by everyone else on campus always bragging about their busy schedules.

It was a dangerous cycle because, even if I didn't want to be busy, I felt like I had to keep up. To be idle was to potentially lose out on a great internship, an impressive leadership experience, or an important contact at a company where I might want to work after graduation. So I overloaded myself as much as possible during the school year but completely checked out over the summer. While most Princeton students swarmed to the professional hotbeds of New York City, San Francisco, and Washington, DC, I went to China. For at least six weeks after I landed in Shanghai, no one I talked to would have any connection to Princeton, which was exactly what I wanted. Time and space to think.

But the summer after graduation, I brought Robert with me. We taught a monthlong public speaking course together at a university in Jiangxi Province. At the time, I knew having Robert around would probably color the decisions I made in China about how my life would go when I got back to the States. But then, I thought, maybe the decisions were supposed to be colored. I wanted us to spend the summer together. I wanted him to understand this place I escaped to—to meet my past students, to share simmering vats of spicy hot pot, my favorite Chinese dish, and to build a new class community with me.

Before I went to China, there were two big decisions on the table: where I'd live when I got back to the States and whom I'd live with. Starting in September, Robert would be working in DC, but I knew that Olivia and Denise—along with a lot of my other friends from college—would be living in New York. I don't think I ever really considered not going with Robert to DC, but I told myself that I did. I was sensitive about being the girl who followed her boyfriend to a random city right after graduation.

When people asked me "Why Washington?" I usually made up some other reason—"It's as good a place as any," or "New York makes me anxious." At Princeton, I minored in gender and sexuality studies. I didn't want my feminist friends to think less of me, especially the ones heading out for a year alone to save orphans or trafficked women in rural Malaysia or Bangladesh. But in China with Robert, it was easy not to worry about them and the judgments they might make.

The other decision—whom to live with—was more difficult. Robert wanted us to move in together. He made a lot of good arguments, the best one being the fact that we'd already lived together for a large part of my senior year. Six months after he graduated, Princeton hired Robert to coach the university's mock trial team. He rented an apartment off campus, but his practice sessions often ended late, and he'd stay in my dorm room. That year, I lived in a tiny single. If we could tolerate sharing one key and one hundred square feet for a few days a week, he said, we were ready to lease an apartment.

Still, I hesitated. The prospect of signing a lease with Robert felt different from living in the same dorm room. We'd be committing to cohabitation for at least a year. There would be furniture buying involved. If we decided to break up, one of us couldn't just walk out the door. The landlord would give us lots of complicated paperwork. We'd have to decide who got the strainer and who got the spatula.

Right from the beginning, my relationship with Robert was serious. In the months that preceded it, I put us both through incredible pain and anxiety as I decided whether to end my previous relationship. When we finally became boyfriend and girlfriend, there was no starting slow, no happy-go-lucky honeymoon period. We'd both already given up a lot for this relationship, so we couldn't pretend we didn't have high expectations for where it would lead. After we'd been dating a few months, I decided to spend a semester in China. Again, we went through some seriously unhappy times—missing each other; opting out of the drunken, carefree hookups that our friends were having all around us—for the sake of our relationship. We got through it but, again, it raised the stakes. At one point or another, we both definitely thought, "This thing better turn out to be worth it."

This prolonged intensity was a big part of the reason I hesitated when Robert asked me to move in with him. I knew we already leaned heavily on each other. I didn't know how *not* to lean heavily on him. And I worried that, if I didn't take this opportunity to create and inhabit my own space, I'd never be able to survive on my own.

Around the same time I was making this decision, Alex told me she thought most people spent their first year after college trying to fill the void left by moving away from such a tight-knit community. She knew a lot of graduates who, in their first year out, latched onto one particular person. That person, she said, replaced the group of friends they had living right next door in college, adding security and stability to their lives.

"But I think the goal is eventually to fill the void with yourself," she said. "This year is the transition. You can't get to that independent place right away."

That resonated with me. If I lived with Robert, I thought, I might never learn to fill the void with myself. I wanted to make my own decisions and trust my own opinion more than anyone else's—and I knew that the closer I got to Robert, the more difficult that would become. When I considered the possibility of us living together, I also had my mother's voice in my head: "You're too young. You think you know what you want, but you don't. You need time to be on your own, to learn how to be an independent person."

TOWARD THE END OF OUR SIX WEEKS in China, I sent in a deposit on a room in a nine-person group house in DC. The plan was for Robert and me to live in different group houses relatively close to each other. That way, we'd each have our own space and the chance to make our own group of friends. I'd convinced myself this was the responsible choice. The two of us aren't the most social people—we'll live happily as introverts unless forced to do otherwise. At the same time, though, we are both keenly aware that sometimes it's good to be forced to do otherwise.

After deciding to follow Robert to DC, I recognized the importance of safeguards: mechanisms in place to ensure that, even if we broke up, I'd still have a life, a place to eat, a place to sleep, and friends. People told me I was crazy to live with eight roommates—to deal with so many people's dirty dishes and stray pubic hairs. But to me, the house was a safety net. I loved Robert, but I couldn't let him consume my whole life. The roommates advertised weekly house dinners, group parties, and many shared bottles of wine. I knew it would be hard, losing the community I had at Princeton. Without an office job—spending solitary days in coffee shops—I didn't know how to meet people. But this house solved that problem. Putting myself in a situation where I couldn't not make eight new friends seemed like a promising start to adult life.

■ ◆ ■ ◆ ■

When they arrived in Redmond, Alex; her brother, Ben; and his wife, Tory, unpacked nine computers, two iPads, and three iPhones. Ben immediately dumped almost all of this hardware—plus monitors, tangled mounds of unidentified cables, funky-looking concave keyboards, USB cords—onto the dining room table: their new office. Tory unpacked most of the rest of the stuff because Ben decided they couldn't waste any more time. He told Alex they needed to start work the next day.

The real estate company had hired Alex and Ben to work on an independent programming project. This company had decades' worth of data stored in all kinds of places. This data included information like how many square feet were in a particular building, how much a building cost, and what broker made a deal with what client. Alex and Ben put this data through an ETL (Extract, Transform, and Load) process and created an API (Application Programming Interface), a mechanism Alex described to me as a secure way to deliver data safely to the consumer. They cleaned and organized the information so that anyone in the company who dealt with the data could easily find what he or she needed. The goal was to give employees access to all the different sources of information so they could analyze it and use it to inform future decisions.

At the start of the project, Alex and Ben didn't even think it would work. A lot of the data was really old, stored in strange formats that made it hard to manipulate. Because of the company's tough security regulations, Alex and Ben had to spend months just trying to access the data. They also had to cater to thousands of employees, who all wanted to view the data in a different way.

"We're working on a project we essentially know is going to fail," Ben said. "They should have thirty people on this job, and we have two."

From the beginning, Alex felt a lot of pressure to perform well. First, there was the possibility that the CFO would cut their funding. Most of the executives were comfortable with the way their company had always done things, she said, and resisted any change that might make them obsolete. If they didn't have regular and significant proof of progress, she felt sure they would abandon the project—and she and Ben would be out of a job.

But Alex also had the added pressure of knowing she would never have gotten this job without her brother's help. At Princeton, she majored in history. What she knew about coding she'd mostly taught herself. For this kind of job, she was fairly certain the vast majority of companies required a computer science degree. But Ben had put in a good word for her, so she felt like she had to prove herself to the company and to him. That meant working nonstop from eight in the morning to nine at night during the week, learning new programming techniques on the weekends, and not leaving the house for days at a time. Ben would make sure she was awake in the morning and advise her on what time to go to bed—a schedule specially calibrated to allow for maximum productivity. When I visited a few weeks after Alex moved to Redmond, Ben texted her while we were out on Friday night: "You can stay out as late as you want."

"I think Ben wanted the new setup to be like an intense coding boot camp, where you program all day, every day," Alex said. "But the thing is, when you go to those camps, you eventually get to go home."

Even though Alex was working as hard as she could, she knew she wasn't performing as well as Ben wanted her to, and she didn't know how to improve. Ben wasn't a teacher. He would either explain something once or not at all. When he was coding, his eyes bored into his computer screen with an intensity that made Alex afraid to interrupt him with whatever inane question was halting her progress, so she would regularly spend long periods of time trying to figure out something he probably could have resolved in two minutes.

After nine on weekdays, Alex got up from the dining room table and retreated to her bedroom—to call Bethany, work on her thesis, read, and usually watch a string of cat videos on YouTube. But she always had her programming books open on her desk, ready to start feverishly annotating pages if she heard Ben coming upstairs. If Ben didn't find her working, she worried he might not think she was invested in her job.

Before I met Ben for the first time, I imagined him as a kind of cruel dictator figure. But after spending my first few days with him, I realized that whatever dictatorial leanings he has (and he does have quite a few) come from a hyperintellectual intensity, not any unkindness. He has a tendency to become deeply interested in things to the point of obsession. I once offhandedly mentioned to Ben that Robert and I might take a weeklong hiking trip. His response was to usher me over to his computer and spend the next half hour browsing through Google images of every mountain within five hundred miles of Seattle, narrating the pros and cons of each range and peak. Every ten minutes or so, he'd turn around suddenly and ask, "Is this okay? Are you interested?" He caught himself being obsessive in a way that made me think a lot of people had called him out on it before. When something has his full attention, he has a hard time considering or empathizing with other people. He was fixated on the programming project. I don't think he intentionally ignored Alex's feelings; he just didn't dwell on them because, in his mind, they didn't relate directly to the project's success.

Having Ben as her boss reminded Alex of what it was like to have her dad as her javelin coach. In high school, Daniel took complete ownership of Ben's and Alex's track-and-field careers. It was his way of getting them out of Byron, a town in Arkansas with a population of 2,850 people. At Byron High School, the only college flags displayed outside the guidance counselor's office were from in-state schools: University of Arkansas at Monticello, Southern Arkansas University, University of Central Arkansas, Arkansas State, and Arkansas Tech.

When Ben and Alex were young, Daniel read an article in an airline magazine about Ivy League schools, the gist being that if you wanted your children to be successful, you had to do everything in your power to get them into one. That article prompted Daniel's two-pronged plan of attack: when Ben and Alex were in junior high, he enrolled them in Stanford University's intensive online math classes and purchased an array of shots, weightlifting equipment, and javelins. Alex eventually had to quit drama club, because her dad said she couldn't be a nationally ranked high school actress. Track-and-field events—specifically relatively obscure track-and-field events—on the other hand, would allow her to excel individually and get noticed.

After Alex started throwing javelin and training as a heptathlete, Daniel stopped being her dad and became her trainer. At dinner, he chastised Alex for not eating enough protein. He woke her up every morning at 5:30 A.M., drove her to the high school track, and blew a whistle when she wasn't running fast enough. Alex could never do anything on weekends, because almost every Friday, her dad packed up their old station wagon and drove her across the country to another track meet. He saw time spent with friends as time wasted because it did nothing to move Alex closer to their shared goal. If Alex didn't yield to her dad's demands, he'd accuse her of not caring about her future. She stayed in the school library for as long as possible every day after class, just to be in a place where her dad couldn't watch her.

"It was the weirdest thing," Alex's mom said. "Alex and I would be sitting in the living room, watching a show, having a good time. Then she'd hear her dad's car pull into the driveway and she'd run to the closet in her room. She didn't want him to see her watching TV, not studying."

In her first few months in Redmond, Alex sometimes slipped up on the phone with Bethany, calling Ben "Dad."

"There was definitely something to that," Alex said. "Even though they're just two years older than me, it felt like Ben and Tory were my parents and very disappointed in everything I did. I was a teenager again."

Like the one between father and coach, the line between brother and boss started to blur. Alex felt guilty whenever she wasn't doing something productive and directly related to the programming project. She couldn't escape to school, so any time Ben gave her a break from work, she drove ten minutes down the road to have a sandwich or a cup of coffee at Panera. Leaving the house,

Alex liked to imagine she was making a prison break. Panera was noisy and smelled strongly of feta, but it was outside the house and that made it a sanctuary.

▪ ◆ ▪ ◆ ▪

As soon as Olivia arrived in San Francisco, Leon started talking about the possibility of breaking up. He said he needed to be fully present in San Francisco, and their relationship made that difficult.

"When I'm close to you, I feel like I always have to take care of you," he said. "It's hard for me to do that right now."

Olivia wanted to prove to Leon that he didn't have to take care of her—that she could even take care of him. At Princeton, Leon had always tried to convince Olivia to be dominant during sex: to take control and demand whatever she wanted. She never liked doing that because it didn't feel natural. She was too conscious of her body. But now, Olivia desperately wanted to make Leon happy. On her third night in San Francisco, Olivia came up with a role-play that would give her control of the situation. Leon would get stoned—his reflexes would slow, and he'd lose his ability to analyze every little thing—and she would tell him what to do.

As soon as Leon rolled a blunt and started smoking, Olivia got anxious. When he first mentioned breaking up, a few hours after she got off the plane, she hadn't allowed herself to be sad because the possibility hadn't seemed real. She'd convinced herself that, with a week of one-on-one time, they could repair their relationship. But as Olivia watched Leon take hit after hit, his eyes small and red around the edges, she began to resent him. She felt like she was the one putting in all the effort, trying to make things good again. Leon had disengaged. He wasn't participating in their relationship. It was like he'd already decided she wasn't worth messing up his new life in San Francisco, or even distracting him from it.

"Why can't you just be with me?" Olivia asked. She tried to sound authoritative, to make the question more of a demand than a plea. But Leon recoiled.

"What are you doing?"

"What?"

"You're messing it up," he said. "You're breaking the fantasy."

"No, I'm not."

"You are. You're being the weak and needy one." He paused. "Are you drunk?"

"What? No! No, I am not drunk."

"Yes, you are. That's why you're getting so emotional about this. I thought we agreed you were going to stay sober so you could stay in control."

"I am sober. When would I even have had time to get drunk?"

Leon pulled out a piece of paper and a pen. "I want you to write 'I am not drunk' ten times."

"You're being ridiculous. I'm not going to write that."

"Fine." Leon rolled over, his back to Olivia. "Let's just go to sleep."

Olivia wasn't drunk, just humiliated. She wished she could have given Leon the kind of sex he wanted. All she'd needed to do was stay in control of the situation for half an hour. Olivia knew she'd just confirmed all of Leon's reasons for not wanting to be with her.

Olivia couldn't sleep, so she watched him. When she stopped to admire Leon physically, she always wondered why he'd settled for her. Leon had a rock climber's body, toned by years of scaling mountains in Colorado and almost every building on Princeton's campus. If he hadn't spent most of his time at Princeton brooding in his single room alone with his math theory textbooks, Olivia knew a lot of girls would have been interested. Now that he was developing what seemed to be a great social life in San Francisco, she was sure he could do better.

THE NEXT MORNING, Olivia and Leon biked downtown. When they stopped, Olivia realized she didn't have her bike lock. After watching her struggle to find a solution alone for a while, Leon suggested they lock their bikes up together.

"I wonder—if I wasn't here, what would you have done?" he asked.

Olivia felt like Leon was gathering evidence of her helplessness, compiling a list he would pull out at the end of the week when he decided to break up with her.

Olivia knew she could be independent. She was just going through a difficult period. She thought Leon should have recognized that. He should have believed in her enough to know that this was temporary, that soon she would find a job and a place to live and get her confidence back. A good partner was supposed to be supportive—someone you could fall back on when you were going through a hard time, not someone who kept a running tally of your failures and moments of weakness.

"I would like to say that I am a strong, independent woman," Olivia told me a few days later, back in New York. "And here was this person who was incredibly important to me, telling me that I was not. That killed me."

After they locked up their bikes and started walking, Olivia turned to Leon and said, "Actually, I think we need to break up."

"Yeah, okay," Leon said. "Let's do it."

■ ◆ ■ ◆ ■

After three weeks exploring Europe, Michelle boarded a plane home to London. She would spend the next two months there with her parents, her brother, and her best friends from high school.

"Imagine if you had a diary that you wrote in every day for two months," Michelle told me. "All your values—everything that's most important to you—is in there. Then you close it up and go away for a year. You don't even look at it. When you come back and read it again, it totally revitalizes you. For me, that's going back to London."

On the Euro trip, Michelle spent all her time with her parents. It had been family dinner followed by bed (or dejected Reddit browsing) every night—no sneaking out, no meeting up with French guys she met at a bar. But back in London, she could effortlessly slip back into the habits she'd honed in high school: staying out until four in the morning and lying to her parents about spending the night with guys. Back when they both lived at home, Michelle's older brother, James, had never missed a day of school and regularly spent his Saturday nights at home studying. Michelle, on the other hand, had acquired her first fake ID by age fourteen. At her all-girls prep school—where everyone wore matching starched oxford shirts, tweed blazers, kneesocks, and red ribbons—she demonstrated her favorite sex positions in the cafeteria. The summer and fall after senior year, she secretly slept with both her best friend's older brother and her older brother's best friend. "James was the angel," she said. "My parents weren't prepared for me."

At my own Catholic high school, I was constantly exposed

to stories of people who found themselves again by rediscovering their values. This almost always included someone triumphing over some sort of self-inflicted malady: heroin addiction, teenage pregnancy, hospitalization after drinking too much alcohol. These stories usually came from either current students (finagling their way out of suspension) or speakers my school would bring in from New York. The stories always ended the same way. The wanderer cleaned up her act—usually finding God in the process—and promised to never again stray so far from what she knew was right. So to me, living true to your values translated roughly to celibacy (or at least monogamy), sobriety, and a perpetual state of self-denial. For Michelle, it was exactly the opposite. She'd been a serial monogamist for the past three years. If she'd visited Paris in high school, she wouldn't have spent even one night cooped up in her hotel room. It wasn't that Michelle wanted to revert back to who she was as a teenager—she winced at the memory of lunchtime orgasm demonstrations—but there was something akin to an independent spirit she felt like she had lost at Princeton.

On one of the last nights of the Euro trip, Michelle decided to cut things off with Sam for good. Until this point, Michelle had convinced herself they were going to get back together.

"I thought that after fucking ten more women, he'd realize I gave everything to him," Michelle said. "He'd realize how rare that was. I told myself he'd want to stay with me."

But by the end of her trip, she realized she was probably better off not fixing their relationship. She e-mailed Sam, saying she didn't want to get back together during the two weeks she would spend in New York before heading to Philadelphia—just to make sure she couldn't take it back. As long as she was with Sam, Michelle knew she would be trying to mold herself into his ideal. Now, looking back on their relationship, she felt embarrassed. She'd known all along he wasn't happy. For two years, she'd known he wanted someone different—better.

A few weeks before graduation, Sam had been asleep in bed next to Michelle when his phone started buzzing. It was a text message from Katie Starr, a tiny blond art history major who carted a clunky DSLR camera around campus. Like Sam, she was artsy and alternative in a way that seemed effortless. Michelle knew Sam used to have a crush on her. Probably still did. Michelle opened the message and saw that they'd been talking about her. Katie asked him why he was thinking about ending things when Michelle moved to Philadelphia. He replied, "I just think I can do better."

"I should have left right then and there," Michelle told me. "My heart fucking sank to the middle of the earth. I never told him that I saw that—because what could he say that would ever change the fact that I saw that? So I didn't say anything, and we kept hanging out. It was the most painful thing I have ever done to myself."

Michelle saw London as a new start. As soon as she got off the plane, she called her best friend, Lindsay, who had stayed in London through college and now worked for a music label. Michelle had been friends with Lindsay since she was four years old. They'd gone to school together for fourteen years. Michelle likes to say that the girls she met at Princeton are her sisters, but Lindsay is her wife.

Lindsay looks the part of cool girl maybe even more than Michelle, with long platinum-blond hair she recently released from full dreadlocks. She wears heavy-lidded black eyeliner everywhere she goes and usually has a cigarette expertly twisted between her fingers. She's a knockout, but more grungy rock star than Barbie (in pictures, she likes to close her eyes and stick out her tongue).

Michelle told me, "We're like two dudes, just drinking beer and hanging out." That summer, Lindsay immediately determined that "hanging out" would not include any crying over Sam. On Michelle's first night in London, they went clubbing together. Michelle went home with Jack, a muscled, bearded twenty-seven-year-old who owned his own art gallery—the first guy she'd kissed since Sam.

In theory, Michelle knew she needed a summer of no attachments. If she'd gotten some kind of professional opinion on her situation, she knew she would have been told to lie low and avoid any significant romantic relationships. She didn't like admitting that she entered into a quasi-relationship with Jack, seeing him exclusively for the rest of the summer. But she figured she had to start somewhere. It was a lot to ask herself to instantly transition from three years of monogamy to singlehood. Two months was a lot better than two years. As long as Jack was gone by the time she went back to the United States, she didn't think he posed a problem.

Even with Jack hanging around, Lindsay had more than enough time to impart her wisdom—to remind Michelle of who she was when she wasn't attached to a guy. Right before she headed back to the States, Michelle spent a day tripping on mushrooms with Lindsay. They packed a picnic and walked to one of the most touristy places in the city—the Royal Botanic Gardens, overlooking the River Thames. Within an hour of eating the mushrooms, Michelle felt like the ground and the sky were breathing, moving slowly closer, then farther away. She picked up a cold can of Coke and felt ice tingling in every part of her body. After jumping around and trying to dance with a bird, Lindsay lit incense and put praise music on her iPhone speaker. Surrounded by parents picnicking with their children, they lay down in the grass and meditated.

"Lindsay, what's my spirit animal?" Michelle asked after they lay silent for a while.

Lindsay thought about it—for a few seconds or ten minutes, Michelle couldn't be sure. "Definitely something that has resurgences in energy."

"What do you mean?"

"Well, you always have to hit rock bottom, but then you come again with this whole new wave of energy. It's awesome."

"What about a phoenix?"

"Holy shit. Yes. Michelle, that's perfect. It's like you die and come alive again."

▪ ◆ ▪ ◆ ▪

The MCAT was in twenty-one days, and Denise knew she was going to fail. She wasn't ready, and three weeks wasn't nearly enough time to prepare. But even though Denise had a feeling that her second score was going to be lower than her first, she couldn't not take the test again. Not when her score was the only thing standing between her and the top medical schools in the country. Her original score was good, but she knew it could be better.

A lot of Princeton students would have happily broadcasted their goals for high scores on standardized tests. They would have wanted other people to know about the high expectations they had for themselves. But Denise didn't tell anyone. Not her mom, not her best friend, not Craig, whom she'd been seeing regularly since they met on the subway. Her MCAT and med school aspirations were her most guarded secrets. She'd worked hard to convince her family members that she'd be happy with a school that wasn't ranked in the top twenty. She needed them to believe that so they wouldn't get their hopes up. This made for a lonely July. With her MCAT coming up at the end of the month, Denise was under incredible pressure, but no one else really understood how much.

Since Denise moved to New York in early June, she'd been lugging four MCAT books around in a rolling backpack—physics, organic chemistry, MCAT writing, and one book of general practice tests—but had hardly looked at any of them. She hadn't had time. Denise had been working at her job for only a few weeks, so she still felt like she needed to prove herself. She knew this was stupid—this job would last a year, whereas med school would impact the rest of her life—but she was too proud not to work extra-long hours.

"The person who had this fellowship post before me didn't put in a lot of extra effort," Denise said. "When I shadowed her, she told me to leave if I didn't finish my work by the end of the day. And it's true, we don't get paid overtime. If you don't eat lunch, no one is clapping. The proof is in what you produce."

When Denise's coworkers told her how to do her job, they constantly referenced a girl named Sarah, who had the fellowship two years before Denise. At the primary school, people called Sarah "incredibly hardworking" and said she revolutionized the way they ran the administrative office. Denise wanted to be remembered like that.

When I asked Denise's friends to describe her, all of them individually used the term "role model." She is the kind of student teachers want to write a recommendation for, the kind of friend parents want their kid to have. In everything she does, Denise is eager to win people's respect and make a good impression. But creating a good impression takes time. And that summer, by the time Denise left work at 6:00 or 6:30 P.M., the temptation to go straight to Harlem, collapse onto an air mattress in her empty apartment, and call her mom usually won out. Plans to study for the MCAT got postponed.

But with twenty-one days to go, Denise promised herself that today was the day she would take a timed practice MCAT. No distractions, no pausing for a quick minute to look something up. She needed an honest evaluation of how unprepared she was and what she had to do between now and the test. After she left work, Denise sat on the steps outside her office and scoured Google Maps on her phone for a Starbucks that stayed open till midnight. She needed the Internet, and her apartment still didn't have Wi-Fi. All the stores except the one in Times Square closed at 10:00 P.M., so she headed downtown, even though she knew it would be teeming with tourists. After waiting half an hour to get a table—frantically flipping through flash cards while hovering over two people with empty cups—she logged on to the Princeton Review test prep website. The practice test wouldn't load. Denise sorely wanted to take this as a sign that she was trying to do too much. That she should go home, cry, cancel the MCAT, maybe even postpone med school for another year. But then she thought about the end goal—a score that would make a school like Harvard possible—and called tech support at Princeton Review.

The technician spent forty minutes on the phone with Denise before he apologized, said he didn't know what else to do, and hung up. Denise kept trying, turning the Wi-Fi on and off until she got the page to load. She jumped out of her chair when the test finally materialized on her screen. Surely, she thought, this was the sign she was supposed to notice: hard work and perseverance paid off. She had the MCAT situation under control. And for half an hour or so, that stayed true. But then she started getting question after question that she couldn't answer; she kept having to guess, and this was physical sciences, usually her best section on the MCAT.

"So much fear and panic and paranoia hit me at that moment when I realized the test was in several weeks, and I was going to do worse on the section I'm best at. I was going to fail and not get into any med school. Everything I had done up until that point was useless and I was never going to be a doctor. The hopeless thoughts just went on and on and on and on."

A few minutes later, Denise left Starbucks and stood in the middle of Times Square, her right hand wrapped tightly around the handle of her rolling backpack. It was eleven o'clock at night and people kept knocking her shoulders as they power-walked past. She was thoroughly convinced that she shouldn't have applied to medical school this year. She should have waited. Or maybe she shouldn't go at all. A lot of her best girlfriends from Princeton had dropped the premed track to become nurse practitioners. As NPs, they would have almost exactly the same responsibilities as fully certified doctors, without having to go through med school. They would also have flexible hours and more time for a family. Denise knew that path would be infinitely easier. She imagined herself calling her mom's cell phone and saying, "Mommy, I can't do this."

WHEN WE TALKED a few days before graduation, Denise had been deciding whether to wait another year before applying to medical school. She told me she was scared to give up the narrative she'd built for herself. In the narrative, she went to a top med school, then a top residency. By the time she left residency, she would have enough money to open a center for low-income adolescent women: part health clinic, part leadership school. The clinic would provide services for anything these women could possibly need: gynecologists, psychologists and counseling groups, dental care. But along with great health services, adolescent women would also receive leadership training—instruction on how to succeed as young professionals.

That was the dream, and Denise was terrified of giving up on it. This wasn't about failing other people, because she'd hardly told anyone about her idea for the clinic. Even if it never opened, she worried about her life if she couldn't imagine what it would look like ten, twenty, and thirty years down the road. She understood herself as Denise, committed role model with the passion, drive, and empathy necessary to help—maybe even save—a lot of struggling young adults. Without that narrative for her future, she was scared she'd be lost.

■ ◆ ■ ◆ ■

"Are you sure you don't want to come, A?" Tory asked, stuffing a windbreaker into the top of her hiking backpack.

"Yeah, Alex—seriously, come," Ben added. "The trails on the Olympics will be perfect this weekend."

"It's really okay. My neck is feeling a little stiff today anyway. I'll just stay here and rest."

Ben rolled his eyes. "And stay inside all weekend again? We're in the hiking capital of the world."

Ben could have worked on the programming project anywhere, but he and Tory picked the Northwest because of the mountains.

Every weekend, they donned thermal socks and long underwear, laced up their hiking boots, and drove to a new wilderness destination. They returned Sunday night with camera cards full of gorges, waterfalls, and glacier peaks.

Alex had absolutely no interest. Mountains reminded her of strained backpacking trips she'd taken with her dad and Ben—of giving up halfway through (because of muscle pain she later found out was dystonia) and the subsequent castigation. Usually Alex spent the weekends happily reading at Panera, relieved not to have to face a family dinner at the end of the day. But this particular weekend, Alex decided to stay home. She'd signed up for a thirty-day Amazon Kindle trial and scoured the Amazon store for books matching key terms like "child abuse," "emotional abuse," "parent narcissism," and "borderline personality disorder parent." She'd downloaded thirty books and planned to spend the whole weekend reading.

A few days before, Alex's mom had been admitted to the ICU in Little Rock, Arkansas, with a 103-degree fever. The doctors didn't know exactly what was wrong, but it seemed like she might have overdosed on her depression medication. Daniel called Ben to tell him what was going on but refused to talk to Alex. "I'll just be communicating with your brother," Daniel said, when he finally responded to Alex's calls and text messages. "He can tell you anything you want to know."

Alex knew her dad was being unreasonable. Hiding important information about her mother's health was cruel. She was supposed to be angry with him, and she was angry, but she also felt guilty and responsible—like she somehow deserved to be treated this way by her dad. She couldn't get this idea out of her head. Multiple times a week, Alex asked her girlfriend, Bethany, if she was a bad person. Every time, Bethany would say, "No, of course not," and try to figure out why she was asking.

When Alex first told me about it, I also had a hard time understanding this fear. Alex is kind—genuinely, lovingly kind—in every way. The first time we met for coffee, I made a passing reference to a computer science class that was giving me trouble. A couple hours later, Alex sent me an e-mail that was two pages long, detailing programs that might help me understand—and cultivate an interest in—programming. In every interaction, Alex tries to make sure the other person feels heard and respected. So to me, this idea that she thought she was "bad" just didn't make sense.

As soon as Alex heard Ben and Tory's car leave the driveway, she started to read. For weeks, Bethany had been trying to get her to research emotional abuse and how it affected children. She thought it might help her understand why she felt so guilty all the time. Within a few minutes, Alex found an author who pinpointed the "I'm bad" feeling: "Adults abused as children often see themselves as worthless, crazy, or bad people who have nothing valuable to say or contribute."[26] Almost immediately, Alex identified her dad as an emotional abuser—a narcissist and a controller.

Her dad, Alex discovered, perpetuated what was known as the standard cycle of emotional abuse. He would make Alex feel worthless, but as soon as she starting thinking she deserved better, he would start treating her well again. Alex would then convince herself she'd been overreacting and things really weren't that bad. But just as she began to feel comfortable again, he would say or do something cruel, and the cycle would repeat itself. This hap-

26 Gil, Eliana. *Outgrowing the Pain: A Book for and About Adults Abused as Children* (1983; repr. New York: Dell, 1988), 35.

pened again and again and again. The books made it seem so obvious that she'd been controlled and manipulated all her life. But before now, Alex had never allowed herself to believe that she'd been abused by her father.

"I knew something was wrong with the way my dad treated me and Ben, but I couldn't put my finger on it," Alex said. "I needed the validation first to make sure I wasn't just being sensitive. But then I read the books and it was like . . . Wow. Yes. This is a thing."

Alex read sections from eleven books that weekend. She spent the whole first night sobbing, closing all the windows to make sure the neighbors couldn't hear. It was strange, she knew, that validation would make her so sad, but she felt like she'd lost something important. She figured she was mourning the loss of the childhood she'd always thought she had. As cruel and demanding as her dad had been when she lived at home, Alex had assumed he acted that way out of love. Once, when Ben won a track meet but didn't break his own personal record, Daniel pulled over in a field on the way home and told Ben to throw the javelin until he threw it farther than he ever had before. They stayed in the field until three in the morning. At the time, Alex saw behavior like that as upsetting, but necessary. Daniel pushed Alex and Ben so hard so that they could escape small-town Arkansas and live their best possible lives. Daniel regularly told his children that his influence was what got them into Ivy League schools: "My pushing you is the only reason you're successful." That was how Alex stayed in the emotional abuse cycle for so long. Every time her dad did something mean, she forgave him by rationalizing his behavior. It was because he loved her so much.

In December of her senior year, Daniel sent Alex an e-mail with the subject line "I know." Alex's mom had broken down and told him

Alex was gay, something Alex had shared with her before she left for Princeton in August. Daniel said he'd never been more disappointed and forbade her from ever contacting him or her mom again. Three days later, when she was diagnosed with cervical dystonia, Alex replied to the e-mail. She explained the severity of the disease and asked about health insurance. Daniel said he couldn't help her; he had already taken her off the family health care plan. These actions were especially confusing because of the language Daniel used in his e-mails. His cruelty was subtle. He said things to make Alex feel guilty, rather than angry, absolving himself of responsibility. In one particular message, he told Alex that she was putting him and her mother through unimaginable pain: "Please try to understand that it is all your dad can do just to have a desire to breathe another breath. I am a broken man right now." He told Alex that he didn't blame her, but that he couldn't help feeling sad. At the end of the message, he said, "We are not rejecting you at all, but this is a mystery we simply can't understand."

He would always sign off with "Love, Dad." After reading the emotional abuse books, Alex combed through the e-mails from December. Now she read his kindness and vulnerability as manipulation. Even in the "down" part of the abuse cycle, Daniel said things to try to keep Alex close, never alienating her so much that she wouldn't want to come back.

At the beginning, this worked. Alex agonized over every one of his e-mails, trying to read "I will forgive you" between the lines. She desperately wanted her dad to accept her again, so she adopted the "love-bombing" tactic, promising herself she would send him a steady stream of affection, even if she got nothing in return. Daniel transitioned into the "up" half of the abuse cycle in April, when he started planning the family trip to Europe. But by that point, Alex had started to realize how much his mood swings messed up her life. This time, his kindness wasn't nearly as effective at winning her over.

"The abuse cycle is a bunch of ups and downs," she said. "But when my dad found out I was gay, he did too many mean things in one 'down' period. After that, there was nothing he could really do to make it okay again."

The more Alex read, the angrier she became. Finally, she felt justified in connecting all the dots, making lists in her mind of every awful thing her dad had ever done—to her, to Ben, but also to her mom. Emily had married Daniel right out of high school as a way to escape her home, where, since the age of three, she'd been sexually abused by her father, the town's chief of police. For years, no one believed Emily. When she opened up to her pastor, he told her never to tell anyone else, then tried to sexually abuse her himself. Emily thought everything would get better when she moved out of her family's house and married Daniel, but it didn't. When she finally told him about her father's abuse, years after they got married, he said he never would have married her if he'd known. For as long as Alex could remember, Daniel had tried to control Emily in the same way he controlled her and her brother. He regularly told her that, as the pastor's wife, she had to behave in a very particular way: be at church any time the doors were open, never wear clothes that were too revealing or too expensive, avoid making any close friends. After he found out that Alex was gay, he forbade Emily from seeing her.

After reading the books, Alex made the decision to cut off all communication with her dad, without apologizing for it. She knew this was going to be difficult. Daniel had hardwired Alex to believe that she won love by performing well—by getting straight

As, winning javelin meets, getting into top colleges. As a teenager, Alex had been terrified of trying anything too difficult—like taking a computer science class or even applying to Princeton, scared that everyone in her life would stop loving her if she failed. Because she'd spent her whole life moving through her father's abuse cycle, she felt like she could stop being loved at any moment.

Over the weekend, alone in the Redmond house, Alex realized how much of her self-worth actually stemmed from her dad and winning his approval. That was why she felt like a bad person so much of the time. Through high school and most of college, she gauged her success by how often her dad told her he loved her. Now that was irrelevant. Alex knew it would be tempting to transfer her dad's power to someone new—to Bethany or Ben—but she didn't want to get her self-worth from them, either. She wanted it to come from herself.

■ ◆ ■ ◆ ■

When I met up with Olivia at the Washington Square Park subway station, it took me a few seconds to recognize her. She was wearing cargo pants, a black tank top without a bra, and a backward baseball cap and carrying at least forty pounds of sound and video equipment. There was a hardness in her facial expression that I didn't remember ever seeing when we were at school.

As Olivia led the way to the park—me half running to keep up with her, even with her heavy cargo—she told me about her split with Leon.

"I can't stop to think about it too much. But I'm strong. I'm fucking strong. Right now I feel like I've been hurt so badly, you could literally throw any kind of shit at me and I could take it."

She definitely seemed strong. Her biceps were noticeably bigger than when I saw her last. She'd been going to yoga every day since she got back from San Francisco, taking the most advanced classes at the studio even though she'd never done yoga before.

"You remember that I have a tendency to want to harm myself when I'm stressed, right?" she asked offhandedly as we walked, like I could have forgotten. "Well, now I channel that energy into yoga. I am determined to do every pose even if it kills me."

Olivia told me her strategy for getting over Leon was to make him regret wanting to break up with her—to show him how good she could be without him. To do that, she had to get in shape, find something fulfilling to do, make money, and move into her own apartment. Back in May, Olivia had submitted an application to a documentary filmmaking fellowship at a New York City incubator, a company that helps people develop new projects. The documentary would focus on women in New York City who participated in the drug trade in college. Olivia's plan was to tell the stories of five or six different women, explaining how they sold drugs and circumvented the administration at their universities.

A few weeks before she left for San Francisco, Olivia found out she'd been selected for the fellowship. The incubator would provide her with mentorship, classes, and a workspace for three months, while she worked on her documentary. The fellowship didn't come with any money, but instructors taught classes on how to generate the right kind of media attention and run a successful fund-raising campaign through an online crowd-funding platform. Olivia had been excited about the documentary before she left for San Francisco, but she'd also resented it for keeping her in New York City, far away from Leon. Most people who won the fellowship also had full-time jobs, so she'd spent most of her pre–San Francisco days alone in the incubator offices, missing him. But now that they'd broken up, Olivia was free to take full advantage of the opportunity.

"I've been running around everywhere without breaks since I got back," Olivia said while we walked. "It's crazy. I'll get up early in the morning, film one piece for the documentary, then go to a coffee shop and edit, then go to yoga, then film someone else. I love it. I feel so fucking good." She paused and turned to look at me. "I'm sorry if I'm being too aggressive. I just feel really strong, like not taking shit. I am being more aggressive than you remember, right?"

She was. In the year and a half that we'd been friends, there had always been a guy in the picture, someone she obsessed over and depended on. Now Olivia was adamant about her independence. She insisted on it with a ferocity that made me wonder if she was trying to convince herself it was real.

Around 11:30 that night, we took a forty-five-minute subway ride to Olivia's Brooklyn apartment. On the way, I asked her if she ever felt unsafe, on her own in New York.

"Only in my neighborhood," she said.

As soon as we got off the train, I knew I'd been in an area like this only a few times in my life, and never without a large group or this late at night.

"Walk with me in the middle of the road," Olivia said. "You want to stay where there's the most light."

"How long of a walk is it to your house?" I asked, trying to sound casual and like I wasn't at all nervous.

"Only seven minutes," she said, laughing. "Don't worry, you can do it. I do it every day."

Lying next to Olivia on her air mattress that night, I realized that New York—particularly hanging out with Olivia in New York—made me feel like I was too sheltered and too boring. Both of those feelings came from the same place: self-consciousness about where I was from. Being the girl from suburban Connecticut, the student at Princeton. But I was accustomed to these insecurities. They cropped up a lot. I don't think I would have been nearly as affected by them if Olivia hadn't insinuated that she thought they were valid.

Earlier that night, when we arrived at Olivia's apartment, she told me she didn't think I should move to DC: "You'll just be really sheltered there and you need to be less sheltered. You would grow a lot in New York. I think you need to get away from Robert. He's too safe for you." She clearly knew I'd been uncomfortable walking from the subway. Olivia also asked if I wanted to go to a topless book club in Central Park the next morning, but before I could answer she laughed and said, "But of course you wouldn't want to go to something like that." She was right—I wouldn't—but I wished she hadn't made that assumption.

The next day, I felt like Olivia was judging every facet of my post-graduation life: having a long-term relationship, moving into a group house with a few Princeton graduates, staying on my family's health insurance plan. Her comments implied that I lived in a safe and uninteresting bubble and was unwilling to try existing anyplace else. On the other hand, Olivia was open to trying anything: polyamorous relationships, cheap apartments in unfamiliar Brooklyn neighborhoods, topless book clubs. For the time being, she'd stopped working as a sugar baby, but if the right opportunity presented itself, she told me she was open to starting again. When I brought up something interesting I'd heard on *This American Life,* a radio show with an audience comprising predominantly white, highly educated, middle- to upper-class Americans, Olivia said, "That show is interesting for people like you because it tells stories of eccentric people, but I know those kinds of people personally so it's not that interesting for me."

She kept talking about all the cool people she'd met in New York, most of whom also sugar dated. She spent half an hour telling me about one particular sugar baby she knew who had an affair with her forty-year-old music teacher at age sixteen, then moved out of her family's home and into a warehouse with twelve German models. "That girl has *lived a life,*" Olivia said. "I want to be like that. I need those kinds of stories." A part of me started wondering if I should want those kinds of stories, too—if I was mind-numbingly ordinary without them.

Around four o'clock, I made up some excuse for having to leave. I needed to go somewhere and figure out why I was taking what Olivia said so personally—and why she'd said it in the first place. I ended up in Central Park, holding a book in front of my face so nobody could see that I was crying.

I don't think Olivia was intentionally trying to make me feel bad, but I do wonder if she was trying to mask insecurities similar to mine. For most of her life, Olivia was also sheltered and privileged because of her family. Her dad was a multimillionaire in Malaysia, and she completed her senior year of high school at one of the most prestigious boarding schools in the United States. I think Olivia and I—and maybe Michelle as well—feared this privilege that, to some extent, defined us. Money had never been a major problem in our lives and, in some ways, I think that made us less self-sufficient than many of our less affluent peers. Living on her own in New York, Olivia wanted to struggle, and she wanted other people to know she had struggled. Being around her made me think that I needed to struggle, too.

CHAPTER FOUR

September–October

Do you have any tea?" I asked, holding a pillow tight to my chest and rubbing its silk tag between my fingers.

The woman staring at me from across the room said, "No, I'm sorry, we actually don't."

She wrote a few words at the top of her legal pad and underlined them with a flourish, then continued to stare. I wondered whether the silence was intentional—whether she was manufacturing awkwardness to bait me into saying something noteworthy.

"Maybe just some water then?" I wanted her to get up and stop staring.

"Sure, yes. I'll be right back."

I was already sure that I'd made a mistake by coming to this appointment. It was my first time seeing a psychologist. Somehow I'd assumed it would be more relaxing. More like getting your head rubbed in the sink at the hairdresser's and less like a gynecological exam. I was, after all, paying this person an exorbitant amount of money to make me feel better. Shouldn't I have been overwhelmed by a sense of calm, walking into her office? I'd imagined Zen gardens, candles, steaming mugs of herbal tea, and one of those portable babbling fountains they sell at Brookstone. But this space felt industrial and sterilized, with stark white walls and a large filing cabinet behind the psychologist's desk. I thought about the labeled manila folder she'd probably already made for her new patient.

When she came back, I tried to make small talk.

"How long have you lived here in DC?"

"Quite a while. We just moved into this office, though."

More silence.

"So we can do this one of two ways," she finally said. "You can either start by telling me everything you want me to know—about your background and about how you're feeling now—or I can just start asking questions."

"Um, well, I guess maybe ask me questions? I've never done this before."

"You mean you've never been to a psychologist?"

"No, I haven't."

"Oh, interesting, interesting," she said, scribbling the first note on her legal pad. "Well, what made you come in today?"

"A couple things, I guess. I've been feeling pretty sad lately. A lot of things have been changing and I'm kind of overwhelmed."

I paused, waiting for her to ask another question. She said nothing.

"I just graduated from college in June, and I moved here to be with my boyfriend. I think the biggest issue is the nature of my job. I'm a writer, so I'm alone for at least nine hours every day. I'm just not used to that, and it's lonely."

I paused again. Nothing.

"I haven't made many—or actually any—friends in DC. That's partially because of my job, but I also don't get along with the people I live with. That's especially hard because Robert—that's my boyfriend—has made a bunch of friends. He loves his new roommates, and I'm jealous. It makes me feel like there's something wrong with me, that I've been living with eight people for two months and haven't gotten to know any of them."

She kept nodding and writing for at least thirty seconds after that. When it became clear that I wasn't going to offer anything else, she started asking about my parents and how I grew up. I understood that she wanted to learn my history to put my current feelings in context. But I didn't want to talk about my childhood. I wanted to get right to solving the problem. Before the session, I'd convinced myself that if I was just completely honest with the psychologist, if I used the magic word I was pretty sure now applied to me—"depression"—she'd be able to say some magic words of her own.

But I couldn't be completely honest with her. The whole time, I felt like I was using my "speech and debate" voice—the perky, people-pleasing intonation I employed in high school and college when I needed to convince judges that I was the best contestant in a competition. After a few minutes of talking, I began to view the psychologist as a judge and spent the remaining half hour trying to persuade her that I was perfectly okay. I think I recoiled because she shared so little of herself with me. I wanted to know where she grew up, how she came to be a psychologist, if she was married and had kids. I wanted to feel like I was having a conversation with a person, not an interview with a wall.

At the end of the session, she said, "Well, it seems like starting therapy for you would be preventative. And that's great—we'll deal with any issues before they become debilitating."

Clearly my act had worked. "Um, actually, these feelings are debilitating right now. I cry pretty much every day, and I don't know how to stop."

"Ah," she said, lifting her pen off the page and looking up from her legal pad. "I'm glad you told me. That's good to know."

I HATED THAT MY MOM had been right. When I decided to write this book and every other person in my life was the jumping-up-and-down kind of excited, my mom said she was worried.

"You're so social, Caroline. If you do this, you'll be lonely."

At the time, I didn't think much of this warning. I'd wanted to be a writer since elementary school. For the chance to write a book, I thought, surely I could stomach a few solitary hours in a coffee shop. When we moved to DC and Robert started going into the office from 9:00 to 5:30 every day, I eased myself into solitude by compulsively listening to the Harry Potter books on tape. A book a week, at least. I'd read or listened to the full Harry Potter series at least five times before, but revisiting it was comforting. After four years at college, when all of my closest friends were at most a five-minute walk away, I craved familiarity. I had a few DC acquaintances, but there was no one besides Robert whom I felt I knew well. But I did know Harry, Ron, and Hermione.

The most difficult part of my fall began when I finished listening to all seven books. I guess I could have just started the whole series again, but that felt a little too pathetic. Deciding to reconnect with my favorite childhood characters was something I could laugh off with my friends, but reconnecting with them for the second time in two months was embarrassing. So I found other ways to do the familiar. Every morning, immediately after Robert left for work, I'd watch two episodes of *Gilmore Girls* (a storyline I was even more familiar with than Harry Potter's)—three or four episodes if it was a particularly bad day. I never wanted to try any new restaurants. Instead, I asked Robert to go back to the pizza place we frequented when I interned in DC the summer before, because it reminded me of a time when I was happier. These things calmed me down while I was doing them, but afterward they made me feel guilty, like I wasn't moving forward, like I was stuck in my old college life. I knew that at some point, I would have to let go of the comforting familiarity and try new things, but I wasn't ready for that yet.

I made the appointment with this psychologist when I realized that I now defined a "good day" as one when I didn't cry, and I hadn't had a good day in three weeks. I would try to work in a coffee shop for at least a few hours every day, to be around people—but then I'd come home and start sobbing on my bedroom floor.

Nine hours is a long time to be alone, and being alone was hard, but the physical loneliness wasn't the only thing making me sad. I felt like I'd suddenly lost all the major people in my life. My three best friends from Princeton, Ray, Katherine, and Catherine, were all busy with other obligations—one still at college, one looking for a job, one working overtime on a political campaign. My mom had pretty much stopped talking to me because she didn't agree with my personal and professional decisions. I did have Robert, but he had other people—four roommates he loved spending time with—so he didn't need me nearly as much as I needed him. I would sometimes spend whole afternoons googling phrases like "ways to meet people in DC" and "young professional friend networking DC." But, as it turns out, search engines can't really help you make friends.

I had never been depressed before, but I knew that I was now. My whole body ached all the time. I had trouble sleeping. I was so jealous of Robert's new friends that I would try to limit the time he spent with them. I didn't know what to do, but I knew I couldn't keep dealing with it on my own, so I started scouring the Internet for psychologists. I e-mailed this particular one because I thought she had a nice smile.

■ ◆ ■ ◆ ■

"Nam-myoho-renge-kyo. Nam-myoho-renge-kyo. Nam-myoho-renge-kyo. Nam-myoho-renge-kyo." Olivia rocked back and forth in her chair with her eyes closed and her palms together, chanting the same Japanese words over and over again.

There were twenty other people in the tiny living room in East Harlem, sitting inches apart, reciting the same thing. Some mumbled the words; some shouted them. Some fingered strings of red and brown beads in time with their chanting. Most stared at a shrine at the front of the room: a piece of parchment flanked by flowers and bowls filled with assorted liquids and spices. I sat next to Olivia with my iPhone on my lap, trying to partially cover the screen with my sweater and discreetly read the words everyone else in the room clearly had down a long time ago.

After we chanted for half an hour, we formed a circle with our chairs. The group leader invited everyone to "share testimony." The stories all followed the same basic arc: a group member went through something difficult—one woman had breast cancer, one man had a child with a disease no doctor could identify—but after chanting regularly, thirty minutes every morning and night, their situation improved: chemotherapy started working, the doctors came up with an accurate diagnosis. After each story, everyone in the circle said something supportive—"Thank you for sharing," "We can learn so much from you," "You've been so brave."

At the end of the summer, Drew, one of Olivia's friends at the incubator, had introduced her to Nichiren Buddhism. She went to the first meeting because she thought Drew was cute. She hadn't expected to like it. But then she realized she actually identified with a lot of the Nichiren values. It wasn't anything like the Buddhism she'd grown up with in Malaysia. Nichiren emphasized finding happiness in your current life: if you lived in the right way—if you were a good person—you could find "enlightenment." *Nam-myoho-renge-kyo* literally means "I submit myself to the Lotus Sutra," but Drew told Olivia to instead imagine herself saying, "We believe we can be happy now."

"Nichiren is about helping people become happy and successful," Olivia said. "I like that a lot because that's what I'm here on earth for—to realize my highest potential. That is so intrinsically me right now. I want to realize every single part of me."

Olivia didn't particularly care about the religious element of Nichiren. Unlike all the other people in her prayer group, she didn't believe chanting could solve her problems. She went to the meetings because she liked the people. She called them "neurotically positive." Everyone seemed to genuinely believe that they could make their lives better and that they could help make each other's lives better, too. They were interesting, and right now, Olivia was determined to invest her time in interesting people.

SINCE SHE BROKE UP with Leon, Olivia had been trying to meet as many different types of people as possible. She gravitated toward groups that encouraged some sort of alternative lifestyle, groups with different ideas about what it meant to lead a happy, fulfilled life: the Nichiren Buddhists, the polyamorous community, and the rationalists, a group of people who value logic and reason above everything else. She met a lot of creative types through the incubator, and creative types usually were in with the kind of alternative groups she was looking for.

It made sense to me that, after four years at Princeton, Olivia felt this urgent need to branch out and explore. Princeton isn't a place that really encourages students to be "alternative"—at least not in the way Olivia wanted to be. The school community rewards people who are different—who pursue very specific interests or come from diverse backgrounds—but only if they package themselves in a way the school can understand. A polyamorous LGBT activist could be successful at Princeton, but only if she sought recognition in socially acceptable ways—for example, if she organized an important new program through the LGBT center, marketed that program to other universities, and won a Fulbright fellowship to do research on LGBT rights in some remote developing country after graduation.

Most of Olivia's closest friends from Princeton were heading down traditional, well-trodden paths, working for large and well-established companies. Her classmates seemed to cling to the definitions of success Princeton provided for them, namely wealth, security, and prestige. As a student, Olivia had also bought into these definitions. She'd spent the second half of her senior year furiously sending out applications to the most famous advertising agencies in New York City. At the time, she figured that kind of job would allow her to be both creative and traditionally successful. When all the agencies rejected her, she was devastated.

Olivia knew that, by Princeton standards, she didn't seem successful. The documentary wasn't backed by any major media companies, she had no celebrity endorsements, and, worst of all, she had no money. Almost every day, she posted some variation of the same Facebook status: she explained her documentary and asked (sometimes begged) for money.

To fund the documentary, Olivia had started a campaign through an online crowd-funding organization. Olivia's supervisor at the incubator encouraged her to think of the fund-raising campaign as her salary and select a target amount based on how much she would expect to be paid working for a corporation. So Olivia decided to try to raise $30,000. The problem was that if Olivia didn't collect $30,000 in thirty days, she wouldn't get any of the money. People could pledge $29,500, and she'd still get nothing. Olivia made a comprehensive list of everyone she knew, as well as anyone wealthy those people might have access to. Every day, she sent dozens of e-mails, hoping that some acquaintance from school would agree to talk to his or her wealthy, well-connected parent. Her career hinged entirely on the generosity of others. To the Princeton community, she knew that degree of dependency didn't exactly signal success.

Most of Olivia's friends from Princeton thought she was wasting her time on a documentary that might turn out to be a bust and on a long list of seemingly random experiences totally unrelated to her career. But she didn't care. Every day, she went out looking for something to inspire her. "I feel super high energy all the time," she told me when I visited in September. She loved New York City. She loved the new people she was meeting every day, the alternative lifestyles she was seeking out and adopting as her own. She felt like she was doing everything she could to realize her highest potential. Plus, she was having fun.

▪ ◆ ▪ ◆ ▪

All nine hundred people in the Brooklyn Tabernacle had their heads bowed and their hands in the air. As Denise and I searched for seats in the back, we squeezed past a man the size of a professional linebacker, with tattoos all over his arms, standing in the middle of the aisle, eyes closed, and belting the words to the praise song that reverberated through the building: *"From my heart to the heavens, Jesus be the center. It's all about you, yes, it's all about you."* As soon as we found a place to sit, Denise stood up and started singing. I followed suit.

Almost the entire congregation at the Brooklyn Tabernacle was black, and this particular service—running from eight to eleven on a Friday night—catered to young adults in their early to midtwenties. Someone had clearly tried hard to make the space feel young. The stage was decorated with fairy lights and black banners with the words "pray," "hope," and "love" emblazoned on them in white glitter; ten musicians in low-rise, ripped jeans and polo shirts sang and played instruments onstage. The pastor couldn't have been older than thirty.

"If you're here and you want to make a change, just put your hands in the air," the pastor shouted during a break in the music. "It's a sign of surrender—surrendering to God."

I felt extremely self-conscious, standing next to Denise and the other people in the pew. I was singing and swaying, like them, but I wasn't sure if I really believed the words I was saying. I wanted to believe. I was desperate to feel a little bit of the peace they seemed to find in the hymns we were singing.

Despite my years at Catholic school, I've never been particularly religious. I've had a few moments when I thought that might change, but something always turned me off Catholicism: the ban on female priests, the anti-LGBT rhetoric, the idea that all bad things happen for a reason ("No," I'd always want to say in response, "some things just suck"). Watching Denise, I realized how reassuring it would have been to hand my problems over to a higher power. To let him (or her) worry about how my post-college life would work itself out. I wouldn't need a therapist, I thought, if I felt like I could talk to God and he would listen. That night, I felt jealous of how strongly Denise believed.

As Denise closed her eyes and lifted her arms up, her whole body relaxed. Her shoulders dropped, her face softened. I knew Denise had been under a lot of stress lately. On the subway on the way to church, we talked about her med school applications. It was the beginning of October and she still hadn't finished them. She'd told a couple of people how far behind she was—her mom and a few best friends from school—but their reactions had all been the same: "Don't worry! Just get them in as soon as you can. Your application is so strong, it won't matter."

"They just don't get it," she said to me. Most people Denise knew submitted everything by the end of July. Mid-August, at the latest. Denise knew she probably wasn't going to get in anywhere, even her safety school. Every year, fewer than half the people who apply to American medical schools get in. This wasn't like those times she thought she failed a test and got a B+. But no matter how many times she said that, no one believed her.

After she took her MCAT, Denise shut down. She couldn't

force herself to do any more work. She went out dancing with friends at night and toured New York City with Craig, who was now her boyfriend, on the weekends. Even though she couldn't completely forget the long to-do list on her desk at home, it was easy to justify deprioritizing it. She hadn't allowed herself to have fun for any extended period of time since last Christmas, when she started writing her senior thesis. Since then, the major deadlines had come in quick succession: senior thesis in late April, the first section of all her med school applications in early June, MCAT in late July.

Multiple times a week ever since she moved to New York, Denise had been trying out different churches, searching for the same kind of support she'd felt from her religious community in college. At Princeton, she'd been part of a group that met every Friday night in one of the university's biggest lecture halls. Two hundred students gathered to sing praise songs and listen to lectures by Christian leaders. Later in the week, the group broke into smaller sections for Bible study. Denise didn't agree with its leaders on some political and moral issues, but she still went to meetings because of how connected she felt to other people in the group. Before she joined the group at the end of freshman year, Denise had felt distant from her faith. She saw going to church as just another item on her to-do list, a basic requirement of her Christian identity. That changed when she found the right kind of religious community.

Denise rarely talked to her friends about her problems—she didn't want to burden them or take too much of their time—but she did open up to her Princeton Bible study. At the end of every session, the leader used to ask for prayer requests. When she talked about her struggles in that context, Denise felt less like she was looking for attention. She wasn't offering her experiences to help herself, but to help others. She felt more comfortable being honest with her friends from church, but she also needed the advice only they could give: Trust God. He's got your back. He'll figure it out.

"I was missing that kind of community in a big way," Denise said. "I'm always focused on my plan, and I need other people to remind me that God has a plan, too."

ON HER WAY TO CLASS one day in November of her senior year, Denise got a call from her little brother.

"Daddy's collapsed," he said, hysterical. "There are doctors everywhere at the house and he's not responding."

"What?"

"He's not responding!" David screamed into the phone.

"I'm coming now," Denise said, hanging up. All she wanted to do was run in circles and process what her brother just told her. Her home life felt far away while she was at Princeton, but now suddenly her mind had to switch gears—from figuring out what readings she should prepare for class to how to get to Illinois in the next few hours.

"My legs just somehow moved apart from the rest of my body, my mind, and my sensibilities," Denise said. "Somehow I was on the bus, going to the Princeton train station. Then I was on the phone, booking a flight with American Airlines. Then I was on the plane home, then in a rental car driving to the hospital."

On the hour drive from the airport, Denise prayed. She bargained with God in a way she hadn't in a long time, promising to make changes in her relationship with her father and do whatever she could to be better: "Just please keep him alive." By the time she arrived at the hospital, Denise's father had been sedated. Her whole family was gathered around his bed. Her mom and aunts were on their knees, praying, while nurses ran in and out of the room, grimacing at whatever they saw on the monitors. That afternoon, the doctor told Denise's mom there was an 80 percent chance that her dad was going to die.

At home later that night, Denise sat up with her little sister, Joanna. "Listen to me," she said, trying to regulate her breathing as she stroked Joanna's hair. "Listen to me. We're sobbing and we don't know what to do right now, but I feel like this is going to be a net positive. God is going to get the glory in this situation."

Faith had always been important to Denise. When she lived at home, her family prayed when they woke up, when they went to bed, and before and after every meal. Denise had typically been the one leading these prayers, making sure they were said every day. But even though she'd believed in God, Denise had still seen herself as the one in the driver's seat of her own life. She determined how hard she worked and, consequently, the extent of what she could achieve. When her dad made a full recovery after three weeks in the hospital, however, Denise started to see herself as less significant. She realized God was actually the one in control.

"God has the reins. Any challenges that you think God does not have control over, he does," Denise told me after her dad recovered. "He was there for me, and he always has the reins."

DENISE HADN'T BEEN able to surrender to God in that way for a while. Raising her arms in the Brooklyn Tabernacle, she desperately wanted to get that feeling back. Her father's sickness and recovery had thoroughly convinced her that God had a purpose for everything. A few weeks after returning to Princeton from Illinois, she'd shared her dad's story publicly, in front of her church. She told her congregation that the time in the ICU forced her family to consider what was most important: estranged extended family came to visit, and her father and brother started openly expressing how much they cared about each other. For a while, it also stopped Denise from worrying about what she was going to do after graduation and where she was going to go to medical school.

At her church in Princeton, people shared stories like that all the time. She needed that now. She wished she could go to her Princeton Bible study again. She would tell her friends how late she was with her med school applications, ask for prayers, and then listen as they reminded her what was really important. She enjoyed the service at the Brooklyn Tabernacle—singing with the nationally acclaimed choir, hanging out with a few people she knew from Princeton after the service—but it wasn't the same kind of community. There were too many people. And because there were multiple services every week, she couldn't even count on seeing the few friends she did have in the congregation. Every week, she drifted in and out of a random pew. No one knew what was really going on in her life. No one knew if she missed a week of church. No one would know if she stopped going altogether.

■ ◆ ■ ◆ ■

As Alex walked out of the terminal at JFK, she felt someone jump onto her back and start vigorously kissing the top of her head. Dropping her duffel bag, Alex grabbed every part of Bethany she could reach—her butt, her nose, tufts of her bushy black hair. As quickly as possible, she needed to confirm that her girlfriend's face and body felt the same way she remembered.

"I attribute one of the best feelings I've ever had to that moment," Alex said. "The way Bethany was embracing me—I knew for sure how much she loved me and missed me. I'd been having such a hard time in Seattle, but that feeling made everything okay."

Back in July, Alex had expected three months to pass quickly, but they'd dragged on. Alex hated Redmond. She hated its shuttered clapboard houses in varying hues of white, tan, and brown that lined mazes of quiet cul-de-sacs. Redmond is home to the Microsoft headquarters, an operation that employs forty thousand people. The average resident is in their forties or fifties, with a wardrobe full of Patagonia, a yen for hiking, and an Ivy League–bound child competing in Major League Hacking or the Intel Science Talent Search.

Alex immediately noticed the structure of the streets in Redmond. To stop people from cutting through, only one road leads into the town and only one leads out. The rest are all interwoven inside the Redmond limits. It took only ten minutes for Alex to leave town, but the design still made her feel trapped. The younger contingent of Microsoft employees, most of whom lived in downtown Seattle, escaped on a company shuttle at the end of every workday. After a few weeks in Redmond, Alex started wishing she could get on the shuttle, too.

The house itself felt even more constricting than the town. Even though Alex was paying a third of the rent, she felt like a guest, tiptoeing around her brother and sister-in-law. Ben and Tory's house was immaculate, with high ceilings, shiny steel appliances, and matching cream-colored walls and carpeting; it looked like a show home. Nothing was ever left on any of the surfaces, no knickknacks on side tables or the kitchen counter. If Alex left anything downstairs at night—a sweater, her water bottle, a pair of socks—the items would be neatly piled up outside her door in the morning.

"It was like they were saying, 'Stay in your corner, do what we say, work ridiculous hours. This is your life. This is your box.'"

A few days after she got to Redmond, Alex downloaded a countdown app on her phone, and over the next three months, she watched the number of days get smaller and smaller. Every night, she got one day closer to Bethany and the community she'd developed in Princeton and New York during her senior year.

As Alex had gotten to know Bethany, she'd also befriended all of Bethany's friends—a hyperintellectual crowd of writers, entrepreneurs, scientists, and professors, almost all with master's degrees or PhDs from Ivy League schools. Alex had never before been part of a group that didn't judge her for something—for being gay, for wanting to go to Princeton, for having no money, for being too religious, for not being religious enough. She couldn't believe how easily Bethany's friends accepted her. The first time she met him, Bethany's best friend, George, pulled Alex aside and said, "You're the first person I really like Bethany being with. I'm so glad she finally found you." These people—Bethany's people—were the closest thing Alex had ever had to a tribe. She chose that particular weekend in September to fly to the East Coast because George was getting married. George's friends were Bethany's friends, and Bethany's friends were Alex's friends, so the wedding would be a sort of tribe reunion. No tiptoeing necessary.

GEORGE AND HIS FIANCÉE, Erica, held their wedding at George's parents' cabin in the woods, in upstate New York. The wedding was simple—they got married under four strips of white sheets and fairy lights hung from the eaves of an unfinished barn—but Alex thought it was the most beautiful ceremony she'd ever seen. The wedding party danced into the barn, laughing, following men playing steel drums in green-and-purple jester's hats. Erica carried white wildflowers from the garden and wore a Grecian-style headband made of gold-plated leaves. There was dirt and a lot of bugs, and some people weren't sitting where they were supposed to, but Alex loved that about the wedding. It was the antithesis of the Redmond house. George and Erica didn't care if things were messy or disorganized, because the day was about their relationship, not fancy programs and seating charts. After Erica walked up the aisle, Bethany squeezed Alex's hand and rested her head on her shoulder. The feeling of togetherness and acceptance was so overwhelming, Alex started to cry.

When George read the vows he wrote for Erica, he kept having to stop to catch his breath. Everyone sitting around Alex was crying, too. She interpreted that emotion as a collective nod of approval. This relationship was right, and everyone knew it.

"George and Erica are the kind of couple you meet and know immediately: they are going to do it," Alex said. "They're a great couple. They're going to be great parents. They care about each other more than anything else in the world."

Alex idealized George and Erica's relationship. She wanted every part of it. She wanted their wedding, their supportive family and friends, the easy way they touched each other in public that didn't seem like a performance for anyone else. George and Erica dated for six years before they got married. They were long-distance, and then George moved to Boston for three years—a city he hated—to be with Erica while she went to business school.

Alex wanted her and Bethany to love each other enough to make those kinds of sacrifices. Alex was ready to do that for Bethany. In a year, she planned to move to New York City, probably without a job, so they could be together.

If it had been up to Bethany, she and Alex would have already been engaged. A few months after they started dating, Bethany said, "I'm ready now but I know you're not, so you have to be the one to choose when this happens." Bethany spent her late twenties exploring polyamory while going to graduate school in London. She was still polyamorous but, at age thirty-one, she was ready to start a family. She firmly believed that marriage and children didn't necessitate monogamy.

When Alex first found out that Bethany was polyamorous, she'd been a little skeptical. But after she read a few books Bethany recommended, poly started to make sense. She could never do it herself—she didn't have the emotional capacity to be physically intimate with more than one person at once—but she understood why it was so important to Bethany. Bethany was bisexual, and while she had a stronger emotional connection with women, she had a stronger physical connection with men. Alex had a lot of experience with feeling trapped: she'd felt trapped as a gay teenager in rural Arkansas, and her mom felt trapped in her marriage. She never wanted to make her partner feel that way. As long as she and Bethany set clear boundaries and stayed honest with each other, she didn't have a problem with her having sex with guys. But no girls. Alex could handle Bethany having other physical relationships. Other emotional relationships were something else entirely.

Alex believed that Bethany could be both polyamorous and a loyal wife. She couldn't wait to marry her. Six years younger, Alex knew she should probably wait a few years and have some of her own solo adventures, but she didn't want to risk losing Bethany. While Alex had spent most of her life in a state of loneliness and self-denial, Bethany was accustomed to getting what she wanted. She was the only child of two parents for whom money was no object. She'd gone to an elite private high school in New York City, Harvard for undergrad, and Princeton for graduate school. Polyamory allowed her to fulfill all her romantic desires: if one partner was falling short in some way, she could always find someone else to provide whatever her existing relationship was missing. Being in a long-distance relationship, and waiting to get married, necessitated a state of deprivation that Bethany wasn't used to. So Alex knew she couldn't wait too long to move to New York.

Over the summer, Alex had distracted herself from missing Bethany by planning the proposal. She'd decided to do it a little less than a year from now—in June, at Princeton Reunions. She would start by taking Bethany to all the places that were significant in their relationship: the dorm room where they'd met, the one where she'd lost her virginity, and Bethany's apartment. At the end of the night, they'd cuddle together inside a sheet fort, where Bethany would find *The Strange Case of Dr. Jekyll and Mr. Hyde,* their favorite book, and a note that said, "I love you in Jekyll and in Hyde." Alex had already picked out the ring.

"We're in the giddy stage," Alex said. "It's very reassuring to know I could text her 'Will you marry me?' right now and she would say yes. It's nice to know that she's not going to reject me."

Bethany didn't know when Alex was planning to propose, but at George and Erica's wedding, they talked about their future like they were already engaged. They'd chosen the venue for the wedding and shared a Google Docs list of whom they wanted to invite. They'd decided what they were going to do about last names: combine the two—Burner and Grady—to make "Burdy." And just to be safe, they'd gone ahead and claimed their future e-mail addresses: alexburdy@gmail.com and bethanyburdy@gmail.com. Bethany was Alex's first girlfriend, and they'd been dating only nine months, but Alex didn't think that mattered. She was sure. Bethany said she was sure. That was good enough.

WHEN ALEX LANDED IN SEATTLE, she sat on a bench at baggage claim and looked at her phone for a while before calling a car on Uber. She wanted to delay her return to Redmond for as long as possible.

"So where are you coming from?" the driver asked when Alex got in the car.

"I just flew back from New York."

"God, I'm sorry. Bet you're glad to be back."

Alex didn't say anything.

"I used to live on the East Coast and there's just no comparison. The mountains, the ocean—and people are just so much more laid-back here."

This was one of the things Alex hated most about living in Seattle. Everyone around her was obsessed with it. After living in Redmond for three months and going hiking every weekend, Ben and Tory were convinced it was where they wanted to raise their kids. They constantly made her feel guilty for not taking advantage of what they called the most beautiful place in the country. But Alex didn't want to take advantage of Seattle. She wanted to keep hating it. It would be easier to close herself up in her room and wait for the year to pass.

■ ◆ ■ ◆ ■

"He's not who you would expect me to date. I don't know how to describe him. He's blond and nice. He used to be a Christian. Basically, a happy white guy. I'm only the second girl he's ever had sex with. He didn't have sex until he was twenty-six! Can you believe that?" Olivia asked, laughing so hard she had to spit some of her coffee back into her cup.

Olivia met Michael on a dating website at the beginning of October. He was conventionally and indisputably successful. After graduating from Dartmouth, Michael became a software engineer in California, working for Google and Dropbox while simultaneously amassing a small fortune from Bitcoin, an online currency with a value that fluctuated wildly for a brief period of time. Now he lived in a newly renovated apartment in the middle of Union Square.

"He's pretty boring," Olivia said. "I'm not crazy about him, but he's not crazy about me, either, so it's okay."

"Have you told him that you think he's boring?"

"Yes, he knows, and he's fine with it. Like the other day, I asked Michael whether the people at his company were cool and interesting. He asked me, 'Do I count as cool and interesting?' And he said, 'I don't think I do.'"

"That's so sad! What did you say?"

"I said,"—she paused, giggling—"'You are very thoughtful.'"

"So are you going to stop seeing him then?"

"No! Why would I do that? I love it because it's so easy. Michael is very accommodating. He's so accommodating, it's ridiculous."

"What do you mean?"

"Well, he always wants to hang out, and he also pays for a lot of stuff. He feels like a brother or a father—someone I want to come home to. It just feels great." Olivia explained that they weren't dating, just hanging out. Michael had never heard of polyamory before he'd met her, but he agreed to try it.

Since she met Michael, Olivia had started spending more and more nights at his apartment. In part, she did this because it was convenient. To work on her documentary, she had to be in downtown Manhattan almost every day, but the only place she could afford was at the end of the subway line, deep in Brooklyn. Michael's apartment, on the other hand, was within walking distance to most of the places where she went to film and edit. But Olivia also just liked seeing Michael at the end of every day.

Michael was stable. He went to work every morning at nine and came home at six. He was never late on his rent. He wanted to get married and have kids. He ate meal-replacement bars instead of cooking because they provided a perfectly balanced diet.

"He doesn't cause trouble, he doesn't need much," Olivia told me. "He just lives a good, normal life."

And while lately Olivia had been surrounding herself with people who surprised her—who took risks and challenged her to think about things in a new way—she appreciated having one person around whose actions she could predict. She knew Michael would meet her when he promised to. She also knew exactly where he would be in ten years.

Michael's presence in her life also helped a lot financially. He let her stay in his apartment and paid for about half her meals, taking her out to dinner multiple times a week and keeping her well stocked in meal-replacement bars. Olivia was accepting money from her parents again, but her relationship with Michael allowed her to ask for only half of what she otherwise would have needed to live in New York. She wanted to get a part-time job but couldn't because the documentary was taking up all of her time. At least until the crowd-funding campaign ended, she resigned herself to relying on other people for the money she needed to get by.

■ ◆ ■ ◆ ■

"Yo, Michizzle!" a tall, lanky boy carrying a trombone said, punching Michelle's shoulder. His friend—a tall, lanky boy with a trumpet—watched with wide eyes, clearly impressed.

"Oh god," Michelle said after they passed.

"What?" I asked.

"That guy—he asked me to 'hang out' last week. I said fine, but then he took me to this super romantic café. Now I've made a promise to myself: do not hang out with undergrad boys to do anything but play music. They flirt with any girl they can find."

Later that day, I found out this was not entirely true. "Michelle is known as the super-hot girl at our school," Michelle's friend Mary told me. "All the guys are dying to hook up with her."

When I asked Michelle about it, she reluctantly confirmed this was true.

"I guess I'm kind of a novelty here," she said. "All the guys tell me how 'normal' I am—I know that's a compliment because this school has a reputation for being full of fucking awkward, nerdy kids."

There are two music conservatories within the same one-mile radius in Philadelphia. When classes first started, Michelle was keenly aware of both schools because she knew that, to an outsider, it might seem like she'd picked the wrong one. One school is large, flashy, and commercial—in Michelle's words, "a factory for

Taylor Swift–Mariah Carey hybrids" eager to belt catchy choruses to sold-out stadiums. The other—Michelle's school—is much smaller and primarily concerned with producing music that is progressive and alternative, rather than popular.

The schools seem to resemble their students. The Taylor Swift factory has twenty-one different buildings, the newest of which is sixteen stories tall, made entirely of glass, and lit up at night with dramatic purple floodlights. Michelle's school, on the other hand, has just three—all made of simple gray stone, indistinguishable from others on the street. Inside, the wall-to-wall carpet is dotted with spots of blackened gum. The metal folding chairs are dented, the TVs mounted on the walls are from the late 1990s, and many of the music stands have been reinforced with Scotch tape. Almost everyone at Michelle's school is on a scholarship.

Even though it wasn't much to look at, Michelle felt proud of her conservatory. She loved that it had an entire department dedicated to avant-garde music that bridged jazz and classical. She loved that the curriculum forced her to think deeply about why she chose to write and sing particular notes. She loved that her professors encouraged students to take risks with their music—to improvise and combine different sounds, to play without a hook or a melody.

But as much as she loved her school, Michelle felt like she constantly had to prove she belonged there. Always the most popular girl in her class in middle and high school, Michelle looked and acted like the more mainstream musicians, the pop stars in training. But that wasn't a problem. Good looks and an outgoing personality didn't keep her out of the club at her conservatory. For Michelle, the more concerning difference between her and her classmates was her musical background. At the other school,

Michelle said, all you needed was a good ear to learn music. But at her own, that wasn't nearly enough. The curriculum was highly technical. Most of her classmates had gone to jazz camps every summer. When they were young, their parents (often musicians themselves) enrolled them in advanced music classes, so they were already fluent in jazz theory and technique by the time they finished high school. While everyone else in her master's program went to an undergraduate music school, Michelle had gone to Princeton—and hadn't even majored in music. For years, the vast majority of students at her conservatory had known they would have a career in music. A year ago, Michelle hadn't even considered it.

By the end of September, after a few weeks at music school, Michelle started coming to terms with how far behind she was. At first, it hadn't been readily apparent. Michelle got good grades—As on almost every assignment—but as hard as this was to accept after four years at Princeton, she realized that, at the conservatory, grades didn't matter much. Most students came to class late and never did the homework, and the professors didn't mind. They knew students were spending their time on more important things: playing gigs, recording albums, doing whatever they deemed necessary to develop themselves as jazz artists. Professors understood that, for most people, a graduate degree in music was a way to make connections and get feedback from top musicians, rather than to learn any new skills. But for Michelle, the curriculum was new and difficult. Because she spent a lot of time on her academic work, she could do most assignments as well, if not better, than other people in her class. But if a professor asked her to explain a theoretical concept on the spot, without any time to think about it, she'd usually pause for too long or have to ask a friend for help.

Michelle's spotty musical background was most apparent in her experimental ensemble: a group of eight jazz majors who got together twice a week to improvise, monitored by a professor. Of all her classes, this was the only one almost everybody prepared for, probably because the professor, Jim Sharpe, was one of the most renowned and well-respected professors at the school. Clearly a vestige of Woodstock, he had long, curly gray hair and wore casual, loose-fitting tunics. Michelle called him "one of the big guns."

Experimental ensemble was different from any musical group Michelle had ever been a part of. Most of the time, the different instruments—saxophone, electric guitar, bass, cello, piano, trumpet, drums—grated on one another, creating the illusion that eight people were simultaneously playing the wrong note. Every musician in the circle had a sheet of music with a few notes on it. After they played those notes, they improvised and reacted to one another—speeding up, slowing down, getting louder and softer, taking out certain instruments, adding others—until something sounded good. And eventually, it did.

"Gorgeous," Jim said when the piano and the cello were the only instruments left playing, aggressively gesticulating with both hands. "This duo is gorgeous."

Those kinds of compliments made Michelle jealous. Every day in ensemble, she purposely lost all sense of what was going on in the classroom, closing her eyes and trying to savor each syllable—to say something with each syllable: *"ba da du da du du."* It was incredibly intimate. When I watched Michelle sing in ensemble for the first time, she delivered the last few "*ba da du*s" to the very serious-looking bass player in the back wearing an oxford shirt buttoned up to the top, who promptly turned bright red. Michelle engaged completely with the improvisation, taking the risk that came with losing all self-awareness. But still, Jim had never once said he liked her vocals.

"Jim just fucking shat on me all the time," Michelle said. "He would single me out a lot. He'd say all this stupid shit you don't say to singers, like 'Just *wail*!' That didn't mean anything to me."

One day in early October, Michelle e-mailed Jim to ask how she could improve. She wanted to know what kinds of vocalists she should be listening to. He sent her a compilation of the strangest sounds she'd ever heard a singer make—a series of aggressively articulated consonants and drawn-out vowels. It was weird, but at this point, Michelle was willing to give anything a shot. She was tired of being called out in class for doing something wrong. If this was what Jim wanted, she'd do it. She practiced the noises all weekend and walked into class ready to try them.

Halfway through the session, Michelle took a five-minute solo, imitating the noises she'd heard on Jim's tape. It was embarrassing—she was sure she sounded ridiculous to the other people in her ensemble—but if Jim gave her a compliment, it would be worth it. When she finished, Jim raised his eyebrows, shook his head, and said, "No." He told the class to take out the next sheet of music.

CHAPTER FIVE

November

Around 8:30 every night, I started feeling guilty. I'd hear footsteps upstairs, then the TV, then voices, as my roommates started congregating in the common room. I knew I should have gone to hang out with them—that the socializing would make me feel better than sitting on my bed, watching another episode of a TV show I'd seen before, waiting for Robert to come over. But it would take so much energy. It had been a long time since I'd mingled with a large group of people I didn't know and I'd forgotten about the anxiety. When I hung out with my new roommates, I felt like I had to be "on" every second because everything was contributing to their opinion of me. I would think carefully about everything I said and did before I said or did it, making me far more quiet and withdrawn than usual. This perception of constant judgment could have been all in my head (they probably weren't thinking about me all that much), but I couldn't shake the feeling. I knew it would eventually get better. Once I'd been around them for a while, I'd relax a little more. Hopefully, we would establish that I liked them, and they liked me, so we'd all have reason to be forgiving. If I got too aggressive in a debate or didn't know about some current event they assumed was common knowledge, they wouldn't make a snap judgment about me. They would give me the benefit of the doubt: she's tired, she's been busy, she's just in a bad mood.

This social paranoia was particularly problematic because it made me feel bland. Like a standardized, censored version of my former self. Sometimes when I spend time with a new friend, I'll ask myself, "Am I comfortable enough with this person to make my duck noise?" It's always been my special talent—I puff air in my cheeks and push it out with the corners of my mouth. The subsequent sound is fairly loud and startling, and people are generally amused. But it's weird. Not for acquaintances. Only for friends. The freedom to act and talk and make random noises without thinking was what made me feel close to my friends in college. But at my house in DC, I wasn't comfortable enough to function without inhibition. When we hung out, I didn't say much, which—upon later inspection, back in my room, alone—made me think that I didn't have much to say. After living in the house for a few weeks, I managed to convince myself that I was hopelessly dull and that no one wanted to be friends with me. This feeling was exacerbated by how little I heard from my closest friends. If they didn't want to invest in their friendship with me, I thought, who would?

At the end of October, I went back to Princeton for the first time to judge a mock trial scrimmage. If any one thing defined my four years at college, it was my mock trial team: a bunch of type-A kids in suits who took our task of defending made-up people in a made-up city far too seriously. At the beginning of my freshman year at Princeton, there was a mad rush to join a group: an a cappella ensemble, a club sports team, a fraternity or sorority, a musical theater troupe. These affiliations were especially important at Princeton because they funneled into the eating clubs, which 75 percent of the class typically joined in the middle of sophomore year. To get into most of the clubs, you had to have older people rooting for you. So at first, it was social pressure that pushed me to bond with a group that spanned all four class years. But after that—after I'd gotten into my eating club and felt settled at Princeton—it was easier to just stick with my unit. Even when the seniors in mock trial graduated every year, they passed down their stories—so when I was a senior, the freshmen on my team knew about things I'd done as a freshman, three years before. Especially considering how much most of us changed during college, that feeling of being known was incredibly reassuring.

My senior year, the mock trial team consisted of nine people. My friend Ray was my cocaptain, and, for the second half of the year, Robert was our coach. There were days when the three of us would spend eight hours in the mock trial room, cycling through different members of the team, watching direct examinations, cross-examinations, opening statements, and closing arguments. Then we'd all go back to my room to talk and drink wine until two in the morning. I stopped going out to the eating clubs at night. Screaming over loud music and aggressive beer pong players wasn't nearly as appealing as a quiet night with my unit. We finished my senior year with the American Mock Trial Association National Championship Tournament in Orlando. The year before, our team had been ranked sixty-third in the country. That weekend, we came in second. Standing on the stage in front of hundreds of people, accepting our award with Ray on one side and Robert on the other, I felt intensely loved and accepted. I thought about how I could cry in front of any one of these nine people—I knew they would listen and try to help. I tried not to dwell on the fact that I was the only one graduating.

WHEN THE NEW TEAM CAPTAINS first asked Robert and me to come back to campus, I said I didn't want to go.

"It's too soon," I told Robert. "I don't want to intrude."

"Intrude? These are your friends, Caroline. They want you to come."

I hesitated for a couple of reasons. I didn't want to be the alum who never left campus. I'd never been one of those college students who happily said they were living the best years of their life—I'd always assumed those would come later, after all the studying and preparation. So when graduates came back to campus multiple times a year, I used to see that as a kind of failure. Now I thought about the mock trial team and nationals all the time—and that embarrassed me. I worried that if I returned to Princeton too soon, people might notice just how nostalgic I was feeling.

My bigger concern was whether the team members actually wanted to see me. A part of me knew this was ridiculous. They'd invited us. But no one on the team had done much to reach out to me since the beginning of the new school year. I knew it would be extremely painful if I went back and saw they were a happier and more cohesive team without me—if they didn't want to hang out with me, or, worse, if they felt obligated to.

When I walked into the mock trial room for the first time since June, the whole team was there, setting up for the scrimmage.

Anna, Charlotte, and Nancy—the three freshman and sophomore girls I'd been close with during junior and senior year—screamed, ran over, and hugged me. Big bear hugs.

"We're all going to dinner with you after this, right?" Anna asked, holding my hand and jumping up and down. "Do you want to go out tonight? I can put you on the list at my eating club!"

"If you want to, yes! I'd love that."

"We're all going to dinner," said Taylor, the resident frat guy on the mock trial team. "It's great to see you, dude." He pulled me into a hug. "I'm glad you're here."

I'd tried hard not to get my hopes up about the visit, but I still secretly had pretty high expectations. That night exceeded all of them. We ate dinner, then talked and played drinking games at my old eating club until after three. I'd forgotten what it was like not to be self-conscious. I was just there, in the moment, enjoying the people around me. Laughing. Not thinking about why I was laughing, or the weird sound of my laughing.

TWENTY-FOUR HOURS LATER, I was back in my room in DC. I heard two people run upstairs and then the opening credits of *Cutthroat Kitchen,* one of the many TV shows my roommates regularly watched together. I thought the weekend in Princeton might boost my confidence: remind me of who I was around friends and how to interact with a large group of people. But if anything, it even more thoroughly impaired my social instincts, because now I knew exactly what I was missing. And it felt impossible to achieve with these new people. The comfort I felt when spending time with my mock trial team took years to establish. I was probably going to be in DC for only a year—two at the most—so what was the point?

Whenever I felt lonely, I could just go to a mock trial tournament. The team came down to DC or Baltimore every few months. Surely that would be enough contact to remind myself that I still had friends. Now, I told myself, I could guiltlessly watch reruns of my favorite TV shows on Netflix in peace. Problem solved.

■ ◆ ■ ◆ ■

"Okay, guys. This one's a little weird. I'm not sure what I was thinking when I wrote it," Michelle said, passing out sheets of music to the boys on piano, drums, and bass guitar. "It's got sort of a creepy, old country-western feel."

The piano came in first with a series of chords, then the drums, then Michelle started scatting over the top—no words, just sounds. Siofra, Michelle's vocal ensemble professor, closed her eyes and mouthed the syllables as Michelle sang them.

"Yeah. Dig," the drummer said when they stopped playing. "It makes me feel like watching *Edward Scissorhands*."

"Intriguing," said Siofra. She paused and looked around the room. "What journey are we on?"

"Uh, I don't really know. Do you think it's too much or too weird?"

"Weird? What is weird?" Siofra asked. "The important thing is what the music means to you."

This kind of feedback was possibly even more frustrating than her other professor's harsh, unspecific criticism. Most professors at Michelle's school refused to label something good or bad. They left that up to the student. Michelle knew most students appreciated this element of her school's culture. Unlike a lot of conservatories, there wasn't an obvious hierarchy of the best, most talented musicians. Her school tried to hire professors with diverse musical backgrounds and, by extension, different ideas about what constituted great music. But this musical freedom made Michelle feel like she didn't know what she was doing. Her classmates in the graduate jazz program clearly knew exactly who they were as artists and what kind of music they wanted to create. If they wrote a song that wasn't "them," they could recognize that something was off without a professor's help. But Michelle needed the guidance. She'd just sung a really strange, creepy song—was that the kind of music she should be focusing on? Was that "her sound"? She had no idea.

"With pretty much all famous jazz players, you can hear their music and know who it is," said Max, a friend of Michelle's and a senior at her music school. "That's a big part of how we define success in jazz: How unique are you? Also, is your music valid? Anyone can make something radical, but is it worthy of people hearing it?"

Michelle didn't know how to make something unique and valid. She knew it took time to develop an individual "sound" or "concept," because most of her classmates had been cultivating theirs since middle school. At age fourteen, Max, for example, discovered that he loved Bach, and ever since then, Bach had provided the foundation for his musical identity. Max had been adding to that foundation, incorporating various elements of other composers he admired, for almost ten years. Michelle didn't have a foundation or any time to find one (while middle school Max was listening to Bach, she'd been worshipping pop princess Mariah Carey). Without a clear idea of the kind of music she wanted to create, Michelle felt like an imposter: somebody pretending to be a serious musician in a place where everyone else actually was one.

She wondered again how much of a role Sam, her college boyfriend, played in her decision to go to music school.

"I've been thrown into this cohort of people who see music as their entire life," Michelle said. "Music is what they live and breathe every day, what they've lived and breathed for as long as they can remember. And honestly, I can go for days without thinking about it. Does that mean that I'm not as worthy or that this isn't for me?"

Michelle knew her classmates felt a strong emotional connection to music. For them, it was more than a hobby. More, even, than a career. Most people in the graduate jazz program were far more reserved and introspective than anyone she'd spent time with at Princeton, always preferring to spend Friday night smoking weed with a few good friends and their instruments to meeting people they didn't know. For many of them, Michelle said, music was the only way they could express themselves. But Michelle had never needed help communicating and connecting with other people. Sometimes she felt guilty, because music meant so much more to them than it did to her.

The stakes were also higher for Michelle's classmates. If they didn't succeed in the music industry, they didn't have a whole lot of other options. Their only academic degrees were in music, from conservatories. Michelle, on the other hand, had a BA from Princeton. She also had parents who would be able to help her financially for as long as she needed it. Michelle's mom and dad had always pressured her and her brother to do the unconventional. They said they didn't care if they made money. It also helped that Michelle's dad was a huge jazz fan. He'd introduced her to his favorite jazz musicians when she was a toddler and built a fully equipped recording studio in the basement of their house in London.

"We are privileged enough that you can do what makes you happy," her dad had told her many times. "Don't waste your life on something boring."

When Michelle decided to get a master's in jazz, her parents agreed to support her—to pay her tuition, rent, and all other living expenses—for two years in music school and for at least one year after she graduated. Michelle never talked about money with her friends at the conservatory because, even with the school's generous scholarship program, most were going tens of thousands of dollars into debt to get their degrees, and they weren't likely to be able to pay that back any time soon. Only a handful of the luckiest and most talented musicians at her school would be able to support themselves in the music industry without a day job.

It seemed to Michelle that her classmates approached their music with an intentionality she lacked. They knew exactly what they wanted to get out of school (that was why they were willing to give up so much of their own money to go). She felt like she had as a freshman at Princeton—unmoored from academic or professional goals. Back then, it had been socially acceptable to flounder and wander. The graduate jazz program at one of the country's most competitive music conservatories, on the other hand, certainly didn't seem like the place for trial and error or deep self-exploration. By the time you got to this point, Michelle thought, you were supposed to know what sounded weird and what sounded right. But she didn't, and she didn't know how to learn.

■ ◆ ■ ◆ ■

When Olivia walked into the Palo Alto mansion on Halloween, she was dressed as an ecosystem, wearing a flower-patterned romper, socks embroidered with ducks, and a stripy brown jacket that she'd decided to tell everyone represented a tree. The house was one of the most decadent she'd ever seen, decorated in an old Victorian style, with vintage photographs on the walls and a grand piano in the entryway. She was nervous to meet all the high-profile San Francisco entrepreneurs and software engineers she knew would be at the party. She didn't feel cool enough to be here, particularly when she considered her own bleak career prospects: aspiring documentarian with a trailer, a failed crowd-funding campaign, and no clear path to finishing her film.

"Mason! Guys, Mason's here!" someone shouted over the blaring music as a group of people swarmed around them.

"Dude, we've been waiting for you," another person said before turning to Olivia. "Who's this?"

"This is my friend Olivia," said Mason. "She's from New York, just in San Francisco for a couple weeks. She's awesome. She's a documentary filmmaker."

Olivia beamed, feeling her cheeks start to glow.

"Wow, that's really cool," Mason's friend said. "This guy is the best. He was one of the first investors in our company."

Someone standing in a nearby group of people turned around. "And ours too!"

Alongside Mason, she was immediately ushered into a room at the back of the house, where twenty or thirty people were lying in a dog pile on pillows on the floor, passing around joints and hooking up with each other.

Olivia had met Mason the night she broke up with Leon, her primary, back in July, on a date she set up through OkCupid's website. She'd scheduled the date before the breakup (she and Leon had been trying to get involved in the San Francisco poly scene) and decided that going out with someone new was preferable to staying in Leon's apartment. Olivia ended up crying hysterically as soon as she and Mason started having sex. But Mason comforted her and, after she calmed down, they sat up in bed and talked for three hours. Mason told her all about the San Francisco rationalist community and how being a rationalist changed his life.

Rationalists, by definition, reject anything they don't think is logical. They say they're always thinking about the reasons they make particular decisions, asking themselves what is statistically most likely to maximize their success and happiness in life. If they realize they're being inadvertently swayed by emotion or some kind of social convention, they change their behavior. Olivia told me that a lot of rationalists are polyamorous because they see marriage as something people are just expected to do, not something that will actually make them happier.

Mason was a rationalist leader in San Francisco, the movement's birthplace and epicenter. He had a top job at one of the most prominent rationalist research organizations in the country, and all his friends—his roommates, his (primary) girlfriend, and many of the people at the Halloween party—also called themselves rationalists. When Olivia described Mason to me, she used the phrase "big fucking deal" at least five times. "In this community," she said, "he is a god."

After she met Mason in July, Olivia made a conscious effort to keep in touch with him. They texted back and forth throughout August and September. Mostly, they talked about rationalism—Mason sent her articles and she replied, usually a few minutes later, with a list of questions. Of all the new communities she'd sought out since graduation, Olivia was most interested in the rationalists. She didn't know if she could ever be one herself—she didn't have a strong enough hold on her emotions—but she liked the way they approached their lives.

"In all things, I want to come closest to the truth. I am skeptical about the way human society is told to do things. Rationalists are, too. I am attracted to rationalism because I prioritize truth so much," Olivia told me.

In October, one of Olivia's main reasons for going back to San Francisco was to learn more about rationalism. Another was to pursue a relationship with Mason. Even though she'd been spending a big chunk of her time with Michael, the ex-Christian she met online, lately, they'd agreed to be polyamorous, and she wanted to explore.

THE WEEK AFTER the Halloween party, Olivia went to a three-day rationalist workshop. As soon as she got there, the leaders asked her three questions: What do you have a "burning desire" to do in your life? Why are you not doing that thing? What are concrete steps you can take to make sure you start doing that thing, right now? Olivia called it "well-researched, data-driven self-help." Olivia had quite a few burning desires but picked two: to make her documentary and to be financially independent from her parents. The workshop leaders told her to weigh her options by looking at her life like a math problem.

"They told me that if I took a job that paid a lot of money instead of pursuing the documentary, I had to calculate the cost of that other job," Olivia said. "The cost was that I wouldn't be reaching my full potential. I would be sacrificing my happiness and depriving the world of all I could create. They asked me how much money that was worth."

When Olivia raised only $14,000 through her crowd-funding campaign, her confidence took a major hit. Up until the last day of the campaign, she'd held out hope for a big donor—she'd heard that most successful crowd-funding projects made over half their money in the last twenty-four hours—but none came. Almost all her donations had been from friends, each for less than a hundred dollars. Olivia wanted to keep working on the documentary, even without the money. That had always been her backup plan. But ever since the campaign failed, that option had started to seem a little indulgent. She worried the documentary wasn't actually as special and important as she'd thought. Olivia had been thinking about doing something more mainstream for a while—maybe reapplying to work at an advertising agency, or going back to Malaysia to work for her father's construction business. The problem was that, right now, the two "burning desires" she talked about at the rationalist workshop seemed mutually exclusive. If she gave up on the documentary, she could probably become financially independent. If she didn't, she would have to keep relying heavily on her parents and Michael.

But at the workshop, and over her next few weeks in San Francisco, the rationalists convinced Olivia to keep believing in the documentary. They were always talking about "finding your potential" and "contributing to the world." Olivia knew she couldn't contribute to the world at a big company in New York. That situation would be just like college.

For as long as I knew Olivia at Princeton, I saw her struggle academically. Most of these problems stemmed from the fact that her English still wasn't perfect—she'd occasionally use the wrong word or broken grammar—so writing papers or essay tests was much harder for her than it was for her American classmates. At best, Olivia felt like she could do an assignment almost as well as everyone else. After she struggled to complete her senior thesis, turning it in almost a month late, her self-esteem was shaken. She felt like she would never be able to contribute to the world from the United States in any meaningful way.

The documentary gave her a purpose. She loved filming, interviewing, and piecing footage together. And she was good at it. Her subjects told her that. People who watched her trailer told her that. For the first time since she left Malaysia, she felt like she was doing something other people couldn't, and she didn't want to go back to feeling useless. The rationalists assured Olivia that she could, and should, make herself useful.

"I became so secure in San Francisco because I got so much positive feedback about the project from Mason and other people in the rationalist community. When someone like Mason tells other people at a party that you're a cool person and do cool work, that's all you need."

RIGHT BEFORE OLIVIA LEFT San Francisco, a large film and television development company called her and expressed interest in turning her documentary footage into a miniseries. The company sent over a contract. Even without advice from a lawyer, Olivia knew the terms weren't great. The company would require her to give up all the rights to her work, and it would pay her only $2,500 upfront. Olivia would have thirty days to write eight episode summaries for a potential miniseries. After that, the company would review her work and decide if it wanted to move forward with the project. If it did, Olivia would be a codirector. If it didn't, she would be barred from producing any creative material related to the subject matter for at least six months. A few of Olivia's lawyer friends warned her that the language in the contract was suspiciously vague and could potentially prevent her from doing anything with the material ever again.

During the three weeks with the rationalists, Olivia had been working on an action plan: a list of changes she wanted to make to her life in New York. The first step was to spend less time with Michael and more with people she felt she could learn from, particularly Mason and her other rationalist friends. The second was to finish the documentary project. The third was to become financially independent as soon as possible. Before the call from the media company, Olivia thought she was going to have to choose between her second and third goal. But if she took the deal, and the firm decided to green-light her project, she could conceivably support herself and continue her film career. That seemed like her best shot at achieving her fullest potential.

Olivia agreed to the company's terms. As soon as she got back to New York, she began the thirty-day trial period.

■ ◆ ■ ◆ ■

"We're in Champaign!" Denise yelled as they drove past the three big blue buildings on the outskirts of town. This was her tradition. Since she was a toddler, she'd pointed out these buildings every time she crossed the border into Champaign, Illinois.

"I can't believe how time flies," Denise's mom said. "You know, if you go to this school, you will be taught by some of the same teachers who taught me, in the same classrooms. Amen, that would be something."

Denise and Nahvet arrived at the University of Illinois at Urbana–Champaign with three hours to spare. This was Denise's first med school interview, and she wanted to make sure she had time to relax and prepare. But once they arrived, instead of continuing to grill Denise with potential interview questions, as she'd done on the ninety-minute trip from Springfield, Nahvet insisted they take a drive around town.

Around the same age Denise was now, Nahvet flew from Cameroon to Champaign. Nahvet had won the African Graduate Fellowship, a scholarship sponsored by the United States Agency for International Development and the African American Institute that sent three African students to universities in the United States. Every year, three hundred of the best students in the country applied. Nahvet had never been out of Africa, and she assumed things like this automatically went to the worldly, rich children of diplomats or businessmen. When she got the scholarship, she feverishly started applying to schools in the United States, eventually choosing the University of Illinois over Cornell because she had a friend there. By the time Denise was born, Nahvet was one of the top students in her class. When she went into labor, she brought her statistics assignment to the hospital; before going home the next day, she stopped by the math department to turn it in.

"Do you remember which apartment was ours?" Nahvet asked Denise as she pulled into the graduate student-housing unit where they lived while Nahvet finished her PhD.

"7105 Apartment 404, Oakwood Circle," Denise sang in the rhythm she remembered from when her mom made her and her brother memorize their address. The units at Oakwood were simple. It was the kind of sprawling three-story structure with outdoor stairs typical of a low-cost hotel you'd find off the interstate. Like a dorm, the walls were white cinder block; the floors, a

speckled tan linoleum. Nahvet had bought all the furniture from past graduate students when they moved out. But even though the space was somewhat dull, Denise remembered her years at Oakwood as loud and colorful. Her mom's African friends—other graduate students—were always filing in and out of the apartment, inviting her to graduation parties, asking her to be the flower girl at their weddings, cooking jollof rice and grilled tilapia for the gatherings the African community at Champaign hosted every Friday night.

"I owe who I am today to this school," Nahvet told Denise as she drove.

Denise had watched her mom—and a dozen people she now called aunts and uncles—graduate from the University of Illinois. Almost all of them were first-generation Americans. This school had been the first stop in their new life in their new country.

"It was a very full-circle experience," Denise later told me. "It was weird to think: this is *my* interview, this is me going on to *my* schooling, after seeing so many other people in my life study and graduate from here."

But as much fun as she had driving around with her mom, checking out all the places they used to go together, Denise was keenly aware of the fact that a circle started and finished in the same place. She wanted her parents to be able to look at her life—her academic and professional trajectory—and feel like she'd moved forward. Even though her mom clearly loved taking her around Champaign, Denise felt sure Nahvet would be disappointed if she ended up here for medical school. Last year, Denise wouldn't have guessed she'd even be interviewing at the University of Illinois. She would have assumed she'd have too many other options. The only state university she'd applied to, the University of Illinois was

Denise's safety school. But now, it was one of only two she'd heard back from. This late in the year, that was a bad sign. Most of the other Princeton people she knew who were also applying to medical school had already lined up more than ten interviews. They were already turning schools down.

THE ILLINOIS INTERVIEW WENT WELL. Denise thought she gave good answers to the questions and, as she was walking out, one of the administrators made an offhand comment that started with "When you come here . . ." So she felt fairly sure she'd get in. But that didn't make her feel a whole lot better. She didn't want to think about telling people that the University of Illinois was the only school that accepted her.

Denise regularly asked herself, "Who are 'people'?" Who did she worry was going to think less of her when she didn't get into Harvard? Who was she afraid would stop loving her? At Class Day, surrounded by fifteen relatives in Bamenda gowns, she'd been mostly scared of failing her family. But realistically, she knew that her mom, dad, siblings, and aunts and uncles wouldn't stop loving her if she didn't get into a top medical school. They would be disappointed, but they wouldn't expel her from their fold. It seemed like her Princeton friends, on the other hand, associated with only the smartest and most talented people. One of her two best friends, Cameron, still a senior at Princeton, was the president of the undergraduate student government. The other, Sandra, was starring in an off-Broadway show.

At Princeton, the super-high achievers tend to stick together. They start companies together, apply for joint fellowships together, live together when their prestigious summer internships take them to the same cities. I've heard people say this happens because, even as undergrads, Princeton students think about networking; they don't want to waste their time hanging out with people who won't be useful to them in the future. There are definitely people like that at Princeton—freshmen who scan through their class list, highlighting people with famous parents they want to befriend—but I don't think they're the norm. I think the superstars gravitate toward one another because their personalities mesh well. Denise, for example, is driven and intensely goal-oriented in a way that's hard for a lot of people to understand. Whatever the reason, these superstar groups exist, and at Princeton, Denise was a part of one. She worried that if she didn't get into a top med school, her friends would realize she didn't actually belong.

At Princeton, Denise had thought about where she wanted to go to medical school. It was impossible not to. When you had to get yourself through two semesters of 8:30 A.M. organic chemistry, you had to think about the end goal. There were three schools Denise liked to dream about over all the others: Harvard, because that was where her dad had wanted her to go for undergrad; the University of Pennsylvania, because she did a summer program there; and the University of Chicago, because it was close to home. After she got her second round of MCAT scores back, the first two schools started to seem extremely unlikely. But Chicago was still possible. A long shot, but still possible. Denise had been thinking about UChicago since high school, when she spent every weekend doing service work on the South Side of the city. Denise planned to do a lot of community service during med school—she wanted to volunteer at hospitals and free clinics, applying what she learned in class while providing health care to people who couldn't afford it. She already knew the communities she'd be working with in Chicago and what issues were most important to those communities. The University of Chicago was a familiar place, a three-hour drive from home, and a top-ten medical school. If she went there, she would have both comfort and prestige.

After the Champaign interview, Nahvet drove Denise back to the Chicago airport. As they pulled up to the departures terminal, Denise thought about how badly she wanted to see this building again. Soon.

"Mommy, I really don't know when I'm going to be back. I don't think I'm going to get any more interviews."

Nahvet smiled like she was in on a secret plan Denise knew nothing about. "Oh, you're gonna be back. Don't worry."

■ ◆ ■ ◆ ■

When I drove into Byron, Arkansas, I passed two signs. The first read POP 2,851. Five times its size, the second informed me that I was entering the HOME OF JACKIE SANTORO, MISS TEEN USA 2005. After one more minute on the state highway, I hit the center of town: a gazebo and a perfectly square brown lawn, surrounded on all sides by strips of mostly empty shops. Of the thirty storefronts, there were only three open businesses—vestiges of a once-booming paper mill town: a family steak house, a clothing boutique where most merchandise was marked down 80 percent, and a shop with the words "Thrift Store" painted on the window in slanted, off-center bubble letters. Just beyond the square was the town Sonic, a tobacco outlet, a self-service car wash, a Dollar General, and the First Baptist Church, where a sign outside the front door reminded me that A GREAT GOD IS DOING GREAT THINGS.

I visited Byron because it's where Alex grew up. Her father preached at the First Baptist Church from the time she was twelve to the time she turned seventeen. Byron was the kind of place where the bartender might tell his boss, who might tell your aunt, who might tell your mom, that you'd been out drinking the night before. Everyone knew everybody else. If you were the preacher's daughter, that meant there was always someone watching. This kind of attention would have stifled any teenager, but for Alex—who grew up knowing she was gay—it was terrifying.

"I was afraid to buy Converse shoes," she said, "because I thought that might tip them off."

In sixth grade, Alex's two best friends, Lexi and Kim, were both future beauty queens, one a future Miss Arkansas. One night at Lexi's house, after everyone else had gone to bed, Lexi and Kim asked Alex if she wanted to "experiment." She said no but watched them kiss and touch each other in places she knew people weren't supposed to touch each other until they got married. Lexi and Kim said things like "I've never done this with anyone else," and they talked wistfully about what they would do together if one of them was a boy. Alex felt sure that, if she kissed Lexi or Kim, they'd somehow know she actually fantasized about it—that to her, it was much more than a silly experiment. She stopped hanging out with Lexi after that. Instead, she began obsessing over academic work (even though she was already at the top of her class) and acquired the first of a long string of middle and high school boyfriends.

"Alex used to have really good girlfriends, but then she stopped seeing them and I didn't understand why," Alex's mom told me. She paused, biting her lower lip and staring down at the table. "I think she had crushes on these girls. But because she was in south Arkansas, that was just not okay. She knew they'd put the rebel flag around gay people and hang them."

Alex got used to hiding. She got good at it. With her dad roaming around, keeping an eye out for any questionable behavior, her house was the most dangerous place of all. As soon as she came home, Alex would go into her room, shut the door, and then go into her closet and shut that door as well. She'd pull back the hanging clothes and nestle herself between long coats and dresses.

Alex was well aware of the irony of being in the closet in a closet. But in Byron, that small, confined space was liberating. It allowed Alex to have the thoughts she was scared other people would detect anywhere else. She wanted to keep a journal, but she knew her dad would find it. So she wrote notes to herself inside the old shoe boxes her mom stored behind the clothes in the closet, where she felt sure no one would ever look.

"When she was studying for a test, I would hear her in there, reading things out loud in different accents . . . British, southern," Alex's mom said. "I would go in the closet with her and say, 'Why do you go in here?' She'd say, 'I just like my closet.'"

Eventually, the isolation of the closet got to be too much. Alex needed to know there were other people who identified with what she was going through. She started asking her mom to drop her off at the library to study. Once she watched her car drive away, Alex would head straight for the LGBT section—which, in Byron, Arkansas, was all of half of one shelf. Alex particularly loved the book that Ellen DeGeneres's mom wrote about her daughter coming out and how they navigated the experience together. It made her feel like she and her mom could have a relationship like that one day.

Once Alex's dad sprung for faster Internet, Alex discovered the online community that existed for teenagers struggling with their sexuality. She learned about openly gay people living happily in other parts of the country—with great jobs, a partner, and kids—through videos associated with Dan Savage's It Gets Better Project, a nonprofit that works to combat LGBT teen suicide.

These things—the closet, the library, the Internet—made the hiding bearable. But if she hadn't seen a way out of Byron, Alex knew they wouldn't have been enough. College, she felt sure, would make everything better. She was working so hard at school and at javelin so she could leave Byron and go somewhere far away. Even if she didn't come out immediately, she knew she'd meet all sorts of people—people she hadn't known since she was born—whose worlds were far more interesting and accepting than rural southern Arkansas.

AFTER THREE MONTHS living in Redmond, Alex felt like she was back in Byron. Her bedroom in Ben's house was her new closet; her computer, her portal to a better life; her future in New York with Bethany, her way out. Before she moved to the Northwest, she promised Ben she'd live there until the middle of June. When she got home from George and Erica's wedding, Alex started a new countdown on her phone: the number of days until she could move out of the Redmond house.

Alex made her first appointment with a psychologist a few weeks after I did, three days after she got back from the wedding. The psychologist, who specialized in LGBT issues, didn't say much during the meeting. He listened to her describe her relationships with her dad, her brother, and Bethany. At the end of the hour-long session, he gave Alex one piece of advice: "It sounds like you need to get out of that house. Seven months seems like a long time to wait." Alex knew he was right. She needed space from Ben, and space for herself. She just didn't know how to get it without destroying her relationship with her brother.

The counseling office was in Capitol Hill, a neighborhood in downtown Seattle known for having one of the highest percentages of gay and lesbian residents in the country. After her appointment, Alex decided to wander around. Capitol Hill felt like a college town for grown-ups, with plenty of cheap, independent fast-food joints, thrift stores, and bookshops. Here, the businesses she saw all the time—like Rite Aid and Chipotle—looked completely different, with retro neon signs and storefronts designed to resemble old-fashioned movie theaters or soda shops. She thought it was funny that, in order to do business here, these chains had to at least pretend to be niche and independently owned. But what Alex loved most about Capitol Hill was how proud it was to be gay-friendly. Walking around for two hours, she passed four same-sex couples holding hands. Almost every business—even the chains—displayed some kind of rainbow flag or badge. For the first time since George and Erica's wedding, she felt completely safe. Unconditionally accepted.

When Alex walked into the Redmond house that night, Ben was waiting up for her.

"How'd it go?" he asked.

"Really well, actually. I stayed in the area for a while afterward. I love Capitol Hill."

"What did the therapist say?"

Alex had gone back and forth about whether to tell Ben where she was going. In the end, she decided to be honest because he already knew that something was up. Since the wedding, she'd been sullen and completely closed off, spending every free minute in her bedroom. Alex assumed Ben just hadn't been ready to ask what was going on, worried that her answer to "What is wrong with you?" would be too emotional.

"The therapist said it's very normal to have tension between us, to be living together and working together and be brother and sister. He said that just two of those would cause tension. He also offered to help me find housing resources when I move out."

Ben waited at least a minute before saying anything. "Well, do you want to move out now?"

Alex had been hoping he'd ask this question but never thought he actually would. "Yeah, actually. I think that would be great for our relationship."

"Okay, that's good."

"Really?"

"Yeah, that's fine if it's okay with the landlord. I'll e-mail him tomorrow morning."

THAT CONVERSATION HAPPENED on Thursday. By Saturday, Alex was sleeping in her new apartment on Capitol Hill. After signing a lease late Saturday afternoon, she parked her car, walked around the neighborhood, and flopped onto her new mattress. Her sheets were still in Redmond and she had to roll up a hoodie to use for a pillow, but she didn't care. On Sunday she would go back to the Redmond house, pack up her stuff, vacuum her room, and officially move out.

"When you're in the closet—literally or figuratively—there is such a void that needs to be filled: years of repression and self-loathing and keeping yourself in check and being overly self-aware and trying to keep safe. When you're finally free, you want to fill this huge void and make up all the years you've lost. Living in Redmond, I was trapped again. I needed to get out and be in my own space and make up for the years that I lost. For me, that meant moving to Capitol Hill and doing things that would help me understand what it means to be gay. I just needed to feel free."

CHAPTER SIX

December

By the beginning of December, my relationship with my mom had been reduced to a stiff, mostly one-sided text message conversation. She would send a few words every couple of days: "I got an A on my psychology test" (when I didn't even know she'd enrolled in a psychology class) or "You need to call your grandmother." In my freshman and sophomore years of college, I used to call her twice a day, every day, just to talk.

I usually didn't respond to the texts because responding seemed to endorse this new phase in our relationship. Yelling was one thing. You had to care about someone to tolerate the kind of emotionally exhausting battle of wills we used to engage in on a regular basis. A stilted exchange of text messages, on the other hand, signaled no deep attachment, no prior relationship. It was like my ex-boyfriend casually saying hello at a social function with mutual friends. In those situations, I always wanted to shake him. I wanted to jump around waving pictures I still had on my phone somewhere and say, "Don't you realize how fake this is? We have history. You know me. Say something that shows that you know me." It was always painful to have that kind of interaction with someone I knew. With my mom, it was excruciating.

Christmas was supposed to fix these problems. My parents and I planned to spend the holiday at my sister Milly's house in England: a neutral environment full of distractions—train sets, board games, and my six-year-old nephew—and people my mom and I couldn't comfortably yell at each other around. I'd convinced myself that England would be different from all the interactions we'd had that fall. We'd be face-to-face for a whole week. We'd talk about her classes and my life in DC and make gingerbread houses while "White Christmas" played in the background.

When I walked into my house in Connecticut, thirty minutes before we were supposed to leave for England, I found my mom on the phone with the airline, trying to change her flight. She wanted to push her trip back three days because my grandma was sick, and she didn't want to leave her.

My mom is a worrier. Even though she has siblings in the area, she doesn't trust anyone else to care for her mom as well as she does. So I knew that if she didn't get on the plane with my dad and me, she probably wouldn't come at all. I understood why she wanted to stay—eight years before, my mom was in England when her father died—but Mom told me the doctor said Grandma was healthy enough for her to leave. I knew it was selfish, but I wanted her in England with me. We planned this trip in September, and I'd put a lot of faith in its healing power.

I sat down in the kitchen and tried to calmly explain to my mom why I wanted to spend Christmas with her so badly. "I've been going through a really hard time lately—a really lonely time. I need you right now. I really need you to be there. Please."

I'd never said anything like that to my mom before. I never had to, because, until recently, she always had been there, anticipating how and when I would need support before I did. When I started dating Robert, my mom began distancing herself from me: calling less, visiting Princeton less, then finally saying things like "You're not my daughter anymore." She saw me moving toward Robert and away from her, and followed my lead. After she created distance, I created more—each of us seeming to need the other less and less. I was pretty sure that moving away was some kind of power play on her part, but I always worried that my mom actually didn't love me as much as she used to. Soon after I left for college, she also went to school to get her bachelor's degree, reconnected with her high school friends, and then started the process of divorcing my dad. Even after she decided not to go through with the divorce, she would regularly laugh and say, "I'm an independent woman now." Maybe, I thought, she preferred her new, independent life to the one with me in it. So I drifted further away and pretended not to care, while she did the same. When I begged my mom to come with us to England, I was scared to shatter the tough-girl image I'd tried to create for myself, but I was sure it would be worth the risk. We'd fought a lot over the past couple of months, but when she heard how much I needed her, I expected her to come.

"I can't, Caroline," she said. "Grandma needs me here."

I recoiled, got up from the chair, and turned away. I felt my cheeks heating up. I was embarrassed and suddenly completely vulnerable.

"I promise I'll come in two days," she said. "You'll still be getting over your jet lag, and I'll be there. Okay? I promise."

"I'll stay here then. I'll switch my flight, too, and we'll fly to England together." I figured I'd already exposed myself, so I might as well pull every string available in a desperate effort to make this work.

"No, you can't do that. You need to go now."

"Why? Because you're not coming at all, are you?"

"Yes, I am. I will. I promise."

"No, you won't," I said, my voice breaking audibly now. "You don't care about me at all."

I ran up to my room, breathing heavily as I leaned against my door and slid down to the carpet. She wasn't going to come to England. She was going to spend Christmas in Connecticut alone, and she didn't even want me to stay with her. She wanted to get rid of me. When she created distance between us, it wasn't a defense mechanism. I was just less important to her than I used to be.

I heard my dad crying and yelling at my mom downstairs. "You don't care about Caroline!"

I bit down hard on my tongue. My dad agreed with me. For the past few years, particularly since I found out about the divorce, my dad had backed me up in almost all Mom-related situations. After a particularly difficult phone call or aggressive string of text messages, I'd call him, sometimes crying, to debrief. "I don't know what's going on with your mom, Caroline," he'd say. "It doesn't have anything to do with you or Robert. Try not to worry about it." I imagine this is probably the role siblings play for each other: offering some much-needed perspective on parental behavior. He also helped me see when I was overreacting and when I actually had reason to be upset. So when he accused my mom of not caring about me, I knew it wasn't just in my head.

I waited in my room, texting Robert a play-by-play of my parents' fight, until my dad knocked on my door and told me it was time to go. As I walked out the front door, my mom said good-bye and tried to give me a hug.

"I'll be in England in three days. You won't even notice I'm not there."

"Grandma might get worse. What'll you do then?"

"I'll come to England no matter what. Okay?"

I still didn't believe her. Part of me knew I wasn't being rational—of course my mom still loved me, and she probably would come to England—but I couldn't be sure. I needed proof that she cared.

"If you don't come, I am never speaking to you again." As soon as I said it, I wished I hadn't. I knew it made me sound like a petulant child. I should have just hugged my mom and left. But I felt an intense need to convey how much this trip meant to me because she wasn't getting it. I needed an ultimatum to make it clear: If she didn't come, she didn't care about me. If she didn't come, I didn't think our relationship would ever recover.

On my third day in England, I woke up to a text from my cousin. "You okay? Your mom called last night. She said grandma has pneumonia so she won't be going to England."

■ ◆ ■ ◆ ■

"Hiya! Is Jack around?" Michelle asked the guy standing at the door. She'd been back in London for two days before coming to find Jack, her love interest from the previous summer, at his new art gallery—just long enough, she thought, not to seem like she'd been pining. She wanted to surprise him.

Michelle had been fantasizing about coming home to London

for Christmas since she started school in September. Maybe it was because she didn't know people that well yet, but her friends at school all seemed so serious, completely consumed by their music. When she hung out with them on weekends, the interaction typically devolved into getting high, sitting on the floor, and talking somberly about what their music meant to them. Now she felt a lot like she did after her summer Euro trip: desperate to hang out with her best friend, Lindsay, and be stupid and spontaneous. Maybe trip in the botanical gardens again, or just drive around London in the car with the windows rolled down, making up nonsensical rap songs. Those were the times when Michelle felt most like herself. In London, she knew she wouldn't feel like an imposter anymore.

"Nah, he's out," the guy said.

Michelle knew who this was. She'd seen pictures. His name was James Evans, one of the featured painters at Jack's gallery.

"I've seen your face before," he continued. James peered at Michelle with an intensity that made her look down at her chest to make sure none of the buttons on her blouse had come undone. James's eyes looked like they should have been a snake's: slits so small she could see almost no white, just dark green behind thick, black, rectangular glasses. The two of them were completely alone. Michelle had seen the hours on the gallery door. She knew it wouldn't open for another two hours.

"He's not here, but do you want to come in anyway? I can show you around." James watched Michelle as he rolled up the sleeves of his oxford shirt, exposing arms covered entirely in tattoos: a fork lifting a clump of spaghetti, a teacup overflowing with diamonds, a butcher's knife.

"Wow, this place is incredible," Michelle said as he led her through a hallway and into the main room of the gallery.

"It doesn't take much to please you, does it?"

She laughed. If he wanted to ratchet up the sexual tension, she was happy to help. "That's what I want you to think."

The gallery was simple and unpretentious, with stripped plaster walls and unfinished cement floors. All the furniture was modern and top-of-the-line—glossy oak or black steel—creating the illusion that the exposed walls and floors were art, purposely preserved to be admired alongside the paintings on the walls.

Michelle walked around the room, lingering on a few canvases, pretending to focus on them.

"Do you ever think about whether art and sex are related?" she asked James without looking up.

"Absolutely," he said. "They're both about provoking pleasure. You have to understand how to properly tease someone's senses."

This was an entirely new experience for Michelle. James knew that she wanted to have sex with him. Michelle knew that he wanted to have sex with her. And they both knew that they knew. It was refreshing.

"I can go there, but not many other people are willing to," she told me. "James was totally on the same page."

Michelle tended to pursue introspective, emotional guys who were too timid to make the first move. She was almost always the first one to say something explicitly sexual.

"What are you doing now?" James asked, after half an hour of aggressive flirting.

"Nothing."

"So what's the go, miss? Want to come back to my place?"

"Sure, yeah," Michelle said.

"Before we go," he said, "I should tell you that I have a girlfriend."

James explained that he was polyamorous. He had a girlfriend—a primary—but they agreed to sleep with other people. The two of them had operated that way for years. He said he'd been in a few serious, long-term relationships in his early and midtwenties but always ended up cheating.

"This is how I approach my women—they need to know everything. If they're not comfortable with me being in a relationship and sleeping with a lot of different people, then I don't pursue it."

"Well, I'm down," Michelle said immediately. She'd never thought too much about polyamory. Back in June, I told her about a poly convention Olivia took me to. She found the idea interesting but said she'd never be able to do it herself. She said she'd get too jealous. But now, after six months of being single, Michelle thought poly sounded like a pretty good option.

"Just out of curiosity, how many women are you sleeping with right now?"

"Four."

She loved how unflinchingly honest James was being with her. She loved how unashamed he was of his sexuality. He clearly knew what he needed to feel satisfied, and he was upfront about it. No games. No pretending to be in some way unavailable so the other person would want you more.

FOR THE NEXT THREE WEEKS, Michelle saw James almost every day. He taught her all about poly—why he did it, and what rules he set for himself to make sure he did it right. He introduced her to his girlfriend, and the three of them talked about their relationship over coffee. A few days before she left for the States, Michelle bought *The Ethical Slut*, a book on how to adopt a polyamorous lifestyle, written by two second-wave feminists who had been openly poly for most of their lives.

"When I first started reading it I almost cried with joy," Michelle said. "It was like, oh my god. Everything that I've felt in my relationships—desire for other people, all the feelings people told me were wrong—totally make sense."

Maybe, she thought, the strict exclusivity was the reason her previous relationships had failed. She'd felt restricted. Whatever boy she dated, there were always things she craved, sexually or emotionally, that he couldn't provide. Michelle always assumed that state of deprivation was necessary—just part of being in love and, ultimately, of being happy. But the book taught her that love wasn't finite. If she was in a relationship and started to love another person, that didn't mean she loved her initial boyfriend any less.

Polyamory, Michelle thought, would also stop her from letting any one guy take over her life, as Sam had. She wouldn't be able to mold herself into anyone's perfect image, because there would be more than one guy and more than one ideal. If she became polyamorous, she could take advantage of all the good stuff she got from relationships—emotional connection, companionship, sex—without having to deal with any of the bad.

Even though Michelle couldn't seriously continue her relationship with James once she left England, she promised herself she'd experiment with polyamory in Philadelphia. She knew she'd probably have to look outside her school, because her classmates took their relationships almost as seriously as their music, but she'd figure it out. Her goal was to emulate James's approach to sex and romance. She would be honest and upfront about what she wanted, then do whatever felt good.

When Michelle first told me about her foray into polyamory,

I was surprised. Before that, I'd assumed poly was a small, niche ideology—a way for daring, somewhat stability-averse people like Olivia to experiment with their sexuality. Sitting next to Olivia at the poly convention we went to last May, I saw myself as fundamentally different from every other person in the room. I wanted a serious boyfriend, a husband and children, and a guarantee that it wasn't all going to go away if my partner met someone else he might like better. Surely, I thought, that kind of security was something most people hoped to have in their lives. But when I saw Michelle in January, I started to question those assumptions. When she told me she wanted to be polyamorous, she wasn't just talking about having a few of the casual, open relationships people played around with in college. This was the lifestyle she wanted to adopt from this point forward, the one she thought would make her happiest.

■ ◆ ■ ◆ ■

Alex couldn't concentrate. It was a Friday night in mid-December, and she was in her apartment reading a programming book. Her face suddenly felt tired, and her right eye started to close. This was different from the usual heaviness she felt on her eyelids when her body was telling her to sleep. She physically could not keep the eye open. Alex went into her bathroom and stared at herself in the mirror. All the muscles right of her nose had slackened. One corner of her eye and the right side of her mouth turned down. It was like the entire right side of her face had crumpled under some invisible weight.

Alex didn't know what to do. It was too late to call Bethany on the East Coast, and her brother, Ben, always went to bed early.

She thought about dialing 911 or taking a cab to the ER. She briefly considered that she might be having a stroke, but ultimately decided this probably wasn't an emergency, just bad news. Maybe the doctors had misdiagnosed her. As difficult as dystonia sometimes made her life, Alex felt lucky to have it. Every time she visited her neurologist, she saw his other patients in the waiting room—patients with mind-altering illnesses—and imagined what it would be like to lose the ability to process thoughts in the way she did now.

By the time Alex went to see her doctor on Monday morning, the drooping had spread to her right hand and leg. After poking the weak muscle areas repeatedly with a needle, the neurologist told Alex she just had a particularly intense kind of migraine—which, like dystonia, would affect only her body.

"Is it related to dystonia?" Alex asked, relieved.

"In some way," he said. "It might just be a side effect of your medication. But it could also mean the dystonia is spreading." This was one of the most frustrating parts of having dystonia: it was extremely rare, so even specialists left her with a lot of questions.

"I'm going to give you some steroids, but we'll just have to keep an eye on it."

"Well, if you said to keep two eyes on it, we'd have a problem—but I can keep one eye on it!"

The neurologist laughed while Alex looked at herself in the mirror. She thought she kind of looked like a basset hound, but it wasn't that big of a deal. If her brain was healthy, she could handle looking weird for a while.

After the appointment, Ben picked Alex up in Capitol Hill and drove her to Redmond, where she spent the rest of the afternoon on the couch, wearing a patch on her right eye, wrapped in layers of the REI clothing Ben and his wife, Tory, wore hiking. She tried working on her laptop, but the patch made her see double and she couldn't force herself to fixate on tiny pieces of code. Every few hours, Tory knelt down beside her and put drops in her eye.

Since Alex moved out of the house, Ben had asked her repeatedly to spend the night in Redmond. She'd never had this kind of migraine before, but dystonia caused a host of other problems that made it difficult to function. Ben understood Alex's disease probably better than anyone else. Usually he just had to look at her, and the swelling in her neck, to know she needed help. Once every twelve weeks, Alex got a Botox injection in her neck, which stopped the cramping and relaxed her muscles. But after a while, the injections wore off, and one shot every three months was all her insurance would cover. The last week or two before a treatment, Alex had a hard time moving around. Anything that involved turning her head, like driving, became impossible. Sometimes she couldn't stand or sit upright and had to work on her laptop in bed. On the worst days, the pain was so bad that she had to take high doses of Valium, muscle relaxers, or L-dopa and couldn't work at all. So Alex stayed with Ben whenever the Botox stopped working, sometimes for as long as two weeks. Tory took Alex to all her doctor's appointments and cooked dinner every night she slept over.

ALEX HAD ALWAYS FELT like she needed to prove her disease to other people. Particularly during the five months between when she started showing symptoms—migraines that lasted three weeks and neck pain so debilitating she couldn't hold her head up for more than fifteen minutes—and when she finally got her diagnosis, Alex didn't think anyone would believe she was actually sick. She insisted on bringing her professors notes from her doctor, explaining her symptoms and reasons for missing class, even after they said it wasn't necessary. When she had to cancel an interview with me in November of our senior year, she e-mailed me the doctor's note, along with the message: "I want you to know that I take your work seriously, I'm just having a really hard time getting out of bed."

Before she was diagnosed with dystonia, Alex's biggest fear was that the doctors wouldn't find anything wrong with her. She knew this was probably because, growing up, her dad regularly called her mom a hypochondriac. When Alex was in first grade, her mom began battling severe depression. Whenever Alex's mom said she didn't feel well, Daniel would say the depression was her own fault and imply she was making it up.

"My dad would say, 'She's depressed, she's on all these meds, she's always sick'—and he'd blame her for being unreliable and unaccountable. When I feel sick, I think I'm unreliable and unaccountable. I feel like I need to prove there is actually a limitation that explains why I am having a hard time keeping up with something." It didn't help that when Alex finally got the dystonia diagnosis, three days after her dad found out she was gay, Daniel refused to believe the condition was serious.

Ben, on the other hand, never questioned Alex's illness. Immediately after hearing that Daniel denied her health care, he deposited $10,000 into Alex's bank account, enough to pay for the MRI and several months' worth of medication. After she took L-dopa for the first time, Alex stayed at Ben's house in Philadelphia for a week because the doctor said she had to be watched 24-7.

"Ben and Tory are my rocks," Alex said after her health scare in December. "They take care of me. I don't know what I would do without them."

By the end of the year, Alex had started to appreciate Redmond as a refuge, and Ben and Tory as her ultimate support system. Nothing could make her live there again full-time, but she realized how lucky she was to have two people who cared so much about her health living twenty miles up the interstate, particularly when one of them was her boss. Anyone else probably would have fired her by now. She'd taken too much time off. But Ben was patient. If she said she was sick, he never asked whether she could still work. He told her to sleep and see how she felt the next morning.

A FEW DAYS BEFORE CHRISTMAS, Alex flew to New York City to spend the holiday with Bethany. The first two days were a lot of fun. They drank Scotch with Bethany's dad and barhopped until three in the morning. But on the third day, Alex woke up feeling like she couldn't move. She'd slept nine hours but still felt physically exhausted. She could feel her right eye starting to droop again. That day, she slept until three in the afternoon. The next day, until four. Sometimes this happened when she was stressed, or when she tried to do too much without enough rest (especially important for dystonia patients because tight muscles loosen when you sleep). At first, Bethany took care of Alex, canceling their plans, making her tea, watching movies with her in bed. But when they had plans to catch a train to Connecticut at seven in the morning and Alex slept till the afternoon, Bethany became visibly annoyed.

"Come on, Boo Cat. My cousins really want to see us. They want to see you."

"I'm so sorry, babe. I just can't do it. I wish I could. I want to."

"Okay. I mean, it's fine. I know you can't help it." But then she walked away, turning on the TV in the living room as Alex tried to fall back to sleep.

■ ◆ ■ ◆ ■

When Denise walked into the Harlem Church of Christ for the first time, she scanned the congregation, looking for her friend Dr. Sharon Johnson. She'd been trying out new churches since she got to New York, but so far nothing had stuck. Her Princeton friends all went to churches that were too big: Brooklyn Tabernacle, First Corinthian, and Hillsong. Their choirs won Grammys and their pastors oozed charisma, but their services lacked intimacy. Thousands of people filed in every Sunday. Denise felt totally anonymous, sitting among them.

At the beginning of December, Denise met Dr. Johnson at the hospital where she worked two days a week. Dr. Johnson had the life Denise wanted: she was thirty years old, just out of residency, and working at a hospital in New York. She was married with kids and spent her free time mentoring young women. When Denise mentioned she was looking for a faith community, Dr. Johnson told her about the church she'd been going to for ten years: a nondenominational congregation of two hundred people that encouraged all members to study the Bible together in small groups once a week. It sounded just like Denise's church at Princeton.

Denise didn't see Dr. Johnson anywhere, so she took a seat near the back. Toward the end of the service, the woman sitting next to Denise started coughing loudly. Without thinking about it, Denise put her hand on her back, and she smiled.

After the service ended, the woman turned to Denise. "Hey there, I haven't seen you before," she said. "Is this your first service here?"

"Yes," Denise said. "Dr. Johnson invited me."

"Dr. Johnson? Wonderful. I've been coming here a long time. My husband is the pastor. Are you studying the Bible with anyone, honey?"

When Denise said no, she wasn't, but would like to start, the woman told her about the church's Bible study specially for single women. She offered to drive her to the next meeting.

Denise started going to the Harlem Church of Christ every Sunday. Each week, more and more people recognized her and gave her their phone numbers. After the service, they asked her how she was doing—actually paused, made eye contact, and listened. She usually stayed in the church lobby for at least an hour after worship, and then went to brunch or a movie with some of her new friends. Three times a week, she met with a group of four women her age to study the Bible.

Denise's new friends at church helped her stay connected to and confident in her faith, but she also appreciated them because they didn't go to Princeton. Before she joined the church, all her friends in New York had been Princeton grads. She hated talking about med school with them—particularly as the rejection letters started rolling in—because their expectations were so unreasonably high. She wanted people who wouldn't judge her for getting her applications in late, people who would see admission to any medical school as an achievement.

Denise liked having her boyfriend, Craig, in her life for the same reason. He'd never met his father, and grew up in Harlem in foster care. For him, "success" was having enough money to eat, sleep in a safe place, and eventually provide for a family. Not fellowships, six-figure salaries, or prestigious acceptance letters. He was also older—thirty-three, eleven years older than Denise. "He's just separate," Denise said. She waited months before introducing him to any of her Princeton friends, because a part of her wanted him to stay that way. He told her he thought she had what it took to get into Harvard, but it wasn't something he assumed would happen. If she went to a state school, he would be just as proud of her.

ON NEW YEAR'S EVE, Denise hosted a party at her apartment in Harlem. By midnight, her small one-bedroom was packed with people from all different stages of her life: her cousins, friends from high school, friends from Princeton, Craig, and new friends from church. Most of them ended up staying over—two on the couch, two on a twin-sized air mattress, three in her bed. Denise slept on the floor.

Denise had always been a floater. She didn't have a clique at Princeton—there was never one group she always texted before going out on a Friday night. Denise liked that about herself. She never felt bored or stifled by the people around her. But sometimes the floating got a little lonely. When she left Princeton for a week after her dad collapsed, it took three days for anyone to notice she was gone. Sometimes she had to remind herself that, even though she didn't have a tight group of best friends, she did have a lot of people who cared about her. They were just scattered.

"On New Year's, so many of the people I love came together," Denise said. "And I was the matriarch, hosting them all. I felt anchored in New York. I'd been there for a couple months, so I knew things. I was saying, 'Welcome to my home, this is where I've been.'"

Looking around at the group she'd assembled—most of them laughing, drinking, and talking with people they'd just met—Denise felt perfectly content. She'd never expected to create this kind of community in New York. She was supposed to pass through quickly—take a short pit stop on her way to the next big thing. When she moved to Harlem, she thought she would make just enough friends to keep her sane while she applied to medical school. She hadn't expected to find such a supportive and intimate church. She certainly hadn't been looking for a boyfriend. But somehow, all of these people had fallen into place. And for the first time in her life, she felt planted firmly at the center.

A week later, Denise flew to Illinois to interview at the University of Chicago.

■ ◆ ■ ◆ ■

Olivia left San Francisco determined to become financially independent. Taking money from her parents made her feel obligated to them, and she didn't believe in family obligation. When I told her I felt indebted to my mom for giving up her career to raise me, she said, "Did little baby Caroline ask her mom to stop being a graphic designer? No." Olivia believed parents had children to make their own lives better: to lend meaning to their existence and to take care of them in old age.

"We owe them nothing," she said.

Olivia was hoping the media company would turn her documentary into a miniseries and give her more money than she knew what to do with. But in the meantime, she'd been brainstorming other ways she could make a little extra cash: learn new computer programming skills, find website design jobs, get hired by a tutoring agency for rich high school students on the Upper East Side. She couldn't wait to tell her dad that she didn't need him anymore. She just had to be sure she was financially secure enough to make the break permanent. When Olivia told her dad she didn't need his money at the end of her senior year, she had to slink back and grovel after a couple of months. She didn't want to do that again.

Two weeks after coming back to New York, Olivia got a Facebook message from her dad. He told her that she was ungrateful and an embarrassment to him and her mother. He said he'd decided not to send her any more money.

Olivia panicked. She was broke and hadn't even started working toward the jobs and skills that were supposed to help her become independent. She'd been too consumed by the documentary. She'd written the episode summaries for the film production company, but the people there had been dragging out the approval process, sending her a series of evasive e-mails. She couldn't even access the $2,500 she got for signing over the rights to her material because of complications with her visa. Now her rent was due in a week and, without her dad's support, she wouldn't be able to pay.

"When he cut me off, it was a wake-up call," Olivia said. "I should have seen it coming—because I'm not doing what he wants me to do, I'm not contributing to him in any way—but I didn't. I planned to have his support for much longer."

She thought about calling her dad and making promises about coming back to Malaysia that she wouldn't keep. She hadn't heard his voice in over a year. At Princeton, Olivia communicated with her parents almost exclusively through Facebook. In her sophomore year, she stopped picking up when they called and, eventually, they stopped trying. Occasionally she missed her mom, but she felt no connection to her dad whatsoever. Eventually she decided that no amount of money could equal the cost of begging him to change his mind.

Olivia's relationship with her parents had been strained ever since she started talking about going to college abroad. Her only goal in high school had been to win a prestigious national scholarship that paid for eight Malaysian students to attend one year of private high school and four years of college in the United States. Every year, the winners of the scholarship become celebrities, attending official state dinners. "If you mention the scholarship, everyone will be like, 'Oh wow, this person is really smart,'" Olivia said. "It's like a stamp, like Harvard." This scholarship became Olivia's obsession. She read English-language newspapers for hours every day and attended prep classes specially designed for the scholarship. At the end of her junior year, she won.

Most parents would have been thrilled. For a high school student in Malaysia, winning this scholarship was a huge deal. But Olivia's father had spent the last thirty years singlehandedly transforming his construction business from a one-man operation into a $100 million company. And soon, he would need someone else to take over as CEO. Olivia's half brother had already left Kuala Lumpur, the city where they'd grown up, to become a monk in northern Malaysia, so Olivia was her dad's only option. If she stayed in America, he would have to hand over the business to someone outside the family.

Olivia might have considered staying in Malaysia if she felt closer to her dad. But for as long as she could remember, he was just a guy she knew who would give her money. He was never at home. When Olivia was little and she asked her dad why he wasn't around, he'd tell her he had to work long hours to support the family. "You wouldn't have such a nice house," he'd say, "if I didn't work this much." When she got a little older, Olivia found out that her dad paid for other women—women much younger than her mom—to live in luxury apartments around Kuala Lumpur. She didn't know the term when she lived in Malaysia, but now she calls him a sugar daddy.

AS SOON AS OLIVIA TOLD MICHAEL, the guy she'd been seeing since September, that her dad was cutting her off, he offered to loan her as much money as she needed.

"How about I just give you ten thousand dollars, and then you pay me back when you can?"

"I can't do that."

"Why not? I'll treat you like an investment. I don't want you to make a bunch of short-term decisions just to survive. You should be looking toward the long term."

Before this, Olivia had never talked to Michael about her financial situation. He knew she wasn't working much and somehow could eat and pay rent, but he never asked where the money was coming from. When Olivia got the message from her dad, she'd immediately thought about Michael. She'd assumed he would offer to help, but there'd been no guarantee. They had been seeing each other for only a few months and weren't even officially dating.

Eventually, Olivia agreed to borrow $1,000 a month and move all her stuff into Michael's bedroom. She would live with Michael until she made enough money to pay for her own place. He shared the apartment with five other guys, but they all worked a lot and were already used to seeing Olivia around. She promised Michael she would clean the apartment and make them Malaysian food every once in a while to keep them happy.

Accepting money from Michael was better than accepting money from her dad, but Olivia still felt guilty about it. She'd told Michael that she didn't want to be boyfriend and girlfriend because she was polyamorous and because he was considering leaving New York soon to work in Taiwan. But if she was being honest, she just didn't really like him that much. He wasn't spontaneous or creative. He watched basketball and was careful to never say anything inappropriate.

"I am always bored with him, but at certain times it bothers me more than others. Sometimes I don't care that there aren't exciting things going on with our relationship because there are exciting things going on in other areas of my life. But when my other areas slow down, I care a lot more."

Olivia told herself it was okay to accept Michael's financial support because he was also getting a lot out of their relationship. She pushed him to try things he never would have otherwise: to go to documentary film screenings, lectures on psychedelic drugs, polyamorous picnics. After growing up in a small town in Iowa and spending his undergraduate years surrounded by friends from a conservative Christian group called Crusade for Christ, she knew he needed someone to show him what he'd been missing.

"I make his life fun," Olivia said.

There was also the issue of Mason, the rationalist leader Olivia met in San Francisco. Between Mason and Michael, there was no contest: Olivia liked Mason more. For weeks after coming back from the West Coast, she stalked him on social media, fantasizing about what it would be like to live with him in San Francisco—to be his primary, or even his secondary. She thought Mason probably pushed her in the same way she pushed Michael. On any given day that she spent with him in San Francisco, he might take her along to a meeting with a Facebook cofounder or a Burning Man–themed art exhibit. Spending time with Mason, she was always under incredible pressure to say or do something to make him think she was interesting enough to deserve his time. She loved the high stakes, the adrenaline rush of trying to win someone she was crazy about.

But after her dad cut her off, Olivia started realizing that she couldn't care that intensely about someone right now. Mason consumed her in a way she couldn't afford to be consumed—not when literally everything else in her life was uncertain. Her infatuation with Mason led to nights when she'd stay up until four in the morning, crying and reading his girlfriend's OkCupid profile. The morning after one of these nights, I met Olivia for coffee. I found her hunched over her computer, not touching her latte. As she clicked through the girlfriend's Facebook pictures, hardly glancing at one before summoning the next, her eyes never left the screen.

"She is everything that I want to be. She is a visual artist and a double math and chemistry major and she goes to Burning Man. If I could erect a statue of the perfect girl that Mason wants to be with, she would be it. And I am not it. I have the potential to be cool and she is cool. If you had to decide between those two, which would you choose?"

To me, it felt like a flashback. Six months ago, Olivia had been looking through pictures on Allison's Facebook profile, telling me why she was the perfect girl for Leon. Since I first met Olivia, I'd noticed that when she really liked a guy, she tended to put him on a pedestal. She would talk him up in conversations with me, making him out to be the smartest, handsomest, and most interesting person she'd ever met. Every conversation would end with her saying the same thing: "I don't know why he's hanging out with me." In her mind, he was doing her a favor. Whenever a guy stopped calling or texting back, Olivia internalized his abating interest as a judgment on her personality and began to doubt herself. She wasn't cool enough. She wasn't interesting enough. The guy had better things to do.

Michael didn't have that kind of power over Olivia. She saw herself as the "cooler" one in the relationship. She didn't worry about Michael leaving, and she never felt like she had to impress him or beg for his attention. At this point in her life, she thought, maybe it was okay to exchange the adrenaline rush she felt with Mason for the stability she felt with Michael. Even if he did break things off, Michael's rejection wouldn't hurt Olivia in the same way Mason's would. She didn't care nearly as much about his opinion.

"There are so many moments when I'm like, 'Wait, can we sign a contract or something? Can you be my dad?' Your dad doesn't have to be super interesting, just supportive."

Olivia told me she liked to "act like a baby" around Michael. She got used to telling him about her problems and letting him solve them. She could relax, knowing that someone else cared enough to stop anything really bad from happening to her.

■ ◆ ■ ◆ ■

The day after I got back to the States, Robert and I drove to my house in Connecticut. As soon as I walked in, I saw the tree: a fluffy Fraser fur that looked like it belonged in a Macy's catalog, decorated with white lights and the expensive glass ornaments my mom bought when we lived in Germany. My eyes went immediately to what was underneath it: at least twenty presents, meticulously wrapped in matching paper, each tied at the top with a pile of tightly curled ribbon. I felt a familiar warm pressure behind my nose, moisture pooling at the bottom of my eyes. There was something about that image that made me feel instantly and intensely guilty. While I'd been in England devising a way to see my mom for as short a time as possible before going back to DC, she'd been here, decorating the house and wrapping presents for me. My grandma was healthy again now, but I knew she'd been very sick, and my mom was right to have been worried.

I was mad at my mom for not coming to England. But even more than that, I was mad at her for never calling to tell me she wasn't coming, for sending cold, unapologetic text messages, and for saying no when I asked to come back a day early to spend Christmas with her. She was pushing me away, and I couldn't understand why. But sitting around the tree, opening present after present she'd picked out specifically for me (and even one she'd picked out for Robert), I started wondering if all that had been in my head. Maybe it was confirmation bias. Maybe I'd interpreted my mom's actions in a way that confirmed the growing feeling of isolation I'd experienced throughout the fall. I desperately wanted to believe I was imagining the problem.

But then I thought about Alex, her dad, and the cycle she'd told me about at the end of the summer. Maybe this was my mom trying to pull me back in when she started to think that she'd pushed me too far. I just wanted to know what was real: the kind words, telling me I looked great in the sweater she'd bought for me, or the snappy texts that she sent on Christmas Eve. I wasn't sure. At that point, I was too lonely and insecure to allow myself to relax around my mom. I didn't know if I could trust her. I had to protect myself. So after Christmas, I decided not to see my mom without a friendly face (usually Robert) and an easy way out (usually Robert's car). All my guards went back up. They would stay that way until I felt ready to stomach another major letdown.

CHAPTER SEVEN

January–February

When I met her for the first time, Tara was wearing a matching red velvet top and floor-length skirt, both embroidered with yellow geraniums. Her wavy dirty-blond hair reached all the way down her back. As we settled into adjacent armchairs, she tucked it behind her ears, revealing long, dangling earrings that looked handmade.

Immediately, I knew that I liked her. She told me about her husband and twin five-year-old boys. She swore. She didn't write anything down. She offered me tea—fancy, organic chocolate rooibos tea—before I had to ask.

When I started telling Tara about my issues—my mom, how lonely I felt in DC—she didn't just nod and furrow her brow like the other therapist. She listened intently but then told me what she thought. My last therapist had alternated between "Hmm, interesting," "What I'm hearing is . . ." and "Well, how do *you* feel about that?" And a little bit of that was fine. Hearing someone else echo my thoughts did help me sort them out in my own head. But an entirely one-sided conversation made me feel like the therapist was being too cautious, like she was afraid she'd get sued if she said something too personal or gave bad advice. With Tara, I didn't just talk about how I was feeling. We came up with a game plan for what I should do about it.

"I mean, I think you need to get out of this group house," Tara said during our second session. Her tone suggested she wanted to end the sentence with "duh."

She was right. I realized how much I needed to move on the drive back to DC after Christmas. I gazed longingly at every rest stop we passed. I wasn't hungry and I didn't need to pee. I just wanted to delay the return for as long as possible.

My bedroom was in the back of my house in DC. To get to it, I had to walk past two other bedrooms and through the kitchen. Standing outside the front door, I would try to gauge the location of any voices I could hear: if they were upstairs in the living room, I could slip by unnoticed. But usually there was someone in the kitchen, and I'd have to engage in five or ten minutes of strained small talk before I could vanish inside my room and shut the door. I hated these conversations. I had to smile, pretend to be interested in what my roommates were saying, and watch them pretend to be interested in me. The exchange was always painfully insincere and reminded me that the relationships I had with these people—the closest thing I had to a community in DC—were nothing like the ones I had with friends at Princeton.

This anxiety was mostly my own fault. Almost all the roommates in the house had been living together for over a year. Most of them were two or three years older than me. They had jobs at international affairs think tanks and assorted nonprofits, and their conversations about the Middle East always went over my head.

At the weekly house dinner, I was sure they noticed how much I stuck out: a college kid who sat in the corner, laughed at jokes but said little—who, when it was her turn to cook, couldn't even figure out how to turn on the stove (I sautéed onions for twenty minutes before noticing they were still cold). The roommates had their own clique, but had I been even a little less compulsively self-aware, I'm sure I could have broken into it. I assumed they didn't want to hang out with me, avoided them, and, in the process, created a self-fulfilling prophecy. I thought they were too cool for me, so that's what they became.

My own physical space has always been important to me. It probably has something to do with moving around every few years as a kid. Everywhere we went, I wanted to paint walls and plant flowers. In sixth grade, I bought an American Girl book about designing your own space, took the quiz at the beginning ("Which room is for you?"), and spent the next month transforming my bedroom into a rain forest. I pinned animal drawings on the walls, covered my bed with a leopard-print blanket, and propped three sticks of bamboo against the wall in the corner. We didn't own the house, and wouldn't be living there long, but I still wanted to make the room into my own personalized sanctuary (and that year, I'd decided I was destined to study tamarins in the Amazon). This habit continued in college. Every September, I'd spend days decorating my room with intricate collages of pictures and postcards that covered an entire wall, knowing I'd have to take it all down again in June. But it was worth it. My room has always been a place where I can relax at the end of a long day. Surrounded by all the things I find comforting, I can take a deep breath and release.

There was no release in the group house. Even after I reached the relative safety of my own room, it still felt nothing like a sanctuary. At five in the morning, I'd wake up to what I called "mice orgies": frantic bouncing and scratching inside the wall, right above my head. The hallway always smelled like the mounds of garbage nine people produced (and usually forgot to take out) over the course of a week, and one of the guys on my hall would regularly walk into my room without knocking to ask me to edit a grad school essay or job application—once when I was in bed watching TV with Robert, twice when I was just wearing a towel.

I'd assumed there wasn't anything I could do about this. I'd signed a contract, and that meant I had to at least finish out the year. I didn't know then that people break leases. As soon as I figured out that they did—a lot—I e-mailed my landlord. In mid-January, Robert and I started looking for a place together.

■ ◆ ■ ◆ ■

Olivia spent the first week of the New Year in Colorado with a seventy-year-old multimillionaire. The two of them flew from New York City in a private jet with a 150-pound Newfoundland. The multimillionaire—Greg—spent most of the flight telling Olivia about his philanthropy.

"I donate tens of thousands of dollars every year to rare turtle conservation. I always try to do whatever I can to protect animals."

Olivia thought about the dinner they'd had two nights before, when she'd watched Greg eat a huge slab of rare steak. She smiled.

"But you know I give even more money to primary schools in Tibet. That's an important part of my new faith. I know I'm following the middle way—everything in moderation. This is how we can be riding on this jet, because of all the money I've donated."

A lot of sugar babies would have responded to these kinds

of statements with intense affirmation: nodding vigorously with sustained eye contact, saying things like "Oh wow," "You're so impressive," or "You're so kind." But as a general rule, Olivia didn't perform. She didn't talk much. If a sugar daddy said something she thought was stupid or offensive, she would usually just smile. Olivia knew the job would have been easier—more lucrative and exponentially more fun—if she allowed herself to become a different person: a person who could relax and enjoy being pampered, without an internal voice that constantly questioned what the sugar daddy said and did. The plane ride would have been so much better if she could have just sat back in her cushioned seat, sipped her glass of wine, and doled out a string of excessive compliments. But she knew everything Greg was saying was bullshit. She wanted to look him in the eye and say, "Dude, if you care about a topic, you have to be logically consistent with it. You can't scarf down steak three times a week and claim to be an animal rights activist." She couldn't say those things and keep her job, but she also didn't want to encourage a hypocrite. If Olivia forced herself to act fake, she knew she might start to question what she valued, and whether sugar dating was actually just a job.

"Because I don't perform—I think that's why my sugar daddies aren't like, 'Wow, I'm in love with this girl,'" Olivia told me. "Instead they just think, 'She's okay, doesn't cause trouble, she isn't expensive, doesn't demand much. She is trustworthy because she went to Princeton.'"

After her dad stopped supporting her, Olivia started sugar dating again. When she broke away from her parents the first time, she'd felt triumphantly independent—even if she was sleeping on other people's couches, she'd been in control of her life, "not taking shit from anyone." Michael's money dulled that feeling, and she wanted it back. It had been almost two months since she started the "trial period" with the media company, but she still hadn't heard anything about the status of her project, so had basically no money of her own. When Greg offered to take her to his ski house in Colorado for Christmas, she immediately agreed. Michael begged her not to go, offering to match whatever Greg was going to pay her, but she insisted. While it was tempting to sit back and let Michael take care of everything, Olivia knew that if she did that for too much longer, it would make her question who she was—probably even more than performing for a sugar daddy.

Compared with other sugar daddies Olivia had been with, Greg wasn't bad. He spent most weeks flying all over the world for business—that month alone, he'd been to Chile, Saudi Arabia, and North Dakota. Greg told Olivia that to break even and maintain his current lifestyle—his ski house, his farm in the ritzy holiday town of East Hampton, his New York City penthouse, his private jet, and dozens of personal employees—he had to make a few million dollars every month. Greg was by far the wealthiest and most extravagant sugar daddy Olivia had ever dated. She was sure that a few days with him would easily offset a few months' worth of living expenses.

Once their plane landed in Colorado, Olivia realized she might actually be able to enjoy some of this trip. The ski house was beautiful, and Greg worked for three or four hours a day, so she had time to herself. The best thing about Greg was that he claimed to be too old to have sex, which meant she only had to give him blow jobs and naked massages. He treated her like a girlfriend, consulting her about the things she wanted to do and introducing her to his family and friends. He didn't even get angry when she told him she couldn't ski—he just suggested they hike together instead. Olivia knew he was probably being so nice because she hadn't brought up payment. She was waiting for him to broach the subject at the end of the week. That way, he could delude himself into thinking she was actually interested in him, and they were a couple.

The first day Olivia spent at the ski house, she walked up a mountain with Greg and his dog in a blizzard. She put on as many layers as she could: leggings, ski pants, multiple sweaters, and one of Greg's extra ski jackets. While it wasn't entirely pleasant to climb a mountain with a steady stream of ice water pummeling her face, Olivia didn't mind. It meant she didn't have to talk to Greg and could just run around in the snow with his dog. At the end of the day, they picked up Greg's sixteen-year-old son at ski school. The son didn't seem to think it at all strange that his dad was dating a girl fifty years younger than he was.

"Everyone around Greg knows he's a sugar daddy," Olivia said. "It's really common. In his circle—Republican, very wealthy, into spirituality and rare animals—this is normal. Pay for women, fine. Pay for women, normal."

Greg didn't bring up payment until the end of the trip, when he handed Olivia a check for $1,500. It was substantially less than she'd been expecting, but she figured Greg had spent enough time on SeekingArrangement to know how to play the game. He probably knew $1,500 was just enough to make a sugar baby come back. And sure enough, a week after Olivia got back to New York, Greg texted her, inviting her to spend the night with him in East Hampton.

■ ◆ ■ ◆ ■

A few weeks after Christmas, Denise got into Emory. She'd gotten yeses from two other schools at that point—the University of Illinois and George Washington—but rankings-wise, Emory was by far the best. If she didn't get in anywhere else, that was where she would go. Denise felt good about Emory. It was a solid option. But she was still holding out for Chicago.

The day after Denise got her acceptance e-mail, Craig called during her lunch break. He hardly ever called from work.

"Hey, I haven't been able to concentrate all day. I'm just wondering . . . how are you ranking the schools that you have on the table? Do you think you'll go to Emory?" he said without taking a breath.

"Uh, I'm not sure. I mean, I think it's definitely at the top of the list of ones I've gotten into so far."

"Okay, well, I'm just trying to think. I want to know that we're going to be strong. Are we going to be solid through this?"

Craig caught Denise off guard. Since she sent in her med school applications, they'd talked only once about the looming prospect of her leaving New York. Making breakfast late one Saturday morning, she'd said, "You know, next year we're not gonna have any more time to just be with each other with no worries." Craig said he'd been thinking the same thing and asked if the University of Chicago was still her first choice. Denise nodded. For a few minutes, neither of them said anything. After that, she'd been afraid to bring it up again.

At the beginning, it seemed stupid to talk about the future because their relationship was so new. Denise knew plenty of girls who factored boyfriends into their career decisions after graduation—but those were college boyfriends, people they'd been dating for two or three years. She'd met Craig in June. As her relationship had gotten more serious, Denise started thinking about how much she wanted it to continue. But by that time, it was November, and she'd already made the decision to apply to only two schools in New York: Columbia, a major reach school, and Mount Sinai, a school she thought she had a pretty good chance of getting into. If the process went as she expected it to, she wouldn't have the option of going to one and probably shouldn't take the option of going to the other.

I understood this particular dilemma very well. I think most girls in our class at Princeton would have advised Denise to go to the best medical school she got into—no question. But I spent four months in a long-distance relationship with Robert during my junior year, and I knew how drastically living apart from your partner could disrupt your life. Studying abroad in Shanghai was a wonderful, once-in-a-lifetime opportunity, but I had a hard time appreciating it. I ended up Skyping with Robert for an hour almost every day. Whenever I had a particularly interesting experience—touring an old Buddhist nunnery, eating some weird food, sustaining a ten-minute conversation in Chinese for the first time—I felt like I was only partially present. Part of my mind was wandering back to Princeton, wishing Robert could be in Shanghai, sharing the experience with me. That longing didn't go away, and it made it hard for me to focus. It also made me promise myself that, unless circumstances were truly extenuating, I'd never do long-distance again.

"I'm still waiting to hear from a lot of schools, so I really don't even know what my options are right now," Denise said, scrambling to string words together after what seemed like much too long of a pause. "Can we talk about this more tonight? I feel like this is a conversation we should have in person."

Really, Denise just wanted to call her mom. She didn't answer big questions like this before talking to her.

"Okay, sure," Craig said. "Right now, though, I just want you to know I'm serious about this. I talked to my HR department, and I might be able to move to a position that would let me leave New York. Probably not this year, but soon."

He'd thought about this, *really* thought about it. Craig had lived in New York his entire life. Everyone he knew was in this city. Denise had no idea what to say.

"Mm-hmm, okay," she mumbled into the phone.

"I'll meet you after work," Craig said. "I love you."

Right after Craig hung up, Denise dialed her mom's number. She needed someone to remind her that she didn't know Craig that well and that six months wasn't enough time to justify thinking seriously about marriage—that six months wasn't enough time to start making sacrifices. She knew her best medical school prospects were outside New York, probably outside the Northeast. But still, she was sorely tempted to figure out a way to stay.

After quickly rattling off the whole story to her mom, Denise took a deep breath. "Mommy, I just don't know what to tell this man."

Nahvet laughed. She did that a lot when Denise asked for advice. Translated into words, Denise thought the laugh might say, "My love, you have no idea how lucky you are." Without ever sounding condescending, it reminded Denise that her mom had the experience and wisdom necessary to put everything into perspective.

"This is funny, you know?" Nahvet said. "Your life is so similar to mine."

Denise hadn't thought about this until now. Her father had moved to the United States while Nahvet was still in Cameroon. At the time, they hadn't even started dating. They'd just written letters to each other.

"Everyone in Cameroon laughed at me," Nahvet said. "They would always say, 'Love does not exist across the oceans.' It wasn't clear how it was going to work at all. There were so many other men trying to charm me. But still, it was always only your father."

"How do you get through that, though? Craig asked me if we were going to stay strong, and I just don't know."

"If it's meant to be, it literally will be."

Denise wished she had her mom's faith. When her dad was in the ICU, her mom had been completely at peace. She prayed by his bedside for twenty hours a day for a week. When people asked how she was doing, she'd say she was trusting in God. If it was time for her husband to pass, she said, she would accept that.

WHEN DENISE RELAYED the "if it's meant to be" message to Craig at his apartment later that night, he wasn't convinced.

"We can't just be passive," he said. "We have to work for this."

Craig was almost excessively earnest, always preferring to say exactly what he meant rather than being sarcastic or joking around. He was so serious so often that Denise generally felt immune to the narrowing of his eyes and the lowering of his voice. But now, for the first time since she met him, she was taken aback by his intensity.

"Hopefully I'll get into Mount Sinai. I liked it there. The public health research isn't as strong, but the education is probably just as good as the one I would get at Emory."

"That's not what I mean. You know you like Emory and Chicago better than Mount Sinai."

Craig thought Denise was brilliant. He told her that all the time. Denise knew he wouldn't let her stay in New York for medical school if she had better options. That made her like him even more. Before Denise could say anything else, Craig smiled, stroked her hair, and said, "I just want you to be wherever you need to be."

■ ◆ ■ ◆ ■

Her first night back in Philadelphia, Michelle went to a jazz show in somebody's basement. She paid a dollar at the door, ducked, and ran down the stairs. This basement concert looked just like all the others she'd been to in Philadelphia: a band in the corner, some makeshift lighting, and maybe fifty people leaning against the walls or each other—swaying, closing their eyes, nodding their heads in time with the music.

She looked around for somebody she knew and spotted Canaan, a freshman drummer, in the corner. She'd played music with him a few times in the fall. A lot of students at her conservatory looked down on music that came anywhere close to country, but in his music, Canaan bridged jazz and folk. She liked that he put his blinders up and didn't allow his classmates' musical choices to impact his own. She'd always thought he was cute but never seriously considered hooking up with him. He was nineteen; she was twenty-three.

But standing alone in the corner of the basement with his arms crossed, tapping his right foot, he looked so shy and awkward. Michelle was suddenly overcome by the impulse to do something to shock him. She walked over, said hello, then stepped toward him so her body was half an inch away from his.

"Are you attracted to me?" she asked, looking down at his chest, which was now rising and falling in rapid succession. Canaan said nothing but nodded his head five times fast.

"You are?" She stepped forward again, this time pressing herself against him.

"Uh . . ." He swallowed. "Yeah."

Michelle took Canaan back to her apartment that night and the two nights after that. After they had sex, they stayed up talking until three or four in the morning. The fourth time they hooked up, she told Canaan that she wasn't looking for a relationship "in the traditional sense."

"I'm really into spending time with you, and I want to see you again," she said, "but I'm figuring things out right now. I'm just not ready to commit."

Michelle loved the time she spent with Canaan but was itching to experiment with polyamory. The last time she'd had sex with two people at the same time, she'd felt guilty about it. After reading *The Ethical Slut,* she wanted to try again, knowing it wasn't wrong. A few days after clarifying the parameters of her relationship with Canaan, she invited Patrick, another guy from school, back to her apartment. It didn't take many nights with Patrick for Michelle to know that if she had to pick just one guy, it would be Canaan. But the great thing about polyamory was that she didn't have to choose.

"They are just two beings who I enjoy spending time with in different ways," she said. "Coming out of so many serial monogamous relationships, this is very empowering."

The problem was that Michelle hadn't been particularly clear with Canaan or Patrick about the nature of her noncommitment. She hadn't specifically said she identified as polyamorous or told either guy about the other. The conservatory was a small place—there were only 120 students in the entire jazz program. Canaan and Patrick weren't friends, but they knew each other.

"I told both of them what I was looking for, and they said that was cool, so I assume they know it's okay for them to hook up with other people." Michelle paused and smiled sheepishly. "I mean, I probably should have been more explicit."

But she didn't really want to be more explicit. Canaan, in particular, was a notorious heartthrob at the conservatory, always surrounded by a gaggle of cute underclassman girls toting flutes or violins. After they'd been hooking up for a few weeks, Michelle's chest started to tighten whenever she saw Canaan flirting with his little posse. She knew she'd eventually have to deal with a partner who was also poly, but she wanted to postpone that experience—and the inevitable jealousy—for as long as possible.

A FEW WEEKS AFTER Michelle finally told Canaan they weren't exclusive—after numerous friends assured her that he probably already knew—she started wondering whether she'd made the right decision.

"The closer we got, the more strongly I felt for him and the more I wanted from him emotionally," Michelle said.

Coming back from England, she'd been determined to have

a lot of enjoyable sex—to take advantage of being single in a way she hadn't in the fall. But as much as she'd enjoyed her time with James, she was starting to wonder whether she was capable of sustaining that kind of relationship over a long period of time. She liked Canaan. She couldn't help it. The conservatory gave them four snow days in January and she'd spent every one of them at his apartment. They'd always emerge from under the covers around noon to make breakfast, then music. Living alone in her apartment, Michelle loved having somewhere to go when there was four feet of snow on the ground, wind howling, and a tree branch knocking against her bedroom window in the middle of the night.

This longing for company—meaningful, emotionally connected company—intensified when her ex-boyfriend, Sam, changed his relationship status on Facebook. Throughout the fall, Michelle had seen pictures of Sam with a girl, but she never knew for sure that he was dating someone new. Then one morning she saw the notification on her Facebook feed: "Sam Stewart is in a relationship." The start date was August 9: one month after they'd broken up, and Michelle's birthday.

"How fucked up is that?" Michelle said a few days after she saw the post. "First of all, who makes Facebook relationship statuses anymore? Who does that? What are you doing? And out of all the days in the year, you had to go and agree that August ninth is your new anniversary with someone else? Fuck you, Sam."

Until now, Michelle had thought she was over him. Occasionally she'd wondered how he was doing and hoped they would figure out a way to be friends, but thinking about him had no longer triggered intense anxiety. The Facebook status brought all those feelings back. Michelle couldn't understand how he'd moved past her so quickly. The first week of August—when she'd still been going home to cry under her covers after a night out with Lindsay—Sam had been in the process of finding a new serious girlfriend. It hurt to know that he was already six months into a relationship with someone else: a beautiful Columbia senior from Ethiopia. Michelle, on the other hand, was in quasi-relationships with two guys she barely knew—neither of whom, by her own design, felt any loyalty to her.

Eventually, Michelle told Canaan that she'd changed her mind. She wanted them to date exclusively, maybe even call each other boyfriend and girlfriend. He wasn't interested.

"When you said you didn't want to be exclusive, my mind-set changed," Canaan said. "I feel differently about you now because of it."

■ ◆ ■ ◆ ■

When Olivia woke up in Greg's East Hampton farmhouse, he was gone. The night before, he told her he had to leave for the office at 6:00 A.M.: "But just walk downstairs when you wake up, and you'll be taken care of." The chef asked Olivia what she wanted for breakfast, and the groundskeeper asked her if she wanted a tour of the farm. After she'd seen Greg's rabbits, pigs, and snakes, the housekeeper offered to drive her to the bus station. Greg's employees clearly knew the drill.

"This was normal business," Olivia said. "Happens all the time."

After the Colorado trip, Olivia started sugar dating again on a fairly regular basis. She told me she did it because she needed the money, but when I talked to Michael, Olivia's primary partner, he said he thought there was more to it than that.

"You could draw a connection to what had just happened with her dad—he had just cut off funding. But I think there was also something about herself. She wanted to be able to do it. She wanted to be the kind of person who could [sugar date], who wasn't afraid."

All year, Olivia had been trying to differentiate herself from her Princeton classmates. She made choices that would scare or intimidate most of them. Generally, I was impressed by Olivia's insatiable desire for risk and adventure. Occasionally, though, I'd worry she was being too reckless. I think Olivia knew that. And I think sometimes she actually liked to surprise me, even scare me a little. Of all the things she'd done since graduation—experimenting with drugs, filming a documentary, trying kink, practicing Buddhism—sugar dating was probably the one with the highest shock value and the one that separated her most dramatically from our Princeton classmates. It was a significant risk. I wondered whether Olivia wanted to prove she was still willing to take it.

▪ ◆ ▪ ◆ ▪

Bethany spent the entire month of January in Seattle. Alex and Bethany had been talking about this particular trip since the summer. None of their other visits had lasted longer than a few days—someone always had to rush back to work or school. January was their chance to relax in each other's company without the pressure of a ticking clock, counting down the hours until one of them had to get back on a plane.

Alex knew January was going to be busy. She had to finish writing her senior thesis. As soon as she did, she'd get her official diploma. The dean hadn't issued a hard deadline, but the New Year was a wake-up call. Her class graduated seven months ago. Alex wanted her degree.

Two weeks after Bethany arrived in Seattle, she called Alex around eight o'clock, while Alex was in the car on her way home from work. Bethany wanted to go out with some of her friends.

"Can we leave right when you get home?"

"Babe, I've gotta keep working on this thesis. I'm just going to pick up food on the way home, but you should go. I'll see you when you get back."

"You suck."

Alex gripped the steering wheel hard. She could hear other people talking in the background: Bethany was already with her friends, so they were hearing everything she said. It was one thing for Bethany to talk to Alex privately about working too much, but now she was disrespecting her in front of other people. Alex knew Bethany would probably start complaining about their relationship as soon as she got off the phone.

"What? Why do I suck?"

"You just suck."

"It's not nice to tell me that I suck just because I have to do my thesis. You know how important this is."

"Okay."

"Okay." Alex paused, hoping Bethany would apologize or at least say that she loved her.

"Bye."

Alex immediately started going over options in her head. Since moving to Seattle, she'd plotted three possible paths for the next few years of her life: plan A was to leave the programming project immediately and move to New York without a job, plan B was to stay six more months and apply to a New York hacker school (an intensive programming boot camp), and plan C was to stay two more years, start taking software engineering classes in Seattle, and finish in New York. All versions culminated in moving across the country to be with Bethany. That ending seemed inevitable.

Alex accelerated, fixated on the farthest point visible on the open highway, and finally allowed herself to consider an alternate ending. Bethany had made it clear to Alex that a life in Seattle and a future with her were mutually exclusive. Alex tried not to like her city, but lately that hadn't been working. She was settling into Seattle. In Capitol Hill, she'd started to collect "regular" places like prized trinkets. When people came to visit, she could take them to her favorite ginger beer shop, vegan restaurant, ice-cream store, or bar that served the best burgers in the city.

Her work life was also getting better. In early January, the real estate company approved an additional $1 million in funding for the project she was working on with her brother. Soon they'd be able to hire consultants and other programmers to shoulder some of the workload. Alex still didn't think she was contributing much to the operation, but now at least she didn't feel like she was holding Ben back. She also knew her programming skills were rapidly improving. Most computer science majors would have taken her job in a second. If she stuck it out for a few more years, she would be able to program at any company in America.

Bethany never wanted to hear about the good parts of Seattle. Though she never said it outright, Alex knew Bethany resented her for having a great day at work or making a new friend on Capitol Hill. Even after Alex started getting along with Ben again, Bethany maintained that he was trying to take advantage of her professionally. When she first moved to Seattle, Alex was pretty sure it comforted Bethany to know she was sad. Now she wished Bethany could just be happy that she was starting to be happy again.

"I usually call Bethany on my way home from work," Alex said. "I spend the first half of the drive talking out loud to myself. I think about the day and say, 'Oh yeah, that was so exciting.' I get the excitement out of my system. Then by the time I call Bethany, I can just say, 'Oh yeah, that was pretty cool.'"

Since she went to New York over Christmas, Alex had started to wonder if maybe Bethany was a little selfish. She had a long list of things she wanted Alex to do, and if Alex didn't do them, or even hinted that she might not want to do them, she would get extremely passive-aggressive: glowering, not making eye contact, answering questions with one-word answers. Almost all their arguments—more like periods of angry silence—revolved around two demands: Alex needed to be more social, and Alex needed to move to New York as soon as possible.

A few nights before the "you suck" comment, Bethany and Alex talked about the first issue. Bethany started the conversation by saying, "I just don't know how we're going to do stuff when you can't go out as much." Alex told her there was nothing she could do—if she wore herself down (as she'd done over Christmas), her face would begin to droop, and her body would start to fail. Bethany pushed back.

"I know I can't get mad, but this is really important to me. All I'm asking is that we go out on weekends and maybe have dinners with people twice a week."

At home in New York, Bethany went out with friends five or six times a week. She drank heavily and regularly stayed up until three or four in the morning. Dystonia made it physically impossible for Alex to keep up with Bethany socially, but even before she got sick, Alex had always preferred staying home. On nights when Bethany was around, Alex wanted to curl up on the couch with her cat on her lap, sip herbal tea, and cuddle. Most of the time, Bethany hated nights like that. She felt like she was missing out.

The question of whether to go out and be social caused a lot of little fights, but Bethany and Alex's worst arguments always happened when they started talking about the future. Alex wanted to keep working with Ben in Seattle for two more years and move to New York when she was healthier and more professionally established, with money saved up in case she needed to pay medical bills out of pocket. Bethany wanted her to move now. Alex understood that Bethany wanted them to be together, but recently she'd started to question why she was the one expected to make the big change. Bethany had been recruited for post-doc programs at the University of Washington, a twenty-minute walk from Capitol Hill. She studied the spread and control of diseases, and Washington had one of the best epidemiology departments in the country. But Bethany wouldn't even consider it. She hated Seattle. Columbia was her dream school, and it looked like she was going to be able to do her research there.

"I keep telling Bethany: 'There is a difference between you taking a risk and me taking a risk,'" Alex said. "'When I stop working with my brother and move to a city that is totally foreign, I let go of Ben, the one person who has always been there, and all my job security. That's a bigger risk than if you come out here for two years to do a postdoc.'"

Bethany was the only person Alex knew in New York, so if she moved, she would have to rely on her for everything. And considering how much Bethany loved her social life, Alex didn't know how much she could even do that. If Alex had a flare-up, she was pretty sure Bethany would stay home with her for the night. But if the flare-up lasted two weeks? Alex didn't know if Bethany's patience and charity would stretch that far. She might get bored, go out with her secondary partner, and leave Alex alone when she needed her most. Ben was family. Alex knew he would take care of her—as a boss and as a brother—because he'd been doing it for twenty-five years. She'd known Bethany for only fourteen months, and that meant she had a palpable lack of evidence.

There was also the possibility of a breakup. If Alex's relationship with Bethany ended after she moved to New York, Alex would be completely alone. When Alex brought this up to Bethany, she laughed it off, saying, "No way, we're not going to break up." But Alex didn't think Bethany really understood what she was getting herself into. Bethany was inclined to do whatever made her feel best in the moment—and in the moment, she wanted Alex to be sleeping next to her in New York. Alex doubted whether she'd actually considered how her illness would impact their future together—how there would probably be weeks when Alex wouldn't be able to get out of bed, and Bethany would have to take care of their kids all by herself. No clubbing, no dinner parties, no fun. At that point, Alex was sure Bethany would resent her. Then it would just be a matter of time before they split up.

"My biggest fear is that I wake up alone in New York City," Alex said, "with a life that I never really wanted."

WHEN BETHANY LEFT for New York, Alex didn't drive her to the airport. They'd stayed up too late the night before talking about their relationship, and Alex couldn't get out of bed the next morning. Bethany said it was no big deal to get a cab, but Alex knew that it was. On the road trip, they'd talked extensively about their ideal conceptions of family—what "family" looked like in the flesh, in real life. This was one of the examples they'd come up with together: family takes each other to the airport.

As soon as Bethany left, Alex started trying to figure out how she felt about the whole situation. She was simultaneously relieved that Bethany was gone and miserable because their relationship might be ending. She also felt guilty. Alex wondered whether she was actually the reason their relationship wasn't working. She'd spent a lot of time on her thesis and neglected Bethany. Maybe, Alex thought, Bethany didn't think she cared about her as much as she used to. Of course she wanted Alex to come to New York—Alex had been acting so distant, Bethany probably thought they couldn't make their relationship work if they weren't permanently in the same place.

A few days later, Alex told Bethany she wasn't playing games. "If it comes down to it," she said, "you're going to win. If it's between Ben and my job and you, you're going to win."

■ ◆ ■ ◆ ■

After a few weeks of living in the new apartment with Robert, one of my friends asked me if I was "nesting."

"It seems like you're really settling down," she said. "When should I expect the babies?"

I was a long, long way from even starting to think about kids, but she was right—I was creating a home for myself. In the short time we'd lived in the new apartment, I'd taken two trips to buy furniture at IKEA, started an herb garden on my windowsill, hosted multiple parties, and baked muffins to give to our new neighbors. I loved my new space. It was small—definitely not designed for more than one person—but that didn't bother me. It had an exposed brick wall and a deck and skylights so that, lying on the couch in the middle of the day, I could feel natural heat on my back. I used to leave the group house no later than ten every morning because anywhere else was more comforting. I'd scope out a coffee shop and plant myself there for at least five hours. But in the new apartment, if I didn't have something particular to do, I didn't feel like I needed to leave. The room was bright, the kitchen was clean, and I could watch TV while I ate lunch without worrying about running into anyone I didn't feel like talking to.

Living with Robert was easy. In the group house he'd slept over almost every night, so we'd basically been living together already. I knew his annoying habits: he never picked his sweaty workout clothes up off the floor; he couldn't tolerate the sound of me eating chips, apples, or carrots. I could deal with those things.

A lot of my friends asked me if I thought moving in with Robert added pressure to our relationship. The first time we fought in the new apartment, I did wonder about the logistics of breaking up: How easy would it be to break this lease? Would we both move out, or would one of us stay? But those thoughts didn't last long. There was already a ton of pressure on our relationship. I'd moved to DC because that was where Robert got a job. We had already been making decisions with each other in mind, planning our lives together two years, five years, down the road. We were serious. The decision to move in together just made that commitment more public.

CHAPTER EIGHT

March

In August, Olivia had told me that the post-grad life I had planned was too boring. If I moved to DC, stayed with Robert, and lived in a house with other Princeton grads, she'd said, I would be sheltered. I wouldn't push myself. I wouldn't grow.

For the next few months, I didn't give this conversation much thought. I wasn't too concerned about growing (figuring out how not to cry every day seemed like the higher priority). But after Robert and I moved into the new apartment, and I settled into a routine, I started to think about it again. I was comfortable and happy, but did that mean I was doing something wrong?

For the vast majority of twenty-somethings who live here, Washington, DC, is a pit stop. Unless you're dead set on a career working for Congress, it's a place you go for a year or two to pad your résumé. Almost every college graduate I knew in DC was already plotting his or her next move: graduate school, a company based in New York City, a year in some remote country. Most "young professionals" found a relatively cheap group house with a flexible lease, bought some cheap IKEA furniture, and joined a dodgeball team with people they knew from college. People solidified relationships with college acquaintances so they'd have someone to hang out with on weekends, but most didn't try to make any new, lifelong friends. All around me, people seemed to be doing what was necessary to make themselves comfortable for a year, but not more.

After a couple of weeks, our new neighborhood felt more like home to me than anywhere else I'd ever lived. Every row house on our street was a different color, with its own garden that looked a little different every time I walked by. I loved the way the bricks on the sidewalk jutted out and overlapped, adopting the shape of the tree roots underneath them. I made friends with our landlady and the vendors at the market two blocks away—Dee at the meat stand liked to make fun of my laugh, and Daniel at the cheese stand always let me sample as many different cheeses as I wanted before I bought a small hunk of the cheapest cheddar he sold. In the new apartment, my days quickly took on a fixed rhythm: wake up, work out, make tea, say good-bye to Robert, write, make lunch, write, make dinner, maybe socialize with some people we'd invited over, watch Netflix, sleep. It wasn't a particularly exciting routine, but after the first half of my year in DC, it was reassuring. I stopped seeing DC as a pit stop and started seeing the city—particularly my new neighborhood—as a place where I could happily spend most of the rest of my life. When I saw parents playing basketball in the alley behind our house with their kids and their dogs, I thought about what it would be like to raise my own family here.

But I wasn't supposed to have that feeling. I was twenty-three. That was, as Olivia had said, the time to explore and take risks.

Certainly not the time to settle down in a row house in an upper-middle-class neighborhood with my boyfriend, pursue the kind of writing career that would keep me in one place, and start thinking about children. I knew that I wanted to do more before I did that. Everyone else my age was moving, trying, planning. No one was putting down roots. Not yet.

If I didn't try something new and leave DC now, I was afraid I never would. So I started to think about my options. Since I graduated, Robert and I had been talking about moving to China for a year. When we left the school where we worked right after I graduated, the administrators invited us to come back to teach during the school year. "Foreign teachers" at the school taught only fifteen hours of class per week, so we knew these jobs would give us time—time to learn Mandarin, time to hang out with students we'd gotten to know last summer, time for me to write, time for Robert to study for the LSAT, the law school admissions exam. Since I went to China for the first time freshman year, I'd always wanted to spend a year there. I kept going back for one- or two-month stints, but it wasn't enough. I could see myself having a career as a foreign correspondent, reporting for an American newspaper from Shanghai or Beijing. But I couldn't do that without being fluent in Chinese, and I couldn't become fluent without living in China for a lot longer than six weeks.

Law school was another option—if my parents had their way, the only option. When I tried to talk to my mom about my writing, she would nod and smile for a few minutes, then find some way to ask when I was going to start studying for the LSAT. If I told her that I might not take the LSAT at all, she'd put on a condescending smile—the one that implied she knew me better than I knew myself—and say, "Caroline, you're going to be a lawyer." I resented this expectation so much that, for a while, I wrote off law out of spite. Everyone else in my life, particularly Robert, told me that I had better things to do than spend three years in law school, and I listened.

But when I moved to DC, I started volunteering for a local domestic violence nonprofit, answering calls from victims who needed lock changes, housing, or help navigating the legal system. I did something similar in my sophomore and junior years of college, and I'd been writing about domestic violence and sexual assault ever since. But working directly with victims again made me wonder whether writing about these issues was really doing any good. The women I talked to on the phone needed skilled, affordable lawyers to help them put together a case more than they needed to read another article about what they were going through.

"I LOOKED INTO taking the LSAT today." I was sitting on the couch, looking up LSAT test dates on my computer when Robert came home from work. "I think I want to take the test in October. But if I do that, I want to start studying now. There's a prep course near here that starts in June. We could take it together."

"What?" Robert abruptly stopped scrolling through Facebook on his phone and looked up. "Really? When did you start to get so serious about this?"

"I mean, you know I've been thinking about it for a while."

"But this is the first time you've really talked about it with me."

"That's not true. I've always said I might want to go to law school."

"Yeah, but it was never a real thing. You always talked about it like a vague possibility."

"Well, I think I want it to be more than a distant possibility now. You're definitely going to go to law school soon, and it makes sense for us to apply together. Then we can try to go to the same school or find two schools close to each other."

"We're not going to get into the same school," Robert mumbled, staring dejectedly at one fixed point on the carpet.

"You don't know that."

"Yes, I do."

Robert was going to be a lawyer. Both his parents were lawyers. He'd known he was going to be a lawyer since he was fourteen years old. I, on the other hand, was not at all sure that this was what I wanted. It was just one of the career paths I had floating around in my head. But my grades in college were much better than Robert's, so we both knew I would probably get into a better school.

"This isn't fair. You're going to have all this time to study for the LSAT while I'm at work." Robert sat on the floor and put his head in his hands. "I'm not going to have any time. You're going to do better than me."

"Are you saying you don't want me to study?"

"Well, I just—no, I'm not. But this is frustrating."

"It sounds like you're saying that you don't want me to do well on this test."

"No, it's just . . ." Robert paused. "You're going to get into Yale, and then of course you're going to have to go to Yale. And I'm going to have to compromise and go to some shitty school."

"No, you're not. I don't care about going to the very best law school. This is what I'm saying—if we apply together, we can both compromise on where we go so we're close to each other."

"If you get into Yale, you're going to go." Yale was the number one law school in the country.

"No, I'm not." I sat up straight on the couch. "You're not listening to me."

"This is the thing I've been waiting for my entire life. I don't want to have to compromise and go to a bad school."

"So what do you expect me to do? Just follow you wherever you go?"

"No," he said. "But I thought that if you were a writer, you'd have more flexibility to move around."

I got up from the couch, ran into the bedroom, slammed the door, and wedged my body into the foot of free space between the bed and the wall.

Even if I didn't end up going to law school, this conversation did not bode well for our relationship. I didn't think I was asking for much—just that we agree on two schools relatively close to each other. In this situation, no matter what happened, we would both have an exciting, new professional opportunity. Even if we ended up at schools that weren't the very best ones we got into, we would still both go to law school. What would happen down the road in our relationship if we had kids? What if one of us had to take a year or two off work to take care of them? If Robert wasn't willing to make this small sacrifice now, he definitely wouldn't be willing to make a much larger one later.

Since we started dating, Robert had encouraged me to write. I'd always thought he was incredibly supportive—posting my articles on Facebook and e-mailing them to people around his office—but now I wondered how much of that support was self-serving. Maybe he wanted me to be a writer because it would give me the flexibility to move around, stay at home, and take care of kids while he spent long hours at a law firm.

I knew I was probably blowing this conversation out of proportion. I knew how important law school was to Robert—he hadn't tried to succeed academically at Princeton, so this was his big chance to prove himself. But still, it scared me. No matter what, I wanted to feel supported by my boyfriend and, eventually, by my husband. I didn't want a relationship that felt like a competition. Sitting on our bedroom floor, I thought about different reasons Robert wouldn't want me to study for the LSAT but kept coming back to one. He didn't want me to succeed.

■ ◆ ■ ◆ ■

"Butcher in a slaughterhouse, cemetery gates clooooosing, bottle of liquor spilling out." The piano played a few ominous-sounding minor notes. Michelle stumbled. After swaying in place for a few seconds, head lolling, she bolted upright and screamed.

"Murder victim!" She took a deep breath while the drummer frenetically struck his symbols.

"Water currents . . . hands leafing through book . . . two ships pass at night . . . pressure gauge rising . . . eeeeeeeeeeee!"

She paused and the band went silent. Her voice dropped two octaves and she stared, straight-faced, at a boy in the front row.

"Hockey player's elbow."

If someone had played this piece for Michelle seven months ago, before she started music school, she would have laughed. She would have laughed harder, watching the twenty people in the audience close their eyes and earnestly nod their heads in time with the band. Seven months ago, she would have called this noise, not music.

But her definition of music was changing. The piece Michelle was performing, "Treatment for a Film in Fifteen Scenes," had no notes, just words. Following her lead, the musicians had to make a split-second decision about the way something sounded—a water current, a telephone, fruit in a basket—and then translate that idea into music. Entirely improvised, the piece became something completely different every time it was performed.

After the concert, people from the audience swarmed around Michelle, congratulating her. One older graduate student came over and shook her hand.

"I've been at this school for seven years, and you're the first vocalist I've seen who has really tried to tackle free improvisation stuff," he said. "That was awesome."

Michelle beamed. "Free improvisation" refers to jazz music that includes a lot of improvisation. To an untrained ear (like mine), this genre of music generally sounds like a lot of banging and wailing. There's no melody—no pleasing, repetitive sequence of notes for the ear to grab on to. Students at Michelle's conservatory took pride in what they called "active listening." They found cohesion and meaning in sounds that, to other people, seemed like nothing.

That "nothing" was quickly becoming Michelle's specialty. At Princeton and in her first few months at music school, she'd generally stuck to playing and writing "straight-ahead jazz": the kind of melody-driven music popular in jazz clubs. But over the last few months, Michelle had started gravitating toward music that was less mainstream. She loved the unpredictable intensity of free improvisation—how the entire piece depended on the connections between members of the band, and how each of them related to the music in that particular moment. She never knew when an improvised piece would climax or how.

"In improvised music, one person in the band decides to take it up a step, and then everyone follows," Michelle said. "You look at each other and it's like, 'Okay—yes. We're going there.'"

The more Michelle moved away from straight-ahead jazz, the more her professors and classmates seemed to respect her. A few weeks before, Jim Sharpe, the ensemble professor who had criticized Michelle all year, gave her his first compliment. She'd brought some of her favorite poetry to class to use as a jumping-off point for improvisation, drawing out and riffing off a few words and phrases. When she finished one particular poem by e. e. cummings, Jim folded his arms, leaned back in his plastic folding chair, and smiled.

"You know, I've been in the worst mood today, but you just revived me. Now, Michelle, you are becoming a free improviser."

Simon, the saxophone player who sat next to Michelle in ensemble, leaned over and patted her on the back. Michelle's friend Max flashed a thumbs-up and a big smile from across the room. Michelle almost started crying. Finally, she thought, *finally*. She was starting to do something right.

FOR A WHILE, these kinds of compliments allowed Michelle to relax. For the first time since she started music school, she felt like she had a concrete goal to work toward. If she kept working on free improvisation, she could eventually claim a unique sound. People at the conservatory would consider her successful.

The problem was that it meant one thing to be successful inside the conservatory and another to be successful outside of it.

Michelle started to worry about how the rest of the people in her life would react to her new music. Now, when nonmusical friends came to see her sing, she felt like she had to preface the performance with a disclaimer: "This is going to be really weird, and it's totally fine if you don't like it."

Michelle knew her parents wouldn't support her decision to pursue improvised music. They'd always told her to do the things she loved, but Michelle was pretty sure that advice came with an unspoken addendum: within reason. At Michelle's senior recital at Princeton, the auditorium was almost full, with 150 people in the audience. At the end she got a standing ovation. Her parents left the recital believing that Michelle could become at least a relatively well-known jazz singer, fulfilled and financially stable. If she became an improvising musician, Michelle knew she would probably never get that kind of recognition again.

"Even if I'm the most successful singer in the genre, I'll still be an absolute random," Michelle said.

She would probably have to work one or two nonmusical part-time jobs and sing at a few obscure jazz clubs a couple of nights a week. If she wanted to be financially independent, she would have to rent a small apartment in a bad part of town. She knew her parents wouldn't want her to live that way. They would probably demand that she change her career or accept financial help. And Michelle didn't want to take money from her parents for the rest of her life.

"I think my parents dream of coming to New York City and seeing me sing at a jazz club, singing the music they like. But I don't think I'm going to end up in that scene. The improvised stuff is more conducive to a dingy basement."

When Michelle performed at the conservatory's vocal concert

at the end of March, she sang two original pieces. The first was inspired by free improv—a seven-minute piece with no repeated sections and three minutes in the middle reserved for improvisation. To me, the improvised section sounded like vocal exercises: a medley of random fluctuating vowel sounds interspersed with the occasional impersonation of a fire siren or an Internet dial-up connection. But the audience loved it. People shouted "Mmm" and "Oh yeah" every time she changed her sound. After Michelle sat down, the classical bassist behind her said she sounded like an exotic bird. This was an educated audience: students and professors who knew what constituted skilled improvisation. She'd seen improvised performances at the conservatory that didn't get audience approval—an agonizing five or six minutes when no one swayed or tapped their feet while the musicians desperately tried to elicit a response. This made her feel like her classmates and professors weren't just praising her because she was trying this really weird thing, but because she was good at it.

Michelle's second piece was traditional, straight-ahead jazz. With a catchy melody and a standard verse-chorus-verse-chorus structure, it was the kind of music she would have been writing if she'd gone to the Taylor Swift factory. The audience seemed to like this piece, too, but Michelle felt like people were judging her for it. She knew her songs didn't make sense together. She knew she sounded like two different artists. She worried her friends and professors at the conservatory might see the second piece as a sellout: a back-up sound in case improvised music didn't work out.

Michelle wanted to move away from that kind of music—leave straight-ahead jazz behind. But after the concert, the second piece was the one she chose to send to her parents. They loved it.

MICHELLE NEEDED TO DECIDE what kind of music she wanted to create. She knew she should have been making this decision on her own. It should have been one of the most deeply personal choices of her life. But she found herself looking to other people in her life—her parents, Jim Sharpe, the people in the audience at the vocal concert—to make it for her. She preferred her free improvisation pieces to any other music she'd ever written, but she didn't know if she was committed enough to the genre to accept a life estranged from the mainstream. She couldn't be sure, and that made her feel like she didn't know who she was. She missed when music was just something she did for fun, rather than something that made her question her whole identity.

The more Michelle thought about the recent swell of approval she'd received from the conservatory community, the more she worried that she was pretending. Maybe she just liked free improvisation because, here, in this bizarre little musical bubble, it won her respect. Maybe her music would change again after she graduated. Maybe then she would hear free improv in the way that she once had. As noise.

She came home late from the vocal concert and collapsed onto the bed in her empty apartment. She picked up her phone and thought about texting Canaan. But they were still just dating casually, and Michelle didn't feel like she could be honest with him about her insecurities. Instead, she opened the Notes app and started writing.

Feeling inadequate

Helpless constantly

Sun burning through my skin

Thought this was supposed to make me happy
Be cool, be cool
Try to be myself, don't know what that is
Guilty and plagued by lack of songwriting skills
Worry about not being opinionated enough
Worry worry worry, release, release
Help
Get drunk
Start again
Not outrageous enough
Not weird enough

■ ◆ ■ ◆ ■

Denise waited until March to tell her bosses and coworkers that she was going to medical school. Officially, her fellowship lasted only one year, but she knew they were hoping she would stay longer. It took months to train a new employee. Denise spent her first three months at the Harlem primary school constantly bombarding her coworkers with questions about the filing system, the school's computer programs, and the phone-call protocols. At the hospital, she went through almost fifty hours of formal training: acting out role-plays with patients and parents, familiarizing herself with the preferences of every psychologist at the hospital, and memorizing hundreds of variations of evaluation questionnaires. Denise was just starting to understand her jobs well enough to be good at them. And in two months, she would be leaving.

"This is such important work, and these organizations can't afford to lose the time and money it takes to train a new person every year," Denise said. "I'm working with all these people who have been here for years and years, and I am the transient one. It's selfish. I'm coming to take the experience from them."

When Denise finally told her managers she was leaving, they weren't surprised. Every year, a premed Princeton student took these jobs, used the time to apply to medical school, then left to pursue a career far more prestigious than the administrative positions they were leaving. Everyone else stayed behind, continuing the same work they'd been doing for years. Denise hated that cycle. As she waited for the last few medical schools to send their decisions, she started to think about breaking it.

■ ◆ ■ ◆ ■

Ben lifted the desktop computer from its cradle of wires and hurled it across the table. Then he picked up the mouse, the veins on his forearm bulging like he was trying to break it into a hundred little plastic pieces. Alex pushed back in her rolling chair, away from Ben, out of their office, and into the kitchen.

She hated when Ben got like this, and he got like this a lot. By now, she could see his tantrums coming. She knew all the signs. His ears were always the first things to turn red. Slowly, red splotches crept across his cheeks, meeting with others inching up from his neck, until his entire face turned into one big, bursting tomato. After that, he usually stopped using English, opting instead for the kind of aggravated growl that might come from the Giant as he chased Jack back down the beanstalk: *"Agghhhhhhhh!"*

"I'm done," Ben said. "I'm quitting." After pacing around the room for a few minutes, hands balled into fists at his sides, he sat back down in his chair. "Can you help me write my resignation letter?"

If Ben quit, Alex would lose her job. Her coding skills weren't nearly good enough for her to continue their project alone, and she didn't have the education or experience necessary to get another programming job. In a few months, she would be totally out of money. No more dystonia treatments, no more Capitol Hill apartment, no more trips to see Bethany.

"Okay," Alex said. "Yes, I can. But first let's talk about why you're upset." Alex knew her best shot at keeping her job was to stay collected, empathize, and calmly try to get Ben to reconsider. "What bothers you about the company?"

"I'm not being treated well. People don't respect me. I'm trying to get this project done, and everyone at the company is making that impossible."

Alex understood why Ben was frustrated. Because the real estate company had been around for so long, the higher-ups required Ben and Alex to go through a lot of clunky, outdated processes to get things approved. At every new stage of the project, they had to re-pitch their ideas to a board of executives, stalling their progress and leaving them very little time to code.

"How does that make you feel?"

"Angry."

When Ben threw tantrums like this, Alex stopped thinking of him as her adult boss. He was a little kid, coming home after being bullied all day at Byron Junior High. Alex never had any problems making friends, and it had always been her job to make her brother feel better. But this time, she had to be careful what she said. She had to help Ben convince himself that he should stay and that it was his idea. If Ben thought Alex was pressuring him, he would see her as another bully trying to get what she wanted and quit.

"I know you are, but try to think about what's behind that anger," Alex said. "Do you feel undervalued? Do you feel like you're not getting the recognition you deserve?"

"Yes," he said, nodding and making eye contact with Alex for the first time since he threw the computer. "I feel undervalued. I feel like they don't care about me as a person, and if I left it wouldn't matter."

"Okay, then you should ask the corporate team if that's true. If it is, obviously you should leave and find something different."

That seemed to get through to Ben. He started typing his resignation letter but agreed to call his manager in the morning before he sent it.

Alex allowed herself to relax. Ben was back on his computer. His face had returned to its normal color. At least for now, she still had a job. But as soon as possible, she knew she had to make some changes—to develop a contingency plan in case Ben failed her.

"The thing that I want more than anything, for a few years, is stability. I don't want to feel like my job could just disintegrate at any time. No more having every day be a roller coaster. No more relying entirely on Ben and his emotions."

For a few weeks, Alex had been researching the post-baccalaureate software engineering program at Oregon State University. Her best friend from Princeton, Jay, was taking the online classes and raved about them. Working with Ben, Alex constantly felt like she was missing something. Almost everything she knew about computers—all the languages and technical coding skills—she had picked up on her own, from online resources and books. When she started at the real estate company, her programming arsenal included a hodgepodge of skills, which, together, barely covered the basics of what she needed to know to work alongside her brother. Talking to higher-ups at the real estate company, she was always uncomfortably conscious of her degree in the history of science and technology. Though she later found out that she was paid far less than people with computer science degrees, at the time Alex thought the company could have hired someone with relevant academic background for the same amount of money. She assumed Ben was the only reason she was still there.

Back in November, when Alex mentioned the post-baccalaureate idea to Ben, he said she was being stupid: she didn't need to go back to school to have a successful career as a computer programmer. After all, he had a degree in economics and was making $230,000 a year. But Alex didn't just want to be a programmer. She wanted to be a software engineer. When she explained the two jobs to me, Alex compared a programmer to someone fluent in a second language and a software engineer to a linguist—someone who not only knew two languages, but also understood why they worked in the way that they did. There wasn't necessarily a large difference in salary—programmers like Ben could still spearhead big, important projects at tech companies—but software engineers seemed to code at a higher level. And if Alex was going to spend the rest of her life working at a tech company, she wanted to know she was just as qualified as anyone else there.

Ideally, Alex would continue to work at the real estate company for at least another year while taking a class or two in her free time. She was learning a lot from Ben, and she needed the money. But if that didn't work out—if Ben left the company—she could continue to bolster her résumé as a full-time student.

WHEN BEN GAVE HER A HARD TIME, Alex usually turned to Bethany, who always seemed to enjoy commiserating with Alex over Ben's faults. But lately, every conversation with Bethany had turned into an argument, usually about moving to New York, and Alex didn't feel like confiding in her. She didn't want to give Bethany another reason to lay into Ben. Alex also worried that, if she opened up to her about her problems at work, Bethany would try to take advantage of her vulnerability.

A few days after Ben's outburst, Bethany told Alex that her feelings for her weren't as strong as they used to be.

"I don't want to break up," she said. "I just want to let you know what I'm thinking."

Alex didn't know what to say. She and Bethany had been arguing a lot lately, but up until now, she thought the problem had been their circumstances—the distance between Seattle and New York, dystonia, Alex's thesis. She'd never seriously considered the possibility that Bethany was starting to love her less.

"What do you mean? Why? When did you start feeling that way?"

"I just really need you to come to New York. I can't deal with the way things are right now."

"This isn't fair. It's too much pressure."

Alex thought about something her mom had said on the phone a few weeks ago: "Baby, after being with your dad, all I know is that it's better to be alone than to be with someone who only loves you when you do what they say." She finally decided to tell Bethany something she'd been wanting to tell her since Christmas.

"I'm angry at you." Alex paused. She wanted to make sure she said the next part right. "We're very different, especially in how we fulfill our desires. My entire life, I've been denying myself what I wanted. I'm used to holding back the desires that I actually want to pursue. But if you want to do something, you do it right then."

"If you're saying that I've been able to get more of what I want in life, then that's true."

"No, it's more than that. I'm not talking about the events themselves. I'm talking about the approach. I can make this long-distance work because I've spent most of my life not being with somebody that I could love. So what's another year? It's painful and, man, it's not what I want to do. But what's another year? But you need to feel good, and this—being long-distance—doesn't make you feel good."

"You're right. I want us both to feel good. And I think the way we make that happen is by living in New York together."

Alex reminded Bethany that she was applying to the online post-baccalaureate program. As soon as she stopped working at the real estate company, she said, she could live anywhere for at least a year as a full-time student. Bethany didn't seem to hear her. She didn't want to talk logistics with Alex. She refused to engage on specific details like where they would live in New York, how Alex would cover medical costs between jobs, or what would happen if Bethany got hired by a university in a small city or town where Alex couldn't find any programming work. She just wanted her in New York, *now*. For the first time, Alex considered the possibility that Bethany just wanted to see what it would be like to live with her full-time, without incurring any responsibility for her health or happiness.

After graduation, when Robert got a job in DC, I didn't mind following him. But I didn't mind only because, if circumstances had been different—if I had a job that required me to settle in one particular city and he had flexibility—I knew he would have done the same for me. In my senior year, I asked Nannerl Keohane, president emeritus of Duke and Wellesley and a professor at Princeton, for advice on balancing a high-powered career with a committed relationship right out of college. I expected her to tell me to focus on my career and wait to factor my partner into my future plans. But that's not what she said at all. Instead, she told me there were periods of time—some at the beginning of her career—when she made significant professional sacrifices to be with her husband. There were other times when her husband made significant professional sacrifices to be with her. Sometimes her husband couldn't say no to an opportunity, and other times, she couldn't. They made it work. That conversation gave me something to aspire to: a relationship with a healthy push and pull, each partner respecting and valuing the other's career enough to occasionally stall their own.

Alex valued her close relationships over everything else in her life. She actually liked the idea of making a grand gesture—like moving across the country—for the person she loved. If Bethany had been engaged with the logistics of the move, more supportive of Alex's health situation, and not completely opposed to making any sacrifices of her own, Alex probably would have caved and moved to New York right away. But Bethany made it clear there would be no reciprocal sacrifices. Her career came first. Alex had to figure out how to fit her life into Bethany's.

"The poly thing," as Alex called it, made the whole situation worse. Every book Alex had read about poly said the same thing: polyamorous relationships need a foundation of trust and respect. But lately, she'd been feeling like Bethany didn't respect her—or at least not as much as she used to. At the beginning of March, Bethany had texted Alex, asking for permission to hook up with a girl that night. Alex texted back, saying it was fine. It wasn't, but she didn't want to tell Bethany what to do. In the fall, she probably would have told Bethany no, but she didn't feel like she had that kind of leverage anymore.

"No matter what, Bethany will fulfill her desires," Alex said. "And I think I've curbed my desires so much, I don't even have that feeling in me. It's not there. It's not me."

For weeks, Alex came home from work every night, cradled her cat, Jekyll, in her lap, and cried. She felt like the days were too long, and she didn't have anything to look forward to. The same fragments of conversations with Bethany played over and over in her head: "I'm not as attached to you as I was a couple months ago . . . No, I don't know why . . . You need to come to New York." She couldn't believe how much of the stability she'd worked so hard to create in her life seemed to be falling apart in the same week. She was on the verge of losing her job—soon to be followed by her health care plan, her apartment, and all the money in her bank account—and the person she'd thought she was going to marry.

Alex knew Bethany was being selfish, maybe even slightly emotionally abusive, but she still wasn't ready to give up on their relationship. Bethany was the only person she'd ever connected to romantically. Granted, she was the first girl she'd ever dated, but still, Alex thought that connection meant something. She had planned the rest of her life with Bethany. They'd discussed everything, from how they would care for their aging parents (invite them to live in their home) to what they would do if Jessie (their first child) had trouble in math (hire a tutor, because they always wanted her to see them as parents first, not teachers).

"I tend to fall in love with the future," Alex said. "It's really hard for me to let go. I've spent my whole life planning for the future because, since I was little, that's where the hope was. I've always thought, 'Well, things are not so great now, but it will get better.'"

If Alex wanted to continue her relationship with Bethany, she knew she needed to visit Bethany in New York as soon as possible. She often thought back to the morning in September when she wrapped her arms around Bethany outside JFK Airport. If she could just hold Bethany, she thought, she could fix this. Alex hadn't budgeted for an East Coast trip until May. She knew she would have to dip into her savings, but she bought the ticket anyway.

■ ◆ ■ ◆ ■

Most days, Olivia hardly left Michael's room. She didn't need to. There was Wi-Fi, a comfortable bed for her to sit on, and food in the refrigerator. She used to work in coffee shops for five or six hours every day—sending e-mails about the documentary, tweeting to potential donors or collaborators—but now she didn't want to spend the five dollars they charged for a latte.

She wasn't depressed, but she wasn't happy, either. Olivia often thought about her October trip to San Francisco. She'd felt so energized all the time—eager to meet new people, to film and make art. In October, she'd actively tried to minimize Michael's role in her life. She recognized that he was too safe, and she didn't push herself to take risks when she was with him. Now she hardly ever spent time with anyone else.

"Maybe I need to accept that life isn't super exhilarating all the time," Olivia said. "Some people use drugs all the time to make it better, and maybe I'll do that. I just don't feel like I'm rocking it or killing it anymore."

Olivia had completely given up on her documentary. After she got back from Colorado, an executive at the media company told her that she was officially green-lighting her project. That meant the company would invest some money in the documentary—hire creative directors to determine whether it was feasible as a miniseries. But Olivia had hardly heard from the media company since.

"I hardly spend any time on the documentary anymore. Someone else tells me what to do, when they tell me anything," she said. "It is out of my control now."

At the end of March, Olivia started binge eating again. She didn't really know why. When she had bulimia episodes at Princeton, the doctors told her she was too anxious or too depressed, and they gave her medication to calm her down or cheer her up. But she wasn't anxious or depressed now. She didn't feel particularly good or particularly bad. She didn't feel much at all.

ALMOST A YEAR BEFORE, in April of our senior year, I visited Olivia in the eating disorder unit at the Princeton Medical Center. When I saw her for the first time, she was sitting on a couch in the floor's central common room with a fleece blanket pulled up to her neck, typing furiously on her computer. Her face was waxy and colorless, and the circles under her eyes were dark in a way that I'd only ever seen signal sudden deprivation—of sleep, drugs, and, in this case, food.

"What are you working on?" I asked after we hugged, sliding in next to her on the couch.

"Job applications."

I raised my eyebrows.

"I can't stop, Caroline. I'm in here wasting time. I don't have a job and I've only got a month and a half left at Princeton. A month and a half before I get shipped back to Malaysia."

"Okay, yes. I get that. But maybe you could just take a few days off? The doctor said you need to rest."

Olivia shook her head. "One sec, I have to type an e-mail really fast because this is going to die soon. They don't let us keep our chargers. They think we're going to strangle ourselves with them."

"Okay," I said, getting up to walk around. Posters with motivational messages from past patients covered the walls of the common room: CONFIDENCE IS FOUND INSIDE YOURSELF and YOU ARE BEAUTIFUL, INSIDE AND OUT, written in rainbow bubble lettering, accented with tiny hearts and flowers. On the bookshelf, there were multiple well-read copies of every book in the *Twilight* series.

Olivia had been bulimic for eight years. Most of the time she was fine, but every once in a while, usually when she was stressed, she would start to binge. She'd known this was a high-risk time—she didn't have a job, she didn't have a visa, and she was nowhere close to finishing her thesis—so she'd tried to spend as much time as possible around other people. Olivia had essentially been living with her primary, Leon, in his dorm for the past month. But it hadn't been enough. Leon couldn't be around all the time, and she found ways to sneak food, then ways to secretly get rid of it.

"Come with me, I want to show you something," Olivia said, shutting her computer.

Olivia's room looked nothing like the others we passed on the wing. Every other room had colorful sheets on the bed, posters on the wall, and pictures of friends and family in frames on the nightstand. Except for a few clothes strewn across the white linoleum floor, Olivia's room was completely empty.

"Leon visited yesterday and brought me this." She balled up her comforter and buried her face in it. "It smells like him."

"I bet it was good to see him."

"It was nice. But he really wants me to stay here longer. He said the only way I'll get better is to stay here for a significant amount of time."

"What do you think?"

"I mean, I know he cares about me, so I trust him. He also told me he wants me to come live with him in San Francisco next year."

"Really? Wow, that's big. Do you think you'll do it?"

"I'm thinking about it. Seriously thinking about it."

I knew Olivia had applied for jobs only in New York. If she followed Leon to San Francisco, she would be entirely dependent on him, at least at first.

"It was so funny," Olivia continued, still hugging the comforter. "Leon came into my room and turned off the lights, then we started making out. Then a nurse knocked on the door and told us to keep the lights on—but we kept making out anyway."

AT THE END OF MARCH, Olivia started browsing apartment listings on Craigslist. She decided it was time to stop relying on Michael. His roommates wanted her out, but she also just wanted to go. She set her maximum price at $600 a month, a laughable limit for an apartment in New York City. She was hoping to rent a couch in someone else's bedroom.

CHAPTER NINE

April

At the beginning of April, Robert and I decided to spend Easter with my mom. I hadn't seen her since Christmas. When I left my house in January, I promised myself that, from that point on, I'd be on my guard around her. I wouldn't trust too much until I felt secure enough to risk getting hurt. I felt secure enough now. The friends I'd missed most in my life in the fall had started to come back. I'd just spent a week road-tripping across the country with Catherine, one weekend on a farm in Virginia with Carter, and another at a mock trial tournament with Ray. I was realizing that I'd probably taken my friends' lack of communication too personally. They'd been busy, but that didn't mean they didn't care.

I was also making new friends in DC, one in particular whom I hung out with a couple of times a week. Sacha graduated from Princeton with me in 2014 and was one of the nine people in my group house. We moved in at the same time in August, but we never really talked until January. Sacha wore all black all the time and never smiled in pictures. She was from L.A. Sometime in September, we were sitting together in our living room when she opened a gift from her mom: a big box of lacy, stringy black clothing. My mom had always outlawed black undergarments of any kind. Watching Sacha unpack her "care package," I remember thinking that I clearly wasn't cool enough to be friends with her.

In January, when some of the other roommates started to give me a hard time about Robert being around our house so often, Sacha jumped to my defense. She also had a serious boyfriend who slept over a lot, and responded to our roommates' complaints with the kind of biting, overtly contentious e-mails I never would have had the guts to send. At first, we went to happy hours together to commiserate over our housing situation. Then we found out we had a lot more in common. We both worried about spending too much time with our boyfriends, we both missed the close friends we'd had in college, and we both had felt incredibly lonely in our group house throughout the fall. For five months, Sacha lived in the room right above mine. After I got to know her, I kicked myself for never walking upstairs and knocking on her door. By April, she'd become one of my closest friends.

All that to say that by the time Easter rolled around, I was feeling pretty confident in the new life I was creating for myself and strong enough to try to make things right with my mom. I arrived at my house in Connecticut before Robert, and I could tell right away that my mom was making an effort to change. As I started unpacking, she said, "You can tell Robert to put his stuff in the guest room." She said this like it was no big deal, but we both knew that it was. Up until now, whenever Robert had stayed at our house, he had slept on the couch downstairs. Offering Robert a bed was my mom's way of letting him out of the doghouse. She was clearly trying, and I appreciated it.

My first night at home was wonderful. Mom and I ordered take-out Thai food. I curled up on the couch and watched *The Sisterhood of the Traveling Pants,* my favorite movie in middle school, while she finished up a paper for her art history class, coming in to ask me questions about structure and style every few minutes. It was the kind of night I missed most from high school.

Everything was perfect until the following evening, when I started making dinner. I was cooking chicken fajitas, a dish Robert and I made all the time when people came over. I was particularly excited to cook for my mom, because when I lived at home, she never let me near the stove. As I chopped the vegetables and sliced the chicken, Mom hovered in the doorway, watching everything I did, clearly ready to come to my rescue at any second. It was a little annoying—I was, after all, twenty-three—but I didn't mind. She'd never seen me living on my own, cooking for myself, and I knew it would probably take some getting used to.

Then I turned on the stove.

"What are you doing?" Mom yelled, running over and lunging for the stove knobs. "You never heat a pan with nothing in it!"

"Yeah, Mom. For this recipe, you do. You have to get it super hot for the fajitas."

I was having a hard time staying calm. One of my biggest frustrations with my mom was that she still treated me like a child. She didn't seem to respect me as a competent, fully functioning adult, and I couldn't understand why.

"No, let me see the recipe."

"I've made this twenty times, I know the recipe," I said, focusing on my breath, keeping it steady. I knew I had a tendency to overreact to things like this—issues that, later, would seem like nothing.

"Where's Robert?"

My mom knew nothing about Robert's cooking skills or experience, but she seemed to think anyone else would be more capable than me. I lost it.

"Why don't you just make it?" I yelled, dropping the spoon I'd been using to stir the salsa on the counter. "You don't think I can do anything."

I told her that, to me, this was a straw that broke the camel's back kind of situation. I was already extremely sensitive to her criticism about what felt like all other aspects of my life, and this put me over the top.

"You're just looking for something to blow up about," my mom said.

"That's not true. This is a big issue," I said. "Do you want us to go home?"

"No, I don't."

"Well, I don't know what to do."

"Maybe we just need some space from each other." I didn't understand how space could make any relationship better, particularly a relationship as important as ours. Space would just make me angrier. It would make me feel like she didn't care.

"Right, okay," I said, not feeling up to begging her to spend time with me, like I'd done over Christmas. "So maybe we should just leave."

"I don't want you to leave."

I tore off some paper towels and cleaned up the mess I'd made with the salsa spoon. "Let's just eat."

"Okay," Mom said. "I'll set the table."

As I put the chicken on the pan, I thought about a questionnaire I'd found while cleaning out my room earlier that day. It was from an old time capsule I'd made with my friends in ninth grade. I'd opened it four years later, right after I graduated from high school. One of the questions was "What scares you most about going to college?" In the space below, I'd scribbled, "I'm scared of leaving my mom." Now I was desperate to feel that connected to her again. I knew our problems were probably just as much my fault as hers, but I had no idea how to solve them. Just spending time together clearly wasn't working.

When Robert walked into the kitchen a few minutes later, he raised his eyebrows and quickly glanced toward my mom, silently asking, "Is it safe?" I nodded. Mom made small talk with Robert, pouring some tortilla chips into a bowl and acting like everything was completely normal.

"So, what would you say your 'beat' is for *The Atlantic,* Caroline?" my mom asked. The question came out of nowhere.

"I guess, right now, it would be college women."

"Aren't you going to be too old to write about that soon? And won't it stop being relevant?"

"I don't think so. I can still write about it. And I'm sure I'll find other beats, too." I couldn't believe it had taken her only fifteen minutes to bounce back and find something new to criticize. "Mom, this is exactly what I'm talking about—constant criticism of everything. Can't you see it?"

"Caroline, I'm not criticizing. I'm just—"

"You are, though, you are. The implication is that—"

"Hey, hey, hey, hey. Now, no need to shout about this." Robert, who until this point had been standing silently in the corner, smiled and turned toward my mom. "Mrs. Kitchener, I think Caroline heard something from you that you didn't necessarily mean. She thought you were implying that her articles weren't important, or that she wasn't going to be employable in a few months. But, Caroline, I don't think that's what your mom meant. I think she just wanted to suggest that you might want to start looking for new, different topics to write about."

Mom nodded. Robert had always said he wanted to mediate the arguments between me and my mom. He thought we talked past each other. I agreed, but I never imagined he'd actually be able to help. But here he was, saying things that made sense, and my mom was listening.

"Would anyone like a glass of wine?" she said, opening the fridge.

At dinner, Mom was quick to refill our glasses as soon as they were half empty. She gave the fajitas way more compliments than they deserved, and we spent the rest of the night watching home movies of me giving speeches in my eighth-grade Latin class. Mom had them filed away in her office, along with every card I'd ever given her, certificates from third-grade writing competitions, and essays she'd fished out of my garbage in high school. Whenever she asked for a copy of a paper or a story I wrote, I used to roll my eyes. She'd always say, "You'll want these things one day." Sitting around our dining room table, sipping wine and watching videos I'd never show to anyone besides the two people watching them with me, I felt lucky to have a mom who loved me enough to record, in meticulous detail, how I grew up.

■ ◆ ■ ◆ ■

As soon as she got to the practice room, Michelle found her sheet music in her backpack, pulled the bench up to the piano, opened the lid, and put her hands on the keys. She could hear people playing music in rooms on either side of her: a couple of flutes on her right, a guitarist from her experimental jazz ensemble on her left. They sounded great. She thought about packing up her stuff and heading home. This was a brand-new song, and she wanted to play it through at least a few times before anyone else had a chance to judge it.

Then, suddenly, the music from the adjacent rooms faded, drowned out by a much louder sound. Michelle's heart started beating faster than she ever remembered it beating before. She could feel the *bum bum bum bum bum bum bum* pulsing in her ears, throat, and temples. To calm herself down, she tried to take slow, deep breaths. But no matter how hard she tried, they came out shallow and ragged, one after the other, in rapid succession. Maybe, she thought, she just drank a little too much coffee that morning. Maybe the practice room was too hot or too stuffy.

But Michelle knew it wasn't just the coffee or the room. She'd heard people talk about anxiety attacks. Before, she hadn't understood what they meant when they described the sudden, all-consuming panic. But she understood now.

"I needed to isolate my feelings and figure out why the fuck I had this complete sense of dread. That's the only way I can describe it—dread."

Michelle looked down at her watch. It was 11:04. She'd never met with the school counselor, but she knew office hours were from 11:00 to 12:00. She shoved her sheet music back in her bag and headed straight for the counseling office.

Walking out of the office an hour later, Michelle ran into Canaan, the guy she'd been seeing since January.

"Hey. I just got out of class," he said. "Are you okay?"

Michelle hadn't looked in a mirror, but she knew her face was red and splotchy.

"Yeah, I dunno," she said, running her hands through her hair and trying to casually smile. "I was in a practice room and I just kind of freaked out. I don't know, I just fucking lost it. So I went to see the school psychologist. That's where I'm coming from now."

Head cocked, brow slightly furrowed, Canaan stared at her for a second without saying anything. "Why?" he asked.

Michelle felt the muscles in her shoulders tighten and her throat starting to close. In that moment, she just wanted a hug from someone she cared about, who cared about her. She'd been in a quasi-relationship with Canaan for four months. He could have provided the compassionate, physical touch she was looking for, but he chose not to.

Michelle knew Canaan was a big part of the reason she'd been feeling so hopeless lately. She'd wanted a deeper relationship since January, but he'd continued to pull back, always stopping just before he did or said something that might suggest commitment. Canaan's hesitation was different from her ex-boyfriend's, Sam's. Canaan never made Michelle feel like he was waiting for someone better to come along. Instead, he told her he didn't want to commit until he was absolutely certain he could follow through, even after she graduated and, in all likelihood, left Philadelphia at the end of next year. Michelle respected how much Canaan valued commitment. She just wished he saw her as someone worthy of obligation.

When I visited Michelle in April, I couldn't help noticing that she didn't really seem to like Canaan that much. Michelle described him to me as "extremely serious, brooding, and dark." I thought this was weird because Michelle loves to laugh—she's always coming up with some crude joke or acting goofy just because she feels like it. When I asked her whether she wanted to date someone she could be silly with, she said, "Oh yes, of course, definitely. But it's slim pickings at my school, let me tell you." Michelle was also quick to bring up Canaan's age—nineteen—and the distance it created between them.

"He's a baby. He can't go get a drink with me, he can't come watch me sing at a bar. It isn't that big of an age difference but it's an important one. We're at completely different points in our lives. He graduated high school in 2013—can we just talk about that?"

Michelle clearly recognized how incompatible they were, but it didn't bother her enough to break things off. Through March and April, she needed the kind of emotional support she felt like she could get only from a boyfriend, and Canaan was the closest thing she had.

But Canaan was only part of the "dread" Michelle described to the school counselor. By this point, she was confident that she wanted to make music—and, if at all possible, free improvisation—her career. At the beginning of the year, she'd been intimidated by how much more everyone else seemed to care about music. By April, Michelle was pretty sure she cared just as much as her classmates.

"Now there is a lot more to lose," Michelle said. "My anxiety went from 'Am I not as intense and invested in this as everyone else?' to 'Oh wow, I'm really behind—I need to catch up because I want to do this.'"

Michelle felt pressure to be creative 24-7. If she wasn't working on her music, she felt like she was wasting time. She knew she needed to do everything she could to take advantage of her professors and classmates: resources that would become much more difficult to access when she graduated in fifteen months. But it was hard. Michelle wasn't used to treating music like an obligation or a job. It had always just been something she did for fun, when she wanted to.

The day before Michelle met with the counselor for the first time, she asked Mary, one of two other vocalists in the graduate jazz program, and Michelle's best friend at school, to hang out. Mary texted back: "Sorry man, I can't. I started writing this song and I wanna keep going. Tomorrow?" This kind of thing happened all the time, and it always made Michelle feel guilty.

"I'm like, okay, cool, you've been writing a song. I've just been riding my skateboard. Dammit, I should have been writing a song."

In their free time, Michelle's classmates were always writing new material, practicing with other musicians, or performing in a local basement show. Most students at the conservatory were immersed in their own musical projects—making an album, playing in a band—that they took far more seriously than any of their classes. Their friends, family, and schoolwork all took a backseat to their music. Michelle wanted to take her music that seriously. She knew she needed to start her own project, outside of school, but she wasn't sure how.

A lot of people had told Michelle that, as a singer, it would be much easier to start her own band than to join one. While it was relatively easy to switch out one guitarist or drummer for another, it was virtually impossible to do the same with a vocalist without completely changing the band's sound. So if Michelle wanted to be in a band, she would have to do all the work: get people together, write the songs, schedule practice, book gigs. But even though she felt more confident in her individual sound than she had all year, she had only two original songs she considered good enough to perform. She needed at least three more to make a set, and she needed a set before she could get a band together.

When Michelle imagined the band she wanted to start, she always unconsciously compared it with Mary's. At the beginning of the school year—a few weeks after arriving on campus—Mary started a rock-jazz band, which immediately became popular in Philadelphia. She played gigs at basement shows and jazz clubs almost every weekend. Mary had one of the best jazz voices Michelle had ever heard and the most impressive résumé of anyone she'd met in the graduate program. Both her parents were singers. She went to an arts-focused high school, then to one of the best undergraduate jazz programs in the country. She'd won multiple major jazz competitions and spent a semester at a famous music academy in Berlin. Mary was able to immediately start a band because she had friends at the conservatory before she even got to Philadelphia—people she'd met at her undergraduate conservatory in Texas, or the Banff International Workshop in Jazz and Creative Music, the most prestigious summer jazz program in the world, where she'd spent the past summer.

"I am so simultaneously elated and bummed by her existence," Michelle said.

On one hand, Mary was her best friend at school. They had a bunch of classes together and frequently collaborated. But she was also extremely intimidating. As two of only three singers in the graduate jazz program, Michelle and Mary were always being compared—the best vocal professor could take on only a few student mentees; the best summer camps, like Banff, had only a few spaces for vocalists—and Michelle felt sure her music paled in comparison. Even now that she cared as much about music as

Mary did, she didn't know how she could ever compete with her. And it was hard for Michelle to feel justified pursuing such a difficult career path when she couldn't even beat out the other vocalist in her school's tiny graduate jazz program.

After her first appointment, Michelle continued to meet with the school counselor every week. The counselor spent most of the time trying to get Michelle to be specific about what was causing her anxiety, to define the "dread." Michelle talked about Canaan, she talked about Mary, but mostly she talked about the fear that, after taking this big risk—devoting all her time to something as obscure as free improvisation—she wouldn't be good enough. She wouldn't turn out to be as talented and creative and special as everyone had always told her she was. She'd have to quit and do something completely different.

■ ◆ ■ ◆ ■

When Olivia and I met for lunch, she drew this on a napkin:

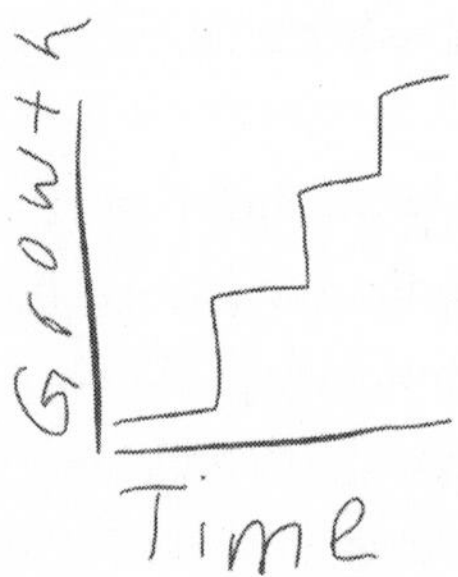

"When I was working on the documentary full-time, I was in the exponential part of the graph," Olivia said. "So much good stuff was happening. But it wouldn't have happened if I didn't decide to sugar date, if I hadn't made the friends that I made, if I hadn't done the documentary, gone to San Francisco, met Mason. That period of exponential growth only came after years and years of accumulating resources—friends, experiences, and skills. I think right now I'm learning stuff, accumulating. I can't deliver another period of exponential growth yet, but that doesn't mean that it won't happen."

Over the last month, Olivia had been slowly moving out of Michael's apartment. She decided not to sign a monthly lease through Craigslist. Instead, she rented couches through Airbnb, spending a few nights in one place, a few in another. Every once in a while, she would crash with a friend. Michael's apartment was still her home base—she kept most of her stuff there, and Michael paid for all the Airbnbs—but now she felt at least a little more independent. Staying in different places also forced her to meet new people. Different kinds of people. She'd missed that. This was what made her feel like she was "accumulating resources."

But it was hard for Olivia to focus on building her future in New York when she knew she had a limited amount of time left in the United States. In September, her visa would expire and she would have to go back to Malaysia. She'd known about this for a while, but she thought she might be able to find a way out of it. When she told her friend Rebecca, another Princeton grad who sugar dated, about her situation over Christmas, Rebecca offered to marry Olivia to keep her in the country. Rebecca had been willing to open a joint bank account and move in with Olivia to make their relationship seem more believable. But then Olivia talked to a few of her friends who were lawyers. They all told her the same thing: even if she married an American citizen, she still had to spend at least two years in Malaysia to get a green card.

If she went back to Malaysia, Olivia felt sure her life graph would completely plateau. After she stopped working on the documentary, Olivia decided that she needed to develop her skills in a variety of different areas: film, graphic design, and coding. She wanted to learn how to operate different kinds of cameras, how to film a commercial shoot, how to code well enough to create her own websites from scratch. Sometime in the future, she would meet someone—hopefully a couple of people—who worked in an industry she found interesting. When that happened, she wanted to make sure she had the skills necessary to get involved. All she needed was the right combination of skills and people—the right resources—to trigger another spike in growth.

If Olivia tried to do the kind of work she wanted to do in Malaysia, she knew what would happen. She would be broke, she'd get frustrated, and she'd agree to work at her father's company. Eventually, she would probably take it over. Then she would be rich, but she would also exist along a permanent horizontal line. That idea made her feel more hopeless than she had in months.

■ ◆ ■ ◆ ■

"Hi, Mommy, I've got another one for you," Denise said as soon as her mom picked up her FaceTime call. "'It is with sincere regret that the Committee on Admissions has completed its selection of the Class entering in September 2015 and has not been able to offer you a place.'" Denise paused and looked up from the letter, giggling. "Can they really not think of anything more original to say? I mean, at this point this is just getting redundant."

Nahvet threw back her head and laughed. This was Denise's

eighth med school rejection letter. Lately, they'd been arriving in her inbox like clockwork, at least one a week.

Before Denise even started applying for medical school, she'd dreaded this part of the process. As a senior in high school, she'd been accepted by every college she applied to. So Denise had built rejection up in her mind: opening the e-mail, tearing up while reading it over and over again, finding out on Facebook that other people she knew had gotten into the school that rejected her, telling her parents and friends that she'd failed. But when the first rejection letter came, she didn't feel nearly as bad as she'd expected to. She read it, called her mom, and moved on. After that, every new letter became a little easier to stomach than the last.

"One rejection I received I was almost gleeful over because it was so nice," Denise said. "They wrote, 'We hope to see you for residency.' I responded, saying, 'Wow! Thank you for sending this encouraging letter! I hope to see you too!'"

Every time she got a rejection letter and didn't cry, Denise felt proud of herself. In college, there were so many times when she'd been paralyzed by fear of rejection. At the end of her senior year, she thought about running for the position of young alumni trustee: the one person from the class of 2014 who would sit on the board of trustees the year after graduation and voice the concerns of the current student body. She couldn't remember the last time she'd wanted anything that much. But she didn't apply—she was too afraid of how hurt and embarrassed she'd be if she failed—and had to vote for one of three candidates she didn't believe would do the job as well. After the election, over a dozen friends and acquaintances told her how much they wished her name had been on the ballot. Denise thought about that decision a lot. She was pretty sure that now, after applying to and getting rejected from so many medical schools, she would make a different one.

The big test for Denise came at the end of April, when she woke up to a text from Matt, her friend at Harvard Medical School. She'd met Matt at a premed summer program her sophomore year and had a little crush on him for a few years afterward. The text was a picture of him with one of her friends from Princeton, Harrison, who had just gotten into Harvard Med. It was admitted students weekend. Looking at the picture, Denise bit down hard on her lower lip.

When Denise worried about how people in her life would view her if she didn't get into a good med school, and thought about exactly who those "people" were, Matt was always at the top of the list, even above her best friends from Princeton. When Denise first met him, Matt had been going into his senior year at the University of Georgia and planning to apply to med school that fall. Denise knew he'd been impressed by her: the sophomore from Princeton with the good grades and incredible work ethic. After the program ended, they exchanged mildly flirtatious text messages every couple of days. When Matt got into Harvard, Denise felt the pressure to get into a good med school more intensely than she ever had before. Matt immediately started talking about the prospect of them going to school together. She warned him that she probably wouldn't get into Harvard, but he refused to even entertain that possibility. "Oh, come on, you go to the number one school in the country," he said, "of course you will." After that, whenever Denise thought about applying to med school, she thought about Matt. She wanted to continue to impress him, to be good enough for him.

The picture of Matt with Harrison confirmed the thing Denise had been dreading. The guy she most wanted to impress knew she wasn't good enough for the admissions officers. And he was just the first to find out she hadn't gotten into Harvard. Soon, everyone in her life—her Princeton friends, younger students she'd mentored, her aunts and uncles—would know about her string of rejections. Last fall, when she'd imagined some version of this scenario, she'd expected herself to completely shut down—to collapse on the floor, cry, and start researching how to go about reapplying to med school the following fall.

"I was waiting for the terrible sting to come, but it didn't," Denise said. "The worst thing that could have happened happened. I did everything I could to prevent it from happening, and then it happened anyway, and it wasn't nearly as bad as I thought."

Denise thought about something her mom told her almost every time they talked about medical school: "People get blessed in different ways." Sometimes she would absentmindedly lapse into comparing herself with people she knew at the very best medical schools. She'd fixate on people like Harrison and make a mental list of reasons an admissions officer would see her as less qualified. Denise considered regret to be the most useless of all human emotions, but that didn't stop her from feeling it. She regretted taking difficult, non-premed classes in college, focusing on extracurriculars, and, more than anything, submitting her med school applications so much later than everyone else.

But then she thought about the life she'd built for herself in New York—her boyfriend, Craig; her church; her new friends. They weren't the blessings she'd been expecting this year, but that didn't mean they weren't valuable. Years down the road, she knew there was a good chance she would consider them far more important than a Harvard acceptance letter.

SINCE SHE STARTED APPLYING to med school, Denise had been counting down the weeks to April 30. Because medical schools had rolling admissions, Denise never knew when she was going to hear back from them. If she interviewed at a school in November, she could get a response a week later or sometime in March. April 30 was the closest thing the med school application process had to an end point. It was the day applicants had to turn down all but one school that offered them a place in their class. If, after that, a school still had open spaces, the admissions office would extend offers to students on the wait list.

On April 30, Denise gave up her spot at every school besides Emory. For the next few weeks, she obsessively checked her e-mail, hoping she wouldn't have to move so far away. Like me, Denise felt rooted in her first post-college home. It was hard for both of us, not knowing whether we would be able to pick up and find that same feeling again somewhere else. At this point, Denise was considering every option that would allow her to continue living in New York: Mount Sinai Medical School, where her application was still outstanding, but also putting off medical school altogether. She liked the idea of staying: in her Harlem apartment, at her job, at her church, with Craig.

■ ◆ ■ ◆ ■

One night in the middle of April, Alex told Bethany that she needed to take a break from their relationship. Earlier that day, she and Ben had a meeting with the CFO of the real estate company. He asked them to start working on a second project and offered them more money. It was a huge promotion. But instead of allow-ing herself to be excited, Alex worried about how she was going to break the news to Bethany.

Back in her apartment, sometime between dialing Bethany's number and telling her about the conversation with the CFO, Alex realized that she needed to end their relationship, at least for a while. A good, loving partner would be thrilled to hear about a major career gain. But Alex knew Bethany wouldn't be. She would never agree to move to Seattle, so a promotion for Alex, if she accepted it, would necessarily mean more time apart. When the words came out of Alex's mouth—"I want to take a break from us"—they surprised her. But she immediately knew she was doing the right thing.

"Boo Cat, are you serious? You just mean a temporary break, right? Just for a day?"

"I don't know."

"No, please. Promise me this isn't permanent."

"I can't right now."

"Why? How can you say that?"

"I need to take a break," Alex said, starting to cry. As angry as she was at Bethany, she still hated causing her pain. "Even when we're together . . . it hurts to love someone and see in their eyes that it's not reflected back."

"But I do love you."

"Not enough. Not enough to make sacrifices—to wait for me to move to New York, or to move out here yourself."

Alex could sense Bethany making calculations in her head, determining whether she should aggressively defend herself, as she normally would, or take a different approach.

"I'm sorry. I just wanted us to be together." It was one of the first times Alex had ever heard Bethany's tone soften during an argument.

"I think you've wanted to break up with me for a while," Alex said. "But you're afraid of feeling pain. Also, I think you're afraid of hurting me. You've been hurting me so much, though. Every time we get off the phone, I feel like you break up with me a little more." Alex paused, took a deep breath, and then whispered, "I feel like I'm a good person."

"You are a good person."

"I feel like somebody could love me more than you do. Maybe."

"This is the best relationship I've ever had. I don't know what's wrong with me."

"I'm really grateful for our relationship," Alex said. "You opened up so many new worlds to me. You taught me a lot about what I want in a relationship and life in general. You gave me the courage to move to Capitol Hill. You took me to my first opera."

Bethany didn't say anything for a while after that. When she started speaking again, her voice was broken. Bethany never cried, so this actually made Alex feel a little better. It proved that, even if Bethany wasn't in love with her anymore, she cared.

"This feels like you're breaking up with me. Please, let's just sleep on it before we decide to take a break."

Bethany was panicking. But by this point, Alex was already in the middle of ripping off the Band-Aid. She knew she would have to take it off eventually, and the process so far had already been incredibly painful. She didn't want to go back.

"This is the decision we're going to come to, whether we make it now or later. I think you know that."

"At least promise me you won't tell anyone. Don't tell Ben or Jay or your mom. Please."

"Okay, I won't." Alex could feel big sobs forming in her chest, and she didn't want to completely lose it on the phone. It would be too easy for Bethany to convince her to change her mind. "I'm sorry, Bethany. I have to go."

As soon as she hung up, Alex took off her clothes, turned the shower knob all the way to the left, stood in a stream of scalding hot water, and cried. She didn't want to go anywhere else in her apartment. Everything in it reminded her of Bethany: the ninja swords they carried on Halloween, the posters of famous scientists they bought at their favorite bookstore, even her cat, Jekyll, because she and Bethany chose her name together. Just a few months ago, she'd been planning to propose and promise to love Bethany "in Jekyll and in Hyde."

Alex was pretty sure that her relationship was over. Or, at least, that it should be over. If it wasn't—if they got back together—it would be because Alex wasn't strong enough to do what she knew was best.

Lately, Alex had started to notice all the similarities between Bethany and her dad. They both issued ultimatums, they both tried to isolate her from the other people in her life, and they both loved her conditionally—as long as she did exactly what they wanted her to do. Most important, they'd both mastered the cycle of emotional abuse. On the phone, Bethany tried to be loving and friendly and pull Alex back in, just like her dad used to do. And it was working. Right now, Alex was sorely tempted to dial Bethany's number, apologize, and try to convince her to forget this ever happened. They'd talked every day since they met eighteen months ago. It would take serious willpower for Alex to resist calling Bethany on her drive to work, or her drive home, or right before she went to bed, like she'd done since she moved to Seattle.

When Alex finally got out of the shower, she put on a baggy pair of sweatpants and a sweatshirt and made some tea. She had the kind of headache you get only from crying. Lying in bed, staring at the glow-in-the-dark stars on her ceiling, Alex tried to reconfigure her plan for the future, without Bethany in it. She wouldn't have to juggle plans A, B, C, and D anymore. She could just have one—maybe two, depending on whether Ben calmed down enough for her to count on him. Without a doubt, she would stay in Seattle. She loved Capitol Hill, and she could finally root herself there without guilt. Throughout the winter, she'd spent most nights alone in her apartment, Skyping with Bethany. But now, she decided, she would go out and meet people—at the park, at the lesbian bar down the street. Maybe she'd even reactivate her old OkCupid account.

Alex would also be able to create a kind of emotional stability in her life that her relationship with Bethany had made impossible. Even though Alex stopped short of depending on Bethany entirely by refusing to move to New York, she knew she'd depended on her too much. For the past eighteen months, Alex's happiness had been contingent on another person, and that necessitated chronic insecurity.

"To feel happy again, I think I need to be able to look myself in the mirror and say: 'You are the person who provides all of your stability and feelings of stability,'" Alex said. "'The people around you bring flavor and happiness to your life, but they are not the source of your happiness. You are the source of your happiness.'"

It would be the first time in her life when Alex felt like she could make her own decisions about her future, without considering anyone else. In high school, she had made decisions based off her dad's plans and expectations; in college, off her dad's and Ben's.

In the past couple of months, she'd been pressured to concede to Bethany's demands. Now she could do whatever she thought was best for herself. She could work full-time at the real estate company for as long as Ben stuck around—and for as long as she felt like she was learning something—then start her software engineering degree at Oregon State.

Sometime at the end of March, after Ben threatened to quit their project and Bethany threatened to end their relationship, Alex realized that everyone in her life had his or her own agenda. Alex had always happily depended on other people to fuel her self-esteem. She'd always preferred having a network to being a floating, individual entity. But so many people in her network had let her down lately that she wondered whether she would be better off on her own.

At work the next morning, Alex held it together for half an hour before starting to sob behind her desktop screen. Ben immediately took off his big headphones and wheeled his chair over to her.

"A? What's going on?"

Even though Alex promised Bethany she wouldn't tell Ben about the breakup, she realized she couldn't spend the whole day around her brother pretending everything was fine. After she described the phone call, as well as the weeks leading up to it, Ben told her to get up from her chair and pulled her into a long, hard hug.

"I am so sorry. You should stay a few days here. I don't want you to be by yourself."

Alex felt a lot less alone after that. Ben wasn't perfect—he threw tantrums and made threats and sometimes acted like a child—but she knew he cared about her. He made her think that maybe she didn't have to choose between being independent and being part of a unit.

Two months after meeting Bethany, Alex had started planning for their wedding and the rest of their life together. Now she shuddered to think about the e-mail accounts they'd made for themselves with the last name they both planned to take when they got married. Surely, she thought, there must be a happy medium between relying on no one and the way she'd relied on Bethany.

■ ◆ ■ ◆ ■

When Michelle first got the e-mail from Banff, she immediately assumed there had been a mistake. The e-mail was just a few lines long and clearly hastily written.

"Congratulations! I am emailing to confirm you have been accepted on to The Banff International Workshop in Jazz and Creative Music."

At least ten students from her conservatory, as well as many of her friends from the music department at Princeton, had applied to Banff. Hundreds of jazz students across the world were competing for just thirty spaces. She grabbed her phone and texted Canaan to see whether he'd heard anything. He'd also gotten an e-mail, but it wasn't the same one. His e-mail apologized for the delay, said the admissions office was still processing applications, and promised to give him an answer next week. Over the next hour, a lot of people who got the same e-mail as Canaan texted Michelle to see if she'd heard from Banff. No one else had been accepted.

It took Michelle half an hour to calm down enough to accept that the e-mail wasn't a mistake and consider what it meant. She would be spending August in the Canadian mountains, training with some of the most famous jazz musicians in the world. If there was ever an opportunity to "catch up" with Mary and the rest of her classmates at the conservatory, this was it.

"A part of me is kind of hoping that no one else goes," Michelle said.

There was nothing that could have validated Michelle and her music more than a Banff acceptance letter. Until now, she'd regarded jazz more as "someone else's thing" than her own. When she lived at home, it belonged to her dad. At Princeton, it belonged to her ex-boyfriend, Sam. Jazz music was always something that people in her life shared with her—that she enjoyed but never took ownership of. But she was taking ownership now. After a year of developing her music, exploring a sound—free improvisation—that was totally different from anything Sam or her dad had ever done, she was being recognized.

CHAPTER TEN

May

"Robert! Robert, wake up." I ran into our bedroom and jumped on the bed. "We got the letters!"

"What?" he said, regaining consciousness significantly faster than he normally did. "Really?"

I handed him my iPhone, the screen open to an e-mail with two pictures attached: our official letters of invitation from Jiangxi Normal University (JXNU) in Nanchang, China.

A few weeks before, Robert and I submitted the paperwork the school needed to consider us for teaching positions. We figured we might as well apply and see what happened, but we didn't think we had much of a shot. The Chinese government had recently implemented a new rule: all foreign teachers were required to have two years of teaching experience in the United States before teaching in China. We had none.

"So I guess we're going to China?" Robert said when he finished reading the invitations.

"I guess we are."

At the beginning, I had been the one pushing for China. I thought that a year abroad, learning a new language and making friends with people with lives entirely different from mine, would be the perfect antidote to the antsy, restless feeling I'd had for the past few months in DC. But then we got the invitations, and the year in China started to feel like it was actually going to happen. That morning, over breakfast and coffee, we talked about when we should buy plane tickets, when we should tell our landlady, and when Robert should quit his job in DC.

As soon as Robert left for work, I panicked. I was finally happy again. No more listening to Harry Potter on repeat, no more hiding from roommates I never talked to, no more spending hours scrolling through last year's mock trial photos. Tara, my counselor, said that in the fall I probably had "situational depression": short-term depression usually triggered by some kind of transition. My transition from college to DC was pretty much over—I had good friends in the area, an apartment I loved, and a much-improved relationship with my mom—but now I was voluntarily signing up for another one. And in China, Tara wouldn't be around to help me get through it.

As comfortable as I felt in China, I knew moving there would be far more isolating than moving anywhere in the United States. In China, Robert and I would have only each other. When I worked at JXNU over the summer, I spent most of my time with my students. But those friendships had limits. I had to watch what I said because I was four years older than they were, and their teacher.

Robert and I were already somewhat codependent. Whenever he wasn't at work and I wasn't traveling, we spent all our time together. It wasn't uncommon for me to go the whole day talking to no one but him. When Robert woke up on a Saturday, he'd ask, "What's the plan today?" Even if we had different things to do, we planned our time around each other. I already worried about how much I relied on Robert, and I knew that in China, I would only rely on him more.

By moving to China, I would also essentially be committing to our relationship for another year. I was happy with how things with Robert had been going lately. We'd talked at length about law school, and I believed him when he said he wanted me to do well on the LSAT. If we moved to China, Robert would take the exam right before Christmas, in Shanghai, and then help me study for it in the spring. We agreed it wasn't worth talking about particular schools until we both had our test scores, and I was sure that I wanted a law degree. But even though we'd worked through that issue, I still felt nervous. I didn't want to put myself in a situation where I might feel trapped.

I'd been preoccupied with this fear of being trapped for a while—particularly after I found out about my parents' divorce. I sometimes thought to myself: What if there was nothing I could do? What if my boyfriend was tricking me somehow, trying to convince me that he was the person I should be with, until we'd been together so long that I felt like I had no choice but to stay? So long that we were married, or had kids. So long that I was older and completely estranged from the world of modern dating. I knew that the next five years—from college graduation through around age twenty-eight—was probably the period of time in my life when I would have the most freedom and flexibility. Even though I loved Robert and had most of our shared life planned out in my head, I still wondered whether, by making such a major commitment so early, and after only one other serious relationship,

I was more likely to feel trapped in the future. This was a fixation of mine, and probably an irrational one. But it still made me hesitant to sign up for a year without options.

AT THE END OF MAY, my mom came to visit me in DC for the first time. I knew her trip was another big gesture—even more significant than offering Robert the guest room at our house. The morning that she came to our apartment, I vacuumed, mopped the floor, lit scented candles, and plumped the pillows on the couch at least three times. I knew she didn't approve of me living with Robert, and I was desperate for the visit to go well.

It turned out I had nothing to worry about. We spent the next few days touring museums, walking through the botanical gardens, and shopping for summer dresses. Mom and I spent the days together, then met up with Robert for dinner. That schedule was something Tara suggested. She encouraged me to spend a good chunk of one-on-one time with my mom—to show Mom it was something I still valued—but also to not hide my new life with Robert. That way, Tara said, my mom could see and share my new routines and relationships without feeling like I was forgetting my old ones.

On my mom's last day in DC, we ate lunch together at a restaurant in Georgetown. We'd eaten at this same restaurant when I was a junior in high school, looking at colleges. It was my favorite part of her visit because I completely let my guard down. We talked the way we used to—the same way I'm sure we did eating there six years ago. I could tell she was genuinely interested in my career, my relationship, and the decisions I was making. She asked about Robert and his prospects for law school. She laughed when

I told her about his terrible GPA, then said, "He's so smart, I'm sure he'll do well on the LSAT." It was one of the first times she'd ever said anything complimentary about Robert, or signaled that she might understand what I saw in him. By this point in the year, I no longer felt like I needed my parents' approval to feel good about myself. I was proud of that. But still, hearing my mom say something positive about my new, post-college life was a major confidence boost.

The September after I graduated, I wrote my mom a long birthday card. I wrote about the time in third grade when my essay was read aloud at an assembly in school. I came home that day saying that I wanted to be a writer. Ever since then, that had been my dream. In the card, I told her that right now, I was living my dream—writing every day, and getting paid for it—and she was the one who made it possible. She'd given me everything: all of her time and energy for eighteen years before I left for college. I wanted her to feel proud of what that time and energy had created.

■ ◆ ■ ◆ ■

At seven thirty on Sunday morning, Michelle woke up to a phone call.

"Hey, Michelle! It's Derek."

It took Michelle a few seconds to register whom she was talking to.

"We met last night"—he paused—"at the recital?"

"Oh, yeah, yeah," Michelle said, rubbing her eyes and sitting up in bed. Derek was an alum of her conservatory who now played in a popular Philly jazz band.

"What are you doing today?"

"Uh . . . nothing, really. Getting over my hangover for the next couple hours."

"Would you want to come sing with my band in Vermont? Our singer just bailed and we've got a gig at a festival there in a couple hours."

Last night, Derek described his band to Michelle as "Italian opera–dance-jazz fusion." It was a fourteen-piece band, larger than any other jazz group she knew in Philadelphia. Michelle had seen them play once and thought their vibe was really cool—a mix between jazz and theater. But the singing was operatic. She'd never done anything like that before.

"Uh, I mean, that sounds awesome, but I'm not an opera singer."

"That's a good thing," Derek said. "Pick you up in twenty minutes?"

Michelle laughed. This was exactly the kind of thing she'd imagined she'd be doing when she applied to her conservatory: spontaneously coming together with people she hardly knew to make music.

"Sure, Derek. I'm there."

When he arrived, Derek was wearing a bright turquoise blazer with a disco-style button-down shirt underneath, frilled sleeves cuffed at the bottom. Shaking his shaggy hair out of his eyes, he threw open the sliding door for Michelle. She clambered over four rows of seats—past guitarists and cellists and violinists—sat down in the back, put on her headphones to tune out the rock music blasting on the radio, and started memorizing. She had three and a half hours to learn eight songs.

Michelle didn't realize how big of a deal the festival was until they arrived at the venue. There were at least two hundred people there—the biggest crowd she'd performed for since Princeton.

The band set up in a room with a cement floor, wood-paneled walls, and industrial lights hanging loose from the ceiling.

"We're on in ten," Derek said as he started tuning his guitar.

"Internally, I was like, 'Oh my god, fuck.' I hadn't actually practiced singing any of the songs," Michelle later told me. "But externally, I was like, 'It's cool, I got this. I fucking love a challenge—that's my shit.' I was like, 'Bring it. Fucking bring it.'"

Before the set even ended, Michelle knew it was the best performance she'd given all year, possibly ever. At the end, the band got a standing ovation. She sounded nothing like the band's original singer, but nobody seemed to mind.

"That was fucking insane," one band member said while they were packing up. "I wish our singer would bail more often."

TWO WEEKS BEFORE the music festival, Michelle and Canaan ended their relationship. She told all her friends it was a joint decision, but breakups were never entirely mutual. When she started the conversation, telling Canaan how sad she'd been feeling lately, he said, "I hate seeing you so unhappy. Maybe we should break up?" He said it so casually, like he was suggesting they go get some lunch.

"I was investing a lot emotionally in someone who wasn't investing a lot in me," Michelle said. "He wasn't even aware that I was investing a lot. That was the heartbreaking part."

When they broke up, Michelle didn't cry. She knew she and Canaan weren't compatible. She'd known that for quite a while, but she still felt sad. She missed the kind of relationship she'd had with Sam, and, in a lot of ways, Canaan reminded her of him. They both thought carefully about everything they said before they said it, they both stayed quiet in a big group of people, they both took their music more seriously than anything else. Even though Canaan frustrated Michelle, his presence had been comforting. Without the option of spending the night at his apartment whenever she felt like it, Michelle's single room in the fancy town house felt lonelier than ever.

The Vermont gig pulled Michelle out of the rut she'd been stuck in since January—a rut that had felt particularly deep since she broke up with Canaan. It got her thinking about why she'd come to the conservatory in the first place and what she should be taking away from it. Standing at the helm of the fourteen-piece band, closing her eyes and leaning into Derek's microphone, Michelle felt happier than she had all year. The Banff acceptance letter gave her validation, but Vermont helped her see music as something fun again, something that wasn't just a source of anxiety but a source of joy. She couldn't wait to go to Canada in August.

■ ◆ ■ ◆ ■

Lying awake in bed alone one night at the end of May, Denise texted Craig. "Should I not go to Emory? Should I take another year off?"

He responded immediately. "Absolutely not."

Denise didn't understand how Craig could be so at peace with the situation. When she got wait-listed at the University of Chicago at the beginning of the month, Denise made the decision to accept her offer from Emory. In six weeks, she would be packing up her apartment in Harlem and catching a train to Atlanta. Craig had a chronic fear of flying, and Atlanta was fifteen hours from

New York City by bus, twelve hours by train. She might as well have been moving across the world.

Denise had been holding out for the University of Chicago, sending a series of letters pleading with the admissions office, because even though it was almost as far from New York as Emory, Chicago seemed a lot closer. Almost all her friends from high school lived in the area, and her family lived only two hours away. Denise knew it would have been exponentially easier to leave one established community for another. At least in Chicago, when she missed Craig and her life in New York, she wouldn't have been alone.

"I knew who my friends were going to be if I stayed in New York, and I knew who my friends were going to be in Chicago," Denise said. "I just don't want to be lonely. I don't want to be lonely. I don't want to be lonely."

Through April and early May, Denise had also been thinking about Mount Sinai Medical School. The official status of her application there was "continued," which meant the admissions committee was still processing her application. Everything she read online suggested that if she sent Mount Sinai a letter of intent, promising to enroll if she was accepted, she would have a much better chance of getting in. After weeks of agonizing, Denise decided not to do that. Emory was a better school for her specific research interests—adolescent medicine for low-income populations—and public health. She also knew that if she stayed in New York and went to Mount Sinai, she'd be doing it because of Craig—because she was scared they wouldn't be able to weather a long-distance relationship. And she didn't want to make a decision this important out of fear.

But now, with just a few weeks left in New York, Denise

was seriously doubting her decision. Every time she committed to something that would make it harder to back out of going to Emory—buying her train ticket, sending in a deposit, signing a lease on an apartment in Atlanta—she became a little more aware of how much she loved New York. She started appreciating parts of her daily routine that she'd never stopped to think about before: waiting for the bus, speaking Spanish with the guys at the hole-in-the-wall taco shop two blocks from her apartment, taking the subway without ever having to look at a map. Denise was proud of how comfortable she felt in New York. But she also noticed how fast her West Harlem neighborhood was gentrifying—just that week, an upscale brick-oven pizzeria had opened next to the corner bodega—and she worried that, when she came back to visit, she wouldn't even recognize it.

"I'm tempted to stay in New York and defer for a year," Denise said. "I keep asking myself, 'Am I ruining my twenties?' You see in the movies—everyone in their twenties is having a ton of fun. Am I running from that happiness if I move to Atlanta?"

She didn't want to leave the people she'd surrounded herself with in New York: her friends from church, her friends from Princeton, and especially Craig. Their relationship meant more to her than any other she'd ever had, and she was afraid of losing him. By the time she finished medical school and residency, Craig would be in his early forties. If she moved hundreds of miles away, she thought, it would be relatively easy for him to find someone new: someone closer to his age who wouldn't be busy trying to change the world over the next ten years. She didn't know if she was willing to risk their relationship just to go to a better med school.

Emory also just seemed so random. It had never been part of

Denise's grand master plan. Before admitted students weekend, she'd hardly known anything about the school. When Denise was accepted, she'd been happy to have a good, solid option for medical school, but she always assumed that's what it would remain—an option. Not her future.

"I was so focused on me not getting into the school that I had determined I was going to go to. In my plan, I was going to get into UChicago—that was my school, everything was going to be wonderful there. I was not focused at all on going to Emory, so I got really insecure."

Denise spent a lot of time talking to her mom and close friends from Princeton about the decision. "Am I going to like Atlanta?" she asked them. "Am I going to thrive there? Am I going to be successful?" They all essentially said the same thing: Emory is a great school; God is sending you there for a reason. Denise knew they were probably right. Emory was statistically a very good medical school, ranking twenty-third in research and twenty-ninth in primary care. The U.S. Center for Disease Control and Prevention (CDC) was right around the corner from campus. Emory med students also worked almost exclusively at Grady Memorial Hospital, which serves some of the lowest-income communities in Atlanta—people who can't find care anywhere else. That was the experience Denise needed to open the kind of adolescent health care clinic she'd spent the past few years dreaming about.

All year, Denise had been trying to be open to God's plan for her future. Since Christmas, her church community in Harlem—particularly the other young women in her prayer group—had been instrumental in helping her do that. She could always count on her church friends to listen closely, empathize, and encourage her to pray about whatever was on her mind. But Denise felt strange talking to them about where she should go to medical school. When she told them she'd decided to go to Emory, they all asked why. Dr. Johnson, Denise's friend and mentor who introduced her to the Harlem Church of Christ, had never left New York. She was born and raised there, had stayed for medical school and residency, and had then found a job and raised her family not far from where she grew up. Dr. Johnson was the only one of Denise's friends at church with career goals similar to her own, and even she didn't understand the impulse to move so far away.

"They're so happy and content with their settled lives—with simple things," Denise said. "They have roots in one place. They don't feel the nagging need to go, go, go all the time."

That feeling of contentment—not constantly trying to have more, to be better—was completely foreign to Denise. She couldn't remember a time in her life when she wasn't striving for something: to go to the best high school, the best college, the best medical school; to win awards or fellowships or fully funded trips to foreign countries. Spending time with the women her age at church, she realized how rarely she paused to reflect on what she had and enjoy it. She had a great life in New York: a steady job, loyal friends, a cozy apartment in a neighborhood she loved, a boyfriend she could see herself spending the rest of her life with. But still, it wasn't enough. When she thought about staying in New York, she felt uncomfortable. Fidgety.

She wished she could find the kind of inner peace that seemed to come so easily to her friends at church, but she couldn't. After spending three years at her highly selective high school and four years at Princeton, alongside some of the smartest and most driven young people in the United States, Denise felt like she had to at least try to keep up with them.

"I've never questioned this movement. My middle school friends didn't understand why I was leaving to go to boarding school. A lot of my boarding school friends didn't understand why I was leaving Illinois to go to college on the East Coast. Now, again, I'm leaving the comfort of where I am."

▪ ◆ ▪ ◆ ▪

When Olivia opened her eyes, Peter was looking right at her. Olivia couldn't stop smiling. She felt like she was simultaneously skydiving and falling in love and drinking a cup of really strong coffee.

"Hey," he said, sitting down next to her on the couch. "Welcome to joy."

Peter looked beautiful. He had huge, almond-shaped eyes and crazy, flyaway hair that looked like a preteen girl had attacked it with a crimping iron. Olivia wondered why she'd never realized how attractive he was before.

Every other Saturday, Peter invited between eight and twenty-five people to his farmhouse in upstate New York. That morning, Olivia had taken a bus from Manhattan. She'd been vaguely interested in psychedelic therapy ever since she realized that Mason, her love interest in San Francisco, and his primary, Sarah, were involved in something similar. A few weeks before, when a friend had mentioned Peter and his weekly meetings, she asked for his contact information.

After everyone arrived at the farmhouse, they all sat down together in a circle on the floor. One by one, the participants stated their "intention" for the meeting, describing something they'd been struggling with that week. Almost everyone was battling addiction of some kind—mostly heroin—and the subsequent depression, anxiety, and isolation they experienced because of it. But people talked about everything, from relationship problems to pressure at work. When it was her turn, Olivia talked about bulimia.

Next, Peter gave out the prescriptions. He had a particular psychedelic drug for every problem. He went around the circle, distributing the substance he thought would give each participant a deeper understanding of whatever he or she was struggling with: how it fit into the person's life and the world. Peter always talked about how everything was connected. You couldn't treat one health issue on its own. He said that was the problem with traditional therapy and medical care—therapists and doctors tried to isolate the problem. They would say, "You have anxiety, so let's solve that." This approach, he said, totally missed the point.

"You can't treat addiction, or anxiety, or depression, or an eating disorder, without changing your relationship with yourself and your relationship with the world," Peter said. "The first step is changing how you interpret your reality."

When Olivia told Peter about her eating disorder, he helped her see that bulimia was just part of a bigger problem. At this point in her life, she felt like she was an unhappy person. If she focused on whatever was making her unhappy—if she tried to change her entire reality—then the bulimia would take care of itself. To change her entire reality, she needed to escape from it for a while. She needed perspective. That was where the psychedelic drugs came in.

Olivia didn't decide to take psychedelics without doing her homework. She spent hours reading about the trials that were being conducted at NYU: renowned doctors and scientists administering psychedelics to cancer patients. The results, these doctors said, were overwhelming. Just one or two doses seemed to cure patients of their anxiety, helping them to calmly accept death and enjoy their last few years or months of life. But still, Olivia was skeptical. A lot of people in online discussion forums talked about psychedelics like they had some kind of magical power. There was magic in the universe, these people said, and psychedelics could connect you with it. Olivia didn't believe in "magic"—she'd spent too much time with the rationalists not to question anything that couldn't be proven—but she figured this new kind of therapy was worth a shot.

"In order to create rigorous scientific proof, you need a lot of time," Olivia said. "I can't wait for that. I have an eating disorder today, I don't want to die from that. I need something."

Even though Olivia still had doubts about the healing power of psychedelics, she trusted Peter. He'd been doing this—administering drugs to people facing major internal struggles—for most of his life. He wasn't a licensed doctor or therapist, and he didn't pretend to be. He was just someone who genuinely believed that these drugs could help people. Peter's parents had both been heroin addicts. For years, they'd been in and out of rehab, going to regular therapy sessions. Nothing worked until they tried psychedelic drugs.

While Peter was the one who actually oversaw the weekly meetings, talking participants through the experience and helping anyone who became anxious or paranoid (common side effects of psychedelic drugs), the whole thing felt like a family business. He lived at the farmhouse with his parents, his wife, and his two young children. The other adults in the family did their part to make the participants feel comfortable. They served homemade soup and fresh food from the farm—vegetables and eggs—while they were tripping. Peter said they did this because "people need to be treated kindly." Olivia felt completely relaxed at the farmhouse, snuggled under a blanket on one of the many couches in the living room. It felt nothing like the cold, metallic eating disorder unit at the Princeton hospital.

WHEN OLIVIA WOKE UP the next morning in Peter's living room, she just lay there for a while, thinking about how she'd felt the night before. She knew she'd been tripping for five or six hours before she fell asleep. She was surprised by how clearly she remembered the experience. Peter had given her something with effects similar to MDMA. She didn't know the exact name. He told her it was regularly used to treat patients with PTSD, because it simultaneously gave you a lot of joy and sharpened your memories. At first, he'd just given her one capsule, a relatively small dose. That felt good: peaceful, like she was floating. But she wanted something stronger. A few minutes after Peter gave her a second capsule, she felt intensely joyful.

"I remember thinking, 'I wish every day was like this.' Instead of feeling anxious, waking up and checking my e-mail, planning my day, I wish I could wake up and be like, 'Yeah, this is life. This tastes so good.'"

That morning, as she recalled the experience, Olivia started to feel hopeful. Before she took the capsules, she had no idea that human beings were capable of that kind of joy. She was the same person she'd been yesterday, before she took the drug, but her perspective on life had shifted. Now that she knew she could achieve that degree of satisfaction, she wanted to experience it every day. The drug gave her something to aspire to. It wasn't that she wanted to take MDMA all the time. She wasn't going to become an addict. But the drug made her determined to reach that state in other ways.

"It made me feel like, wow, I understand how the world works now. I need to get out of this shithole that is my life," Olivia said.

After everyone else woke up—on other couches and beds scattered throughout the farmhouse—they all came together to reflect. Again, they went around the circle, this time discussing how they could integrate their drug-induced epiphanies into their lives.

Olivia still didn't think Peter had given her a magic pill. For a few days, she felt different from the way she had before she went to the farmhouse. Calmer. She felt herself going about her life more slowly, less frantically, and savoring each moment in a way she never had before. After a few days, that feeling went away, but she retained her new aspiration: to reach and sustain the state of joy she'd discovered on the couch at the farmhouse.

Olivia started hanging out with Peter in upstate New York every week or two. She also started meditating every day. She found that meditation could lead her to a similarly joyful state, but it took a lot of practice. The drug was the shortcut. Eventually, she hoped to completely replace her trips to the farmhouse with long, intensive meditation sessions. But she wasn't quite there yet.

IN MAY, I STARTED HEARING LESS from Olivia. When I visited New York to see her and Denise, she didn't respond to my text messages until my last day in the city. She agreed to meet me for lunch but left after half an hour. After that, she started ignoring almost all of my attempts to contact her. For a while I told myself she was probably just busy. But after a month of hearing nothing, I began to think it must be something else.

■ ◆ ■ ◆ ■

"I'm over by the violinist when you get here."

Alex stared at the text for a few seconds before slipping her phone back into her pocket. She'd spent the morning at the salon, getting her hair cut and her eyebrows waxed. This was her first OkCupid meeting, and she wanted to look good.

Alex recognized Andrea immediately. She had long, silky black hair that curled at the bottom, two silver studs in each ear, and a simple black tattoo of intertwining lines circling her right biceps. Her olive-colored skin glowed. Alex watched from behind a vegetable stand as Andrea brushed a few stray hairs out of her face and put on some ChapStick.

Andrea ("yogainseattle83") had messaged Alex ("codewrite267") on OkCupid a week ago. Alex had created an account when she moved to Capitol Hill as a way of making friends, but she hardly ever checked it. Most messages in her inbox came from older women and began with some sleazy greeting. Andrea was the first user Alex had ever responded to. Looking at her profile, Alex could tell they had a lot in common. They liked many of the same things—cats, tea, cooking, blogging—but, more importantly, they seemed to share the same values. After the "I'm really good at . . ." prompt, Andrea had written, "making others feel valued/encouraged/celebrated. I'm a loving, nurturing person and my relationships with others are very important in my life."

When Alex first told me about her plan to meet up with Andrea, she called it a "fig," not a "date." On their OkCupid profiles, Andrea and Alex both made it clear they were only looking for friends. Andrea said she wanted single lesbian friends with time to devote to platonic relationships.

At this point, Alex and Bethany hadn't even officially broken up. Almost every day, Bethany sent a series of pleading messages, saying things like "I wish I could be holding you" and "It hurts so much right now . . . this is what you must have been feeling, I'm so sorry." Alex always responded—she didn't want Bethany to feel alone—but was careful to never say anything that might give Bethany false hope. Because, by now, Alex knew for sure that she wasn't going to let Bethany pull her back in.

"She waited too long and she pushed me too far," Alex said. "I'm already on the other side of the road, walking away. It's done." She just needed to wait for Bethany's emotions to stabilize before she cut off all communication.

When Alex told me all this, I was surprised. A few minutes after she told Bethany she wanted to take a break, Alex recorded a video of herself talking about the decision and sent it to me. She was sobbing so hard that she had a hard time making it through a full sentence. Every time she explained her reasons for wanting the break, or seemed at all confident in the decision, she'd backtrack, ending the thought with "But I don't know . . ." or "Maybe she *is* the one I'm supposed to be with." Alex was so torn up, I was sure it was just a matter of time before she patched things up with Bethany. But a few weeks later, she seemed like she was over it and ready to start something new.

Alex and Andrea spent half an hour wandering around the farmers' market before heading to a nearby bookstore. As soon as they ordered tea and sat down on the balcony, Alex began asking Andrea a series of probing, personal questions. It was her standard practice whenever she met someone new: she made intense, sustained eye contact and tried to get to the bottom of who they were as a person—what scared them, what excited them, what struggle consumed their life more than any other. When Andrea finished telling Alex about what it was like to be bullied as a kid—as the only half-Asian in an entirely white neighborhood—she took a deep breath.

"Wow. I haven't talked about that in a long time."

Alex laughed. "I like to keep it light and breezy."

Next they talked about their past relationships. Alex told Andrea about Bethany, and Andrea told Alex about her seven-year relationship that had ended the year before. When Alex asked questions, Andrea didn't answer right away. She took five or ten seconds to think, looking up at the ceiling or down at the floor, before she started talking. She was clearly taking their conversation seriously. To Alex, that meant something.

"I want to be with someone who talks about the future beyond the more present future," Alex said to Andrea. "Someone who thinks about how we're going to care for our aging parents. Someone who is excited and energized and encouraged by talking about the kind of old ladies we're going to be together."

When Alex said that, Andrea's posture and expression changed—softened somehow. She made direct eye contact and didn't look away. Up until that point, Alex felt like Andrea had been at least partially on guard. Now, finally, she seemed to relax.

"I'm realizing that we've hardly talked about our jobs at all," Alex said after they'd been sitting together on the balcony for almost four hours. "Do you like what you do?"

"Yeah, I mean, it's okay. Pays the bills."

"What would you do if you could do anything?"

"Work for a nonprofit. And I'd like to write a hard copy cookbook—beyond just the e-books that I've published." Andrea worked full-time at a tech company and part-time as a food and health blogger. Every day, she posted original recipes, new workout routines, or tips for daily meditation.

It started to rain, but they stayed on the balcony, talking. Alex couldn't believe this was happening. Andrea was the first person she'd met through OkCupid and the second girl she'd ever been out with on anything vaguely resembling a date. Alex knew she was being a little hasty, but it was hard to imagine this relationship wouldn't work out.

When Alex got back to her apartment, she logged in to her OkCupid account and sent Andrea a message: "It's rare to find a really genuine, kind person. I would love to hang out again." She spent the next hour lying in bed with her eyes closed, trying again to imagine her life without Bethany. It wasn't hard. Before she met Andrea, she felt fairly certain she would be able to find people as compatible—if not more compatible—with her than Bethany had been. But now she knew for sure. There were kind people in Seattle who wouldn't force her to change everything about her life just because it didn't fit perfectly with their own.

As she stroked her cat, Alex said, "Jekyll, this is going to sound crazy, but I think I just met your other mom."

■ ◆ ■ ◆ ■

Before the school year ended, Michelle held her first solo concert—the first independent music project she'd done outside of school.

The last song Michelle sang was one she'd written while she was with Canaan, about the long, lazy days they'd spent together at his apartment during the worst blizzard of winter.

"So I wrote this next song when I was in love," she said. "I'm not in love anymore, so it means something a little different to me now."

Michelle picked up the veil resting on top of the piano and pinned it to her head. If she wore a veil, she thought, she could play the role of innocent bride. The song wouldn't have to be about her failed relationship.

Over the last few weeks, Michelle had spent a lot of time thinking about Canaan and Sam and what she wanted from a boyfriend. She'd realized that, at this point in her life, she didn't need one.

This wasn't exactly a revelation. At the end of last summer, before she left London, Michelle promised herself that she would stay single. After three years of back-to-back relationships, she knew she needed some space to figure out what she wanted, separate from what a guy she loved wanted for her. But then Canaan messed everything up. Just as she was starting to find her sound at the conservatory, she allowed herself to be consumed by another guy.

"Since Sam, I think I've been using men as a distraction," Michelle told me. "Distraction from actually figuring out my purpose at music school."

Michelle wasn't about to stop having sex, but, from now on, she was determined to end any hookup before it got serious. A significant amount of real, boyfriend-less, primary-less alone time would give her the space to carefully consider what she wanted for her future. It would be hard. She knew she'd get lonely. But she also knew it was necessary to prevent another identity crisis like the one she'd had in March and April.

Besides boys, everything else in Michelle's life was finally going the way that she wanted it to. After she got back from Vermont, she wrote a few more songs, then asked around for musicians who might be interested in performing them. The group she assembled for the concert wasn't a band yet, but it had the potential to become one.

"I finally feel like I'm getting my shit together," Michelle said.

She couldn't afford to get distracted again.

■ ◆ ■ ◆ ■

Two weeks before we all headed back to Princeton for Reunions, I called Denise. We realized that we were facing very similar decisions: stay in a good situation, in a good place, surrounded by good people, or give it all up to try for something better. We both suffered from what I call the "Princeton ladder mentality": the idea that staying on one rung isn't good enough—that you should be constantly trying to climb.

"As bad as it would be to regret going to Emory," Denise said, "I think I'm more scared of wondering, 'What if?' It's less scary to me to think about doing something and it being hard at times, because at least I did it."

I felt the same way. Staying in DC and being unhappy would be worse than moving to China and being unhappy, because I'd be imagining all the incredible, once-in-a-lifetime experiences I could have had. If I moved to China, at least I knew what I was giving up. I also realized that, living in China, I would still have options. When I told Tara about my fear of feeling trapped, she said, "It's not like you won't be able to leave." Moving to China, I decided, was worth the risk. That night, I started printing the documents Robert and I needed to apply for our visas.

CHAPTER ELEVEN

Reunions

At 4:30 in the morning on May 29, almost a year after graduation, I was back in Princeton. Only it didn't really look like Princeton. My flip-flops stuck to whatever substance coated the asphalt. Someone had repurposed the hill by the gym as a mudslide. Everything smelled like sweat and Bud Light, and outside the door to my old dorm room, a tree limb sagged under the weight of two pairs of abandoned orange lederhosen.

Normally this place looked like a postcard. In the fall of my senior year, I'd woken up to a film crew shooting a Ralph Lauren commercial on the quad. Models paraded across the lawn in pleated plaid miniskirts and button-up cardigans, carrying smooth leather satchel bags. That commercial captured Princeton in the way the school wanted other people to see it, with perky flower beds lining the sidewalks and the sun peeking out over Nassau Hall.

But tonight, there was no postcard-worthy picture. It was the first night of Princeton Reunions, the largest reunion event in the country, and an excuse for twenty thousand alums to spend three days remembering just how drunk they got in college (very). Almost two-thirds of my graduating class was back on campus.

It was just a matter of time before the maintenance crew arrived and picked up the tens of thousands of cups strewn all over the quads, power washed away the vomit, arranged new swaths of emergency grass, and prepared the campus for another twelve hours of sunlight. By the time all the alums took a few aspirin and staggered out of the dormitories, the campus would be back to the way we remembered it: prestigious and sparkling.

I realized that I was standing in the middle of a pretty good metaphor. At Reunions, most people tried very hard to look perfect. From the minute I ran into the first friend I hadn't seen since graduation, the whole thing felt like a performance. People threw out names of multibillion-dollar companies and top-ten graduate schools like candy, trying to convince one another that they had the ultimate post-grad life.

I'd been going to Princeton reunions since I was a sophomore, and I'd always hated it—the superficial conversations over blaring music, the loneliness of all your closest friends being too busy or too drunk to text you back—but this year was particularly bad. I'd spent most of the day asking the same stale questions—"What are you doing now?" and "What have you been up to?"—and giving the same stale answers. It was the first time I'd adhered to a script with my Princeton classmates since the beginning of freshman year, when everybody asked everybody else the same two questions to break the ice: "Where are you from?" and "Where did you go on OA (the hiking trip we all took before orientation)?" Somehow, we were back to those surface-level questions, that sound-bite understanding of each other. It made me question relationships that, before Reunions, I'd considered worth more than a few minutes of small talk and a hasty promise to catch up more later.

I knew a lot of people in my class had a hard time over the past year: finding jobs, making friends, dealing with relationships that couldn't quite transition from college to the real world. But no one talked about any of that. For three days, everybody smiled and laughed. Everything was gleaming stone sidewalks and bright green manicured lawns.

I still had another day to wait until the part of Reunions I'd been looking forward to the most. Since graduation, I'd been planning for Alex, Michelle, Denise, Olivia, and I to get together for an hour or two to reflect on the past year. I hoped we'd be able to ditch the Reunions scripts and be honest with one another. It was a tall order, particularly because, with few exceptions (Michelle knew Olivia, and I'd introduced Olivia to Alex), none of the girls had ever met.

■ ◆ ■ ◆ ■

Looking out onto a mosh pit of sweaty bodies and sloshing plastic cups of beer, Michelle smiled and took a bow. It was her first time performing at Princeton since she graduated a year ago, and she knew that she'd nailed it. This feeling, she thought, was probably the best measure of how she'd grown as a musician over the course of the past year. The last time she stood on this stage, in the dining room at Terrace, the eating club she'd joined her senior spring, she'd scanned the audience for certain people—classmates in the jazz department, particularly Sam—to see whether they were enjoying the music, and whether they thought she was good. Now all she could think about was moving her voice and body in time with the band.

After Michelle finished the set, as she pushed herself through throngs of people dancing to the next band in the lineup, a guy she'd never seen before tapped her on the shoulder.

"Hey!" He was shouting over the music, but she still had to lean in to hear him. "I just need to tell you—you have the most beautiful voice I've ever heard."

"Thank you," Michelle said, looking from the guy to the door. The guy was cute, but this was the last night of Reunions and the rest of her friends were drunk. She wanted to catch up with them.

"Uh, I'm sorry, I've gotta go," she said. "Nice to meet you!"

Ten minutes later, Michelle was on the second floor of Terrace, drinking with a group of her closest friends from Princeton, mostly fellow musicians. Everyone was congratulating her on her performance. An old classmate said he could hear the transformation in her voice, and a junior she vaguely remembered said she'd inspired her to apply to a conservatory for graduate school. While she was at Princeton, Michelle knew most jazz students hadn't taken her seriously as a musician—because she was a vocalist, because she was a girl in a male-dominated genre—but they were taking her seriously now.

Michelle was busy reminiscing on the full-circle nature of the evening when the guy from the dance floor walked into the room. He came over as soon as he saw her.

"Hi, I'm glad I found you," he said. "I'm Carlo."

Now that Michelle was sitting down, with all manner of substances at her fingertips, she could focus on how handsome this guy was. He had big, dark eyes and thick, wavy brown hair. Michelle could tell from his accent that he wasn't originally from the States—maybe from somewhere in the Mediterranean.

Immediately, Carlo started flirting with Michelle, and she flirted back. After talking for two hours in Terrace, they ran around campus together, holding hands and kissing against the sides of old stone buildings. She knew this wasn't going to go anywhere—Carlo was leaving campus to catch a plane at 7:00 A.M., and leaving the country to live in Italy for the next year in two weeks—but it was a fun way to spend the last night of Reunions. She liked the charged excitement that came with knowing she'd probably never see this guy again.

At the end of the night, Michelle walked Carlo to the train station. When they arrived, he pulled Michelle into a tight hug that lasted much longer than she'd expected it to.

"I really want to keep in touch with you," he said, taking his phone out of his pocket. "I'll text you my e-mail address. Let's write to each other."

A WEEK AFTER Michelle left Carlo at the train station, she was on a plane to visit him in Chicago. They'd been texting nonstop since Reunions. He asked to listen to all her music, then e-mailed her specific compliments for each song. That Wednesday, he offered to pay for her to come to Chicago for the weekend. When she landed, he was waiting at arrivals. There were a dozen roses for her in his car.

"I'm shocked that I have met this person," Michelle told me. "We talk on video chat most days, and it doesn't feel like a burden. It's just really comforting; I feel stronger knowing that there is this person rooting for me."

At the end of June, Michelle decided to forgo her annual trip to England to spend two weeks with Carlo in Greece. When I asked Michelle what happened to swearing off serious relationships for a while, she said Carlo didn't really count. Since he was going to be in Italy for the next year, he wouldn't be able to consume her life in the way Canaan and Sam had. As long as Carlo wasn't physically there, she thought, she would be just fine.

■ ◆ ■ ◆ ■

"Denise!"

"Megan! Oh my god, hey!"

"What have you been up to?"

Denise hated that question. But at Reunions, she got it at least once every twenty minutes. She knew she was supposed to respond with the most impressive-sounding detail about her life. All weekend, she'd been answering with a vague and noncommittal "I've been living and working in New York." But sometimes she'd have to deal with the follow-up: "What's next?"

All spring, Denise had avoided telling people where she was going to medical school. Until the end of May, with everyone but her immediate family, Craig, and a few close friends from Princeton, she'd shrugged off the question, saying something like "I'm still figuring it out. I'll definitely tell you when I know for sure." But she knew that line wouldn't work at Reunions. Too many people there knew about med school deadlines. If she didn't name a school, they would probably assume she hadn't gotten in anywhere.

The prospect of telling people about Emory made Denise nervous for a couple of reasons. She was scared people would judge her for not going to a more well-known school. Because she'd been such a visible leader on campus—organizing social justice clubs and events, winning the award at Class Day—she knew a lot of her Princeton friends and acquaintances assumed she was bound for Harvard or Johns Hopkins. Emory was a great school, but it didn't have the kind of name recognition people at Princeton had come to expect. Denise also worried about how she would respond to the disappointment she imagined she'd feel after she told people where she was going next year.

"I struggle with needing people to validate my decisions," Denise said. "I don't want them to make me second-guess what I'm doing with my life, or make me wonder whether I'm good enough or smart enough or doing something impressive enough."

By Reunions, Denise had already sent her money to Emory. She no longer had the option of changing her mind. She and Craig had organized their visits from July until the following June—at least one per month—and bought tickets to spend fall break together in the Berkshires, in upstate New York. Those plans finally allowed Denise to fully accept her decision. Her greatest fear was that she'd go to Reunions, talk to a few people about next year, and start to doubt herself again.

When Denise took the New Jersey Transit train to Princeton, Craig came with her. At Reunions, he mostly just stood behind her while she talked to people. She'd introduce him to whatever friend she was talking to, then carry on asking and answering the standard questions about post-grad life. But even though Craig didn't say much, Denise felt better knowing he was there, listening. If anyone said anything that upset her, she could find a way to politely leave the conversation, then debrief with him as they walked away.

Denise knew she took people's offhand comments too personally, and Craig was good at building her back up before insecurity set in. On the first day of Reunions, when she told a group of people she'd be going to med school at Emory next year, a girl she barely knew said, "Man, it seems like everyone is going to med school." Denise knew the girl wasn't trying to hurt her feelings, but she felt instantly deflated, like someone had taken away her right to be proud of what she'd accomplished. In everything she did, Denise wanted to be unique and leave a legacy. She hated the idea that she'd chosen a common path for her life—one where she'd never be able to distinguish herself or make lasting change.

"It just makes me think—maybe what I'm doing is not actually meaningful because everyone is doing it," Denise said to Craig as they left the group. "And then some people are going to schools that are better than mine, so it makes me wonder: What's the point of doing anything? Because I'm just one of the many and I'm not actually going to make any kind of difference or impact."

"Slow down. How did you get all that from that interaction? That's not what she meant at all."

"I know she didn't mean that, but I can't help thinking—"

"Listen to me. First of all, not everyone is going to med school. Second, of course you are going to leave a legacy at Emory. That's what you do."

Again, Denise thought about who came to mind when she worried what "people" might think. Over the course of the past year, at one point or another, she'd worried about everyone judging her for not getting into the very best medical schools: her mom, her dad, her brothers and sisters, her friend Matt at Harvard Medical School, her close friend Cameron from Princeton, even Craig. But now, surrounded by former classmates who really were judging each other—sizing one another up with a few cursory lines of small talk—she realized how lucky she was. She had an unshakable unit of people who would continue to love her and think the world of her, regardless of professional success. Her fears came from inside her own head. She was so scared of letting people down that she imagined the people closest to her were saying and thinking two different things: "We love you," when they really meant, "You let us down."

After the "everyone is going to med school" comment, Denise started avoiding situations where she'd be forced to make small talk and hung out almost exclusively with Craig and Cameron.

"Cameron was who I wanted to spend all my time with," Denise said. "I was like, 'Who else did I come here to see again?'"

On the last night of Reunions, Denise lay down on the football field between Craig and Cameron and watched the fireworks. The band played a slow, sentimental rendition of "Somewhere Over the Rainbow" while sparkling gold fireworks dripped down from the sky. The whole weekend, particularly this show, was clearly supposed to make people nostalgic for Princeton and their college years, but it didn't have that effect on Denise at all. She was grateful for her university education, but she would never want to go back and do it again. She much preferred the real world.

In mid-July, Craig and Denise took a train down to Atlanta together. Craig stayed for almost a week, meeting her roommates and lugging Target furniture around her new apartment. When it was time to say good-bye, Denise was surprised by how peaceful she felt. She knew it was going to be hard to live hundreds of miles away from Craig, but for the first time, she felt like she was supposed to be at Emory. She thought about something Cameron had said when she talked to him on the phone a few days before: "You could go to any medical school and make a difference." When he said something similar in February or March, she'd completely dismissed it. But now, finally, she was starting to believe it was true.

■ ◆ ■ ◆ ■

Alex didn't go to Reunions. She didn't see the point. The only person she wanted to see there was her friend Jay, and she was coming to visit Seattle in August. Besides, Alex knew that if she went, she wouldn't be able to stop thinking about her original plan for the weekend.

Alex wanted to propose to Bethany over Reunions because all Bethany's closest friends would be there. She was also going to invite Bethany's parents to come down from New York. The plan had been to ask Bethany to marry her in her old apartment, then go outside, where dozens of people would be waiting to hug her and celebrate the beginning of the next phase in her life.

"Part of the proposal is the celebration that comes with it," Alex said to me in September. "I want Bethany to see that this is the family I want—her family. I want her to see all of us together."

Now Alex and Bethany weren't even speaking. Occasionally, Bethany would send a text or an e-mail with a link to something funny she saw on the Internet, but that was it. Alex was surprised by how little this lack of communication fazed her. She felt like she'd lost Bethany a long time ago—in the months when Bethany became more and more emotionally distant, issued ultimatums, and finally told Alex that she didn't love her as much as she used to.

Over Reunions weekend, Alex and Andrea drove to the beach

on the west side of Seattle. They ate chicken and a salad with homemade dressing, and lay down together on a blanket on the sand. By now, Alex knew she wanted something more than friendship, but she wasn't sure whether Andrea felt the same way. The whole afternoon, Alex couldn't relax. She was painfully aware of her hands and feet and whether they were grazing any part of Andrea's body.

When they got back to Andrea's house, they watched two movies. Andrea got up a lot—to go to the bathroom, to get snacks, to grab another drink from the fridge—and Alex noticed that every time she sat back down on the couch, she moved a little closer. By the last half of the second movie, she was pressed up against Alex, her knees folded in her lap. At the end of the credits, Alex squeezed Andrea's hand. She could feel all Andrea's muscles simultaneously relax.

"I really like you, Alex."

Three days later, Alex texted me with an update.

"Andrea and I are officially dating. She's the one. I have absolutely no doubt. I know it sounds profoundly crazy but I am calling it now. I'm going to marry this girl . . . I think my heart might explode . . ."

Over the next few weeks, Alex was amazed by how easily—and painlessly—Andrea took Bethany's place. After the beach date, she started spending every weekend at Andrea's house in Capitol Hill. Alex felt peaceful there. The walls were stenciled with words like "grateful" and "love" in Hindi, and the open shelves in the kitchen were fully stocked with every imaginable spice and herb. The whole place smelled like lavender and patchouli. On the weekends, their routine was to wake up around eight, make breakfast, sip tea on the porch, work on their laptops side by side on the couch—Alex coding, Andrea writing—decide what they wanted to cook that day, and then head to the grocery store.

When I Skyped with Alex on a Saturday, she was getting ready to make bacon-wrapped filet mignon topped with scallion cashew cheese, with arugula and sautéed portobello mushrooms on the side. Halfway through our conversation, Andrea came in from the kitchen (where I'd been watching her dance around in a T-shirt and gym shorts), put her hand on Alex's back, and placed a mug of hot coffee on the coaster beside her.

"See, she just does this stuff for me without asking." Alex stood up and kissed Andrea on the cheek. "Thank you, babe."

Andrea had the instinct to take care of Alex in a way Bethany never did. When they were together, Andrea would regularly zero in on Alex's neck, making sure that everything looked normal.

"She's always checking on me," Alex said. "When you're dating someone, you wonder: When I'm an old person and this person is also an old person, will she have a desire to care for me? Get medicine for me?"

Almost immediately, Alex started planning for her future with Andrea. One month into their relationship, they talked about how they were going to manage their finances once they got married (with a joint account for mutual expenses, but their own personal accounts, too, for security). They also agreed not to have kids. Before Bethany, Alex never considered having children—she didn't want to risk passing down her dystonia or the emotional baggage she had from her childhood. But then Bethany convinced her to reconsider. They spent dozens of hours talking about how they were going to care for Jessie, their first child. Now Alex was pretty sure she'd made those plans only because she knew that not making them would have been a relationship deal-breaker. Bethany had wanted kids, so she had to want them, too.

In every way, being with Andrea was easier than being with Bethany. They wanted more of the same things and had similar values, and they shared the same physical space. Andrea loved Capitol Hill just as much as Alex did, and she supported the career path Alex wanted in Seattle. In a couple of months, Alex planned to start taking three online classes through Oregon State and drop down to working part-time at the real estate company. If she stayed on schedule, she would have her software engineering degree in two years. Then she would start looking for a job on her own, at a company where she'd be completely independent from her brother. She would have about $30,000 in student loans, but that seemed like a small price to pay for the security of a degree in the field where she wanted to spend the rest of her professional life.

One thing Alex didn't change after breaking up with Bethany was her decision not to start a company with Ben. Even though Bethany hadn't been the right person, she made Alex realize that she wanted to make space in her life for a partner. For most of college, Alex had imagined herself devoting all of her time to a company, working around the clock with her brother to get an original idea off the ground. But now that seemed like a waste of a life.

"If we started a company together, I can imagine Ben saying I had to work weekends, late at night, all the time. I would rather be a middle-class person with an okay retirement than some rich person who had to sacrifice all the way up to my forties to get there. It's like, 'Yay, I'm forty and on a yacht with Andrea, but she didn't know me for the past ten years, so she probably resents me. Woo.'"

Now that he was settling into Redmond, Alex thought Ben

seemed up to starting a company on his own. She wanted to help her brother in whatever way she could—talk him down off the ledge whenever he blew up about something business related—but she wasn't willing to sacrifice everything she wanted for his dream.

ON MY LAST VISIT to see Alex in Seattle, I met with Ben one-on-one. I told him that almost every time I talked to Alex, she described a new, more specific plan for her future. She fixated on how long she was going to work at the real estate company, when she was going to start graduate school, and when she would get her degree. The lengths and dates changed slightly every couple of weeks, depending on how work had been going or the status of her relationship. I also asked if he'd noticed how quickly Alex went from planning the rest of her life with Bethany to planning the rest of her life with Andrea.

Ben smiled.

"If Alex could have the option to have a script for the rest of her life—if she could know everything that is going to happen, and how, and when—she would take it."

■ ◆ ■ ◆ ■

On Sunday morning, a few hours before Michelle, Denise, and I were supposed to meet in a coffee shop a few blocks from campus, I called Olivia's phone. Even though I hadn't heard from her in over a month, I still thought she might come. Princeton was only an hour-and-fifteen-minute train ride from New York City. We'd also been talking about this meeting since the fall, and she'd always seemed excited by the prospect of meeting the other women. Over Reunions weekend, I sent e-mails and text messages telling her where we were going to meet and when. But she never showed.

I knew Olivia was okay because she would occasionally update her Facebook status, usually to publicize some kind of art or music event in Brooklyn. Nothing personal. Nothing that hinted at the reason behind her radio silence. After Reunions, I reached out to some of Olivia's closest friends from Princeton. None of them had heard from her in months.

This wasn't wholly unexpected. When we had lunch in April, Olivia told me she'd been distancing herself from people and things that connected her to Princeton. When I asked why, she said Princeton students had different priorities. Most were too tied to specific career goals, like working at a particular consulting firm or going to a particular law school.

"They're more concerned with what they've accomplished than with the kind of people they are—what mind-set and personal philosophies they have."

When Olivia visited Princeton in October to talk about her documentary, she told me she had no one to stay with. Frank, her best friend during her senior year of high school and at Princeton—whom Olivia had listed as her emergency contact on her college medical forms, and who, the year before, had gathered all Olivia's friends together to discuss how everyone could help her graduate—was on campus, finishing up his senior year. When I asked why she didn't just stay with him, she shrugged and said she hadn't talked to Frank since the summer.

"My lifestyle—sexual freedom, nomadic, not having any

money—it doesn't leave a good taste in his mouth," Olivia said. "Ivy [Club] appeals to him—that is the difference. Ivy doesn't appeal to me. He's going into consulting, I'm not."

In April, Olivia told me it would have been easy for her to also fixate on professional success. She said she could have set her sights on the most competitive design school in New York City and done everything in her power to get in. But she didn't want her self-worth to be so tied to her accomplishments. She knew most of her Princeton friends would have thrown a fit when the documentary deal with the media company started to sour. A typical Princeton student would have found a lawyer to demand more rights to the project, or aggressively networked with other media companies who could take it over. Instead, Olivia said she made the conscious choice to focus on things that were more important. She wanted to surround herself with people who encouraged her to care more about who she was than what she did—people who would help her become a more "interesting, cool, holistic, caring, and good person."

"I want to be friends with people who are more chill in general—more connected to nature, more alternative, more into alternative medicine and yoga," Olivia said. "This makes me slow down and be less neurotic. If I'm surrounded by these types of people, I'm pushed in the direction I need to go down."

Olivia had been separating herself from her Princeton friends, but she hadn't made many new ones, either. The only friend in New York whom she regularly mentioned was Rebecca, the sugar baby Princeton grad who offered to marry her. Olivia idolized her.

"Rebecca never allows herself to feel shame for being a sugar baby," Olivia told me. "She is open about everything that she does, everything that she thinks."

Rebecca had recently published an article in an online magazine about her experiences as a sugar baby. She had also worked closely with Olivia on her documentary and, as far as I knew, they met up in New York a couple of times a week.

"I haven't really talked to Olivia since December," Rebecca said when we spoke on the phone in June. "I think sometime around then, Olivia started going through some stuff because she started getting very uncommunicative."

When I asked if Rebecca knew what Olivia was dealing with, she said no. "That girl never tells me anything. You know what's weird? I have no idea what is up with her family. I have no idea what her beef with them is. I've also heard nothing about this guy she's apparently dating—Michael? I was under the impression he was a friend who was letting her crash indefinitely."

I wasn't surprised by how little Olivia's Princeton friends knew about her life, but I hadn't expected this. If Frank represented everything Olivia was trying to distance herself from, Rebecca represented everything that she wanted to be. But it seemed like Olivia was shutting Rebecca out, too.

I'VE SPENT A LOT OF TIME thinking about Olivia and why she stopped talking to a lot of her friends and me. I know she wanted a different kind of life from the one most of us were striving for. I know she wanted to surround herself with people whose goals and values she admired. But I also think that, when she decided to cut herself off from old friends and change her priorities, she constructed a new identity for herself. I think she wanted people in her new life to see her in a particular way: as a struggling but fiercely independent documentarian, eager to buck social conventions and try anything daring or provocative; as someone who went to Princeton but rebelled against everything that label evoked. Most of Olivia's close friends from Princeton knew a lot about her background: her struggles with her parents, how estranged she felt from Malaysia, her eating disorder. Especially at the end of her senior year, Olivia was intensely vulnerable with her Princeton friends. She had to rely on us (though mostly Leon) to make sure she stayed healthy, turned in her thesis, and graduated. That kind of dependence was fundamentally at odds with the person Olivia wanted to be.

When Olivia started distancing herself from me, I knew it was partly my fault. After what happened on Nantucket, I assumed Olivia wasn't fully capable of taking care of herself. If she was completely alone, without support, I worried something similar might happen again. I think a lot of other people she was close to at Princeton had the same concerns. Those concerns diminished Olivia's autonomy. Olivia wanted to leave all her low points behind. She needed to be around people who believed she was strong enough to independently make the necessary changes to her life.

When I talked to Rebecca and Michael, I couldn't believe how much they didn't know about Olivia. Rebecca didn't know that she came from a wealthy family in Malaysia, that she won a prestigious scholarship that paid for all four years of Princeton, or that she spent her senior year of high school at one of the most prestigious prep schools in the United States. She also didn't know anything about Michael. Before Olivia's dad cut her off, Michael didn't know he'd been supporting her. And before she started having symptoms in February, Michael told me he knew very little about her eating disorder. I wondered if Olivia kept these things under wraps because they interfered with her new identity. She wanted people to see her as independent, financially and emotionally. Her family's money, her elite high school, and the national scholarship got in the way of that.

Back in October, Olivia and I were working together at a coffee shop on the Lower East Side when she looked up from her computer and said, "Can you believe how much better life has gotten for me? And you've seen it all—all the low points. Now I look at myself and think, 'Yeah, I'm actually pretty cool.'"

By distancing herself from her Princeton friends, Olivia distanced herself from those low points. Maybe Olivia hid Michael from Rebecca because she saw him as a low point, too. His role in her life wasn't compatible with her idea of the person she wanted to be. When she embodied her ideal self, she didn't need Michael. She didn't need anyone.

■ ◆ ■ ◆ ■

I woke up early on Sunday morning, and I couldn't fall back to sleep. Eventually, I sat up in bed and pulled out my notebook. I was supposed to meet Michelle and Denise in three hours, but I still hadn't decided what to ask them. I knew I wanted to talk about the people we were when we graduated, the people we were now, and why this year was significant. I wanted to draw some kind of conclusion.

As I scribbled down potential questions, I realized that the end point I'd selected—Reunions weekend—was entirely arbitrary, picked only because, up until now, our lives had been clearly delineated by school. Every year had a beginning (September), an end (June), and a long break in between—an opportunity to reflect on the past nine months, take stock of successes and failures, and decide if and how we wanted to change. Now adulthood extended before us. No end in sight.

Originally, I thought our discussion at Reunions—sharing whatever insights we'd gleaned from our first year out of college—would be the perfect way to end this book. I planned to ask questions like "What have you learned over the past year?" and "How have you changed since graduation?" but once the three of us were sitting together, sipping tea, those questions seemed out of place. They implied that the hard part was over, the transformation from college student to fully functioning adult complete.

We had a long, thoughtful conversation. Michelle and Denise immediately connected, and we talked about the hardest parts of the past year. But it wasn't a conclusion. It didn't wrap up our year with a neat little bow, as I'd expected it to when I graduated. We were still in between stages, figuring out how to adapt who we were and what we knew in college to adulthood. The meeting was more of a check-in than a final reflection: a chance to talk about how things were going and what would come next.

Walking back from the coffee shop, I ran into three people in black polyester robes on their way to baccalaureate. In two days, another graduation would begin, another student would give the valedictory address, another class would pass through the Fitz-Randolph Gate. I returned to Ray's dorm, where I'd been staying for Reunions, and packed up my stuff. After we said our goodbyes and Ray left for baccalaureate, I stuck a Post-it in his closet, next to the tassel he would attach to his cap on graduation: "Congratulations, Ray. This is going to be a hell of a year."

ACKNOWLEDGMENTS

I felt more vulnerable—more sensitive to criticism and judgment—during my first year out of college than I'd ever felt before in my life. I can't imagine how vulnerable I would have felt if someone had been watching and recording my every move. This book belongs, first and foremost, to the four women who let me into their lives and trusted me with their stories. Thank you for your honesty, your courage, and your friendship. I would also like to thank the mothers, fathers, friends, roommates, brothers, boyfriends, and girlfriends who took the time to make sure I saw these four women as they did. This is a richer book because of each of our conversations.

In 2013, I had my first writing job, interning at *The Atlantic*. The articles that I wrote that summer led to this book. Chris Heller, Eleanor Barkhorn, and Bob Cohn encouraged me to write when it wasn't part of my job description.

From the beginning, *Post Grad* was a collaborative project. My editor, Megan Lynch, knew what the book was about before I did. Megan sought me out, believed in my ability as a writer, and reminded me of our shared vision at every turn. Sarah McGrath weighed in on the book at a critical moment, convincing me that I couldn't write about these women without writing about myself as well. At HarperCollins, I am grateful to Allison Saltzman for a beautiful cover, Jeanie Lee and Kyran Cassidy for their helpful comments, Allyssa Kasoff and Sonya Cheuse for their publicity expertise, and Eleanor Kriseman and Emma Dries for fielding my rookie questions with patience and good humor. Thanks also to Miriam Parker, Meghan Deans, and Dan Halpern.

When I started work on *Post Grad*, I knew nothing about writing a book, let alone publishing one. I was excited by the prospect but utterly clueless to the execution. Then Evan Thomas introduced me to the inimitable Binky Urban. Binky was instrumental in formulating the initial concept for the book and giving me the confidence to write it. I am remarkably lucky to have her in my corner.

This book is the product of a string of incomparable teachers, not all of whom I can name here. I am especially fortunate to have been a student of Jayne Collins, who taught me to carefully consider the impact of my words, and William Mottolese, who has treated me like a professional writer since I was fifteen. At Princeton, I benefited immensely from the mentorship of Jill Dolan, Tara Woodard-Lehman, Nannerl Keohane, and Margot Canaday. Above all, I am indebted to my twin guideposts, Evan and Oscie Thomas. They have read the book at every juncture and have gone to bat for me more times than I can count. They give me something to aspire to—in the way they listen, the way they write, and the way they support each other.

Besides keeping me company, my closest friends infused my writing with a sense of urgency and purpose. Our conversations helped me to see that the stories in the book were indicative of something bigger—that everyone struggles after graduation. For their insight and unfailing support, I am grateful to Katherine Ortmeyer, Catherine Ettman, Ray Chao, Sacha Finn, Amber Dreisacker, Corinne Grady, Carter Staub, Wynne Callon, Tariq Adely, Krystle Manuel-Countee, Siofra Robinson, Julie Ertl, Michelle Yakubisin, Nicole Eigbrett, Noam Shapiro, Brandon Holt, Shawon Jackson, Taylor Francis, and everyone on my mock trial team. I did most of my writing in Nanchang, China, thousands of miles away from friends and family. My public speaking class at Jiangxi Normal University—especially my dear friends Xia Xu, Wang YaJun, Wan ZhiXin, Zeng WeiXin, and Xu Na—never let me get lonely.

My sister, Milly, was one of the people in my life most excited about this book. When I spoke with my editor on the phone for the first time, she was pacing around in the next room, waiting for me to tell her how it went. In her absence, Sarah Robbins, Craig Smyth, Andrew Robbins, Cath Harrison, and Charlotte Carnaby have made sure I never lack support or encouragement.

Three years ago, when I got an e-mail from an editor at a publishing house, Robert Marshall convinced me that it wasn't a joke, and that I should probably respond. I am lucky to have someone in my life who could read any sentence in this book and know if I'd changed it. He is my number one fan and my partner in everything.

My father, John Kitchener, has always developed a genuine interest in everything I do, whether it's performing in *The Vagina Monologues* or writing about five twenty-three-year-old women. Though my writing career seemed to come out of left field, he never questioned it. I could not have written this book without his unwavering support.

A talented artist and designer, my mother, Nancy Kitchener, raised me to value creativity. Every time she filed away one of my essays or short stories in a drawer, I became a little more sure that what I wrote was worth reading. As I grew up, she did everything in her power to help me achieve my goals. I could not be prouder now that, as a student at Smith College, she is going after her own.